I0812771

IMAGES
of America

ORANGEVALE

On the Cover: Captured is a rare glimpse into the Landis packinghouse in Orangevale around the late 19th century. (Courtesy Tom Tomich.)

IMAGES
of America

ORANGEVALE

Paul J. P. Sandul and Tory D. Swim

ARCADIA
PUBLISHING

ISBN 978-0-7385-4696-4

Published by Arcadia Publishing
Charleston, South Carolina

Printed in the United States of America

Library of Congress Catalog Card Number: 2006931415

For all general information contact Arcadia Publishing at:
Telephone 843-853-2070
Fax 843-853-0044
E-mail sales@arcadiapublishing.com
For customer service and orders:
Toll-Free 1-888-313-2665

Visit us on the Internet at www.arcadiapublishing.com

Contents

Acknowledgments		6
Introduction		7
1.	Colonization	11
2.	Tilling the Soil	23
3.	A Place to Hang Your Hat	35
4.	The Fruits of Our Labor	47
5.	A Common Cause	57
6.	Getting from Here to There	69
7.	Growing Up In Orangevale	81
8.	Pencils, Books, and Teachers' Dirty Looks	93
9.	The Many Faces of Orangevale	103
10.	Orangevale at Play	115
Selected Bibliographies		127

ACKNOWLEDGMENTS

We are extremely grateful for the many people and organizations that facilitated the completion of this book. Daryl, Jason, and Amber Layland provided their camera equipment to allow us to capture quality images from sometimes dismal originals. Architectural historian Janice Calpo assisted in the editing of our architectural descriptions. Duane G. Sandul provided much needed review and editing, as did Dr. Lee M. A. Simpson, our mentor, who instilled in us the confidence and training we needed to complete this project.

The staff at the California History Room at the California State Library provided valuable assistance, as did Tom Tolley and the staff at the Sacramento Room in the Central Library, which also provided images. Carol Procter and Diane Shakal from the Orangevale Library opened their collection and hosted a "share your pictures" night, which led to the acquisition of more images. Lola Aguilar and the California State Archives helped hunt down valuable resources. Randy Wooten provided us with images from the Pioneer Mutual Hook and Ladder Society. Karen Mehring and Gaynel Wald from the Folsom History Museum opened their collection. UC Davis archivist John Skarstad and fruit label expert Pat Jacobsen also helped.

Residents and friends of Orangevale aided in our quest for images. Betts Flores from the Friends of Orangevale Library, Debbie Poulsen, Becky Maher, and Robert Kegley provided us with contacts. JoAnn Allred, Jean Kelly, Marcia Clark, Naida and Andrew Effinger, Gerald Lammerding, Glenda Lewis, Richard Harke, and Tom Tomich opened up their homes and photograph albums. Likewise, organizations and businesses in Orangevale helped. Jeff Ennis and Brad Tatum of the *Orangevale News* posted a call for images free of charge. Dale and Shirley Baker provided access to the Orangevale Grange's collection. Sharon Wilcox opened up the Orange Vale Water Company's collection and made contact with Fred Tomich, whose collection is unrivaled. Barbara Elliott, secretary for the Orangevale Open Elementary School, not only provided us with images, but also donated the school's precious images and records to the Sacramento Archives and Museum Collection Center (SAMCC). Jean Anne Shenoy and Colleen Hunt, secretaries at Bella Vista and Casa Roble high schools, also opened up the their schools' collections. The Orangevale Chamber of Commerce offered its support and even provided us with an information booth free of charge during the community's annual festival, Pow Wow Days.

We would be remiss, however, not to note the enormous contribution of SAMCC, to whom we donate all author royalties. James Henley, manager, graciously agreed to open up the collection at SAMCC. Likewise, the staff, such as archivist Dylan McDonald and volunteer Lisa Prince, donated their time and expertise. Most importantly, however, archivists Patricia Johnson and Carson Hendricks deserve our biggest thanks for the countless hours and help they provided us. Finally, we could not have finished this project without the love and daily support of our family and friends, specifically, Diana Sandul and Natosha Layland, and David and Karla Swim.

INTRODUCTION

If the man doesn't live there, he probably wishes he did.

—*Sacramento Union*, April 29, 1972

The *Sacramento Union* reported on the growth of the small Sacramento suburb of Orangevale in 1972 and captured the charm of this semirural community by describing some intrinsic desire of outsiders to become Orangevale insiders. Orangevale is just west of Folsom, an old mining town and transportation hub, and east of Sacramento, the California state capital. The *Sacramento Union* continued, "Show me a man with a pickup truck, a gun rack, a cowboy hat and a pair of boots, and I'll show you the spirit of Orangevale." This spirit of Orangevale, the romantic American ideal of a rural community, remains today, even if some of those pickup trucks, cowboy hats, boots, and gun racks have been traded in for SUVs, visors, Nikes, and cell phones. Indeed, the community's spirit, like its history, is strong and alive. One can pass through the streets of an older community, stop and buy some produce from Mr. Tomich as he offers a story from days gone by, and visit the local shops where residents still gather to gossip. Indeed, Orangevale, in "the heart of California," has a history that patterns many beloved small towns across America.

Thousands of years ago, the Nisenan (Southern Maidu) tribe first settled the land that became Orangevale. Maidu culture included living in brush shelters, acorn gathering, and practicing the spirit-impersonating Kuksu religion, a male secret society. The Maidu Indians included the Mountain Maidu of Plumas and Lassen counties; the Konkow of Butte and Yuba counties; and the Nisenan of Yuba, Nevada, Placer, Sacramento, and El Dorado counties. According to A. L. Kroeber in *Valley Nisenan* (1929), the Nisenan were the most prosperous and culturally developed of the three groups and the Maidu had an estimated population of 9,000 in the late 18th century. That number had dwindled to 1,100 by 1910, and, by 1930, the census recorded only 93.

The Spanish and Mexicans had surveyed the Sacramento Valley by the mid-18th century, as had many trappers working along the American River. Nonetheless, Anglo settlement of the area did not begin until the gold rush, which was sparked by James W. Marshall's discovery off the upper American River in Coloma in 1848. Soon miners panned the shores of the American River adjacent to Orangevale along the Mississippi Bar in the Mississippi Township, an area that included all or parts of present-day Orangevale, Citrus Heights, Fair Oaks, Folsom, and Rancho Cordova.

The creation of Orangevale as a settled community resulted from a series of land deals that trace back to California's Mexican period in 1844. According to the Sacramento firm of Buckley and Taylor, in an 1895 survey of all the land titles and transactions involving the area, the Mexican governor of California, Manuel Micheltorena, first granted the land that included Orangevale to Joel P. Dedmond on Christmas Eve in 1844. The land grant, known as the Rancho de San Juan, included more than 19,900 acres. The first land sale occurred in August 1845 to

John Sinclair. Sinclair then sold the land to Hiram Grimes in February 1849 for a mere $5,000. While Grimes officially received a U.S. Land Patent on July 9, 1860, he (and soon others) sold off small parcels throughout the 1850s. In 1861, Serranus Clinton Hastings, California's first chief justice and third attorney general, purchased most of the San Juan grant for $36,000. Hastings eventually sold parts of the land, including portions to prominent business partners Frederick K. Cox, a former California senator, and Crawford W. Clarke, founder of the North Fork Ditch Company. Cox and Clarke eventually sold what they owned to a land company that formed Orangevale. Most importantly, however, Hastings sold land to an Irish farmer, John T. Cardwell, in the 1880s. A contingent of some of Sacramento's most prestigious businessmen, including Valentine S. McClatchy of the *Sacramento Bee*, purchased land from Cardwell and other landholders, and eventually they sold their combined land to their booster organization, the Orange Vale Colonization Company, in 1887–1888.

Five of the company's trustees appeared before a notary public on September 2, 1887, to place their signatures on articles of incorporation. Valentine S. McClatchy, George M. Mott, Thomas B. Hall, Phillip C. Drescher, and Harris Weinstock each signed the document to create the colonization company. They also announced some lofty goals, which included the construction of bridges, ditches, and buildings, as well as the loaning of money to cultivate farmlands. The trustees envisioned the creation of a farming community, yet they had an even grander goal of forming a complex system of suburbs on the fringes of Sacramento's rural landscape, which would include bridges, buildings, and real estate projects. Explicitly, the Orange Vale Colonization Company not only imagined the community as an agricultural paradise inhabited by Jeffersonian small farmers, but also as a thriving suburb of Sacramento where middle-class urbanites could escape the city's buzz. The *Sacramento Union* reported this sentiment in an article written eight months after the formation of the colonization company on May 8, 1888: "There is one especially great advantage to Sacramentans in the opening up and development of these suburban tracts, and that is the facilities afforded business men for enjoying the comforts and privileges of country homes, without interference with their business interests." The article boasted of plans for schools, churches, transportation routes—mainly by railroad—and impressive homes. The trustees of the Orange Vale Colonization Company did not create a mere agricultural colony where farmers simply tilled the soil. More audaciously, they used an agricultural model of suburbanization not yet seen in the Sacramento Valley, a place where agriculture and country life drove the promotion and development of a modern suburb.

The Orange Vale Colonization Company featured 36 businessmen from Sacramento, including McClatchy, Weinstock, Mott, Drescher, and Hall, all of whom served as the original directors. Robert T. Devlin is also credited with being a secretary in 1888, and George Katzenstein, who promoted the creation of the Orange Vale Water Company in 1896, is listed as a director in 1890. These men advertised small land lots to settlers throughout the United States, particularly in Northeastern and Midwestern states, such as Minnesota. They included a morally upright anti-saloon clause for those concerned about principled and proper living. Yet when a national depression, precipitated by the Panic of 1893, brought economic devastation in the 1890s, few migrated to Orangevale, and the company dissolved in 1896.

Sacramento's land-based elite, particularly the two newspapers, the *Sacramento Bee* and the *Sacramento Union*, also sought to promote the city's suburban areas, including Orangevale. Articles appeared intermittently in the two newspapers in late 1890s and the early 1900s, publicizing the growth of suburban areas. Both newspapers went as far as to produce large, spirited booster tracts that, while designed to promote all of Sacramento County, made sure to focus on the city's burgeoning suburban areas, particularly Orangevale. The *Sacramento Bee* published *Sacramento County and its Resources; Our Capital City, Past and Present: A Souvenir of the Bee* in 1894 and the *Sacramento Union* published *Sacramento through the Camera* in 1901. The *Bee*, with McClatchy as an editor, crammed its pages with sensational stories and pictures of Orangevale (some of which are reprinted in this book). Likewise, the *Union* bragged about the community's agricultural productivity and even highlighted William Calder's Orangevale residence, called "The Palms," as an example of the beautiful suburban homes in Sacramento's rural-urban fringe.

Another booster organization, the Orangevale Townsite Company, organized in October 1908 in hopes of profiting from the promotion and sale of land in Orangevale. The company included directors and stockholders B. F. Hulings, John H. Miller Jr., Donald McClain, Robert A. Waring, Ray C. Waring, F. G. Fay, Mary B. Lindley, Clovis T. LaGrave, and Peter J. Shields (the superior court judge in Sacramento best known for his contributions leading to the establishment of the University of California, Davis). The articles of incorporation for the Orangevale Townsite Company mirrored much of the same language used by the Orange Vale Colonization Company 20 years earlier. This included outlining the goals of building houses and infrastructure. The Orangevale Townsite Company spoke plainly, and although it proposed to help farmers, it dropped the facade of an agricultural colony company and declared itself a "general real estate business." The highlight of their endeavors resulted in a sensational pamphlet, the *Sacramento Valley Sunbeam*, published by B. F. Hulings in 1909, with a subtitle, "Devoted to the Interests of Ideal Country Homes." This publication, again like previous endeavors, highlighted both the agricultural and suburban qualities of Orangevale. Despite these collective promotion efforts, Orangevale remained a small, semirural community with a population well under 2,000 until it exploded during the boom years following World War II.

Orangevale, though its name suggests otherwise, produced all types of fruits. In fact, several local histories show that Orangevale emerged as the center of Tokay grape production in the region until the development of Lodi's vineyards. Several articles in the *Union* in the 1880s and 1890s, as well as the publicity tracts produced by the organizations involved with Orangevale, did not limit their praise of the area's soil to its citrus-producing ability but also named just about every type of fruit or nut that could possibly grow under the California sun. Almonds, apricots, berries, figs, melons, peaches, pears, pecans, plums, prunes, and walnuts all grew in Orangevale. Still, orange cultivation in the early years expanded significantly. The Orange Vale Colonization Company organized in 1887 to rival Southern California's booming citrus industry. Although a lot of deciduous fruit trees were planted during the 1880s and 1890s, hopes of competing with Southern California as the citrus center of the world inspired many valley farmers along the eastern foothills to plant oranges. According to Sacramento historian Joseph A. McGowan, more than 250,000 orange trees and 50,000 lemon trees were planted north of Sacramento between 1888 and 1891. The orange trees began to bear fruit about 1893, when four carloads of fruit shipped out from Northern California. The figure jumped to 81 carloads in 1896, 286 in 1897, and 589 in 1898. Orangevale itself shipped 20 carloads of oranges and 200 carloads of deciduous fruits in 1899.

Orangevale, according to local histories, had 500 acres of oranges by 1894 and helped Sacramento County boast about having the best display of budded oranges at the California State Mid-Winter Fair. Orange acreage blossomed to 2,000 by 1915 and reached its peak by 1925. By the late 1920s, however, the community's orange production dropped, mainly because consumers preferred orange juice to whole oranges and because a national law affected the sale of oranges not yet considered ripe. Farmers were further devastated when, in the winter of 1932, a cruel frost swept the Sacramento Valley and killed most crops. This effectively ended Orangevale's period of agricultural productivity, although a few enduring growers, such as Tom Tomich, continue tilling the soil in Orangevale today.

The early, albeit short-lived, farming boom in Orangevale spawned lasting positive impacts, namely the development of other community and social services. For example, because of the need to transport fruit quickly to markets in the east, new bridges were built across the American River to Folsom, as well as from nearby Fair Oaks to a rail line that ran fruit cars and passenger trains to Sacramento. These bridges played a vital role in the later development of commuter traffic to and from Orangevale. Likewise, reminiscences of Orangevale residents in newspaper articles featured in the book *Fair Oaks and San Juan Memories* indicate that Orangevale experienced a building boom at the end of the 19th and early part of the 20th century. Along Greenback

Lane and Main Avenue, a variety of stores and services arose, along with churches, schools, clubs, and a library.

Owing to the growth of community services, transportation, and infrastructure, Orangevale survived the lean Depression years between the Big Freeze of 1932 and World War II. Despite nature's blow, Orangevale's population exploded in the 1950s and 1960s, thanks to the rise of military bases, a shopping mall, and a nearby defense corporation that provided steady employment. Likewise, the construction and widening of bridges on Sunrise Boulevard and Hazel Avenue, the development of highways such as Interstate 80, and improvements to Orangevale's "main street," Greenback Lane, helped sustain growth. To be sure, while Sacramento's dreams of suburbanization did not materialize at the end of the 19th and early 20th centuries, they did create the necessary infrastructure that enabled Orangevale to become a bedroom community for the state capital during the population boom that followed World War II. Indeed, the population increased 725 percent during the 1950s, from an estimated 1,600 in 1950 to 11,600 in 1960. Continuing growth through the 1970s led to a population of more than 18,000 in 1975 and more than 25,000 by the turn of the 21st century.

One

COLONIZATION

Pen cannot describe it nor photograph do it justice; it has to be seen to be appreciated.

—"Beautiful Orangevale," *Farm, Field and Fireside*, May 25, 1895.

Animated claims about Orangevale, such as this one, appeared in numerous publications in the late 19th and early 20th centuries. The promotion of Orangevale by the Orange Vale Colonization Company represents a culmination of the larger promotional efforts by those hoping to boost farming in California. Images of California agriculture during the 19th century focus on horticulture, particularly the state's "glamour crop"—the orange—water irrigation, railroad transportation, and the prominence of the small-farmer and colony systems. Some of Sacramento's most prestigious businessmen formed the colonization company to take advantage of this image of California.

The list of directors for the Orange Vale Colonization Company reads like a who's who of Sacramento politics and enterprise. These "big fish" of the city's relatively small pond were responsible for the formation, promotion, and development of Sacramento's rural-urban fringe. They included Valentine S. McClatchy, Thomas B. Hall, Harris Weinstock, George M. Mott, and Phillip C. Drescher. McClatchy served as the business editor of the *Sacramento Bee*; Hall founded the wholesale grocery store Hall, Luhrs, and Company; Weinstock developed a successful department-store chain, Weinstock, Lubin and Company; and Mott and Drescher helped establish the Sacramento Chamber of Commerce in 1895. Together these businessmen, along with other prominent stockholders, organized land-development companies, water companies, and railway companies; drafted Sacramento's City Charter; and formed the Sacramento Chamber of Commerce and Sutter Club. These connections included links not only to the mayor of Sacramento, but also to the governor and huge corporations and institutions, such as the Southern Pacific Railroad Company and the California State Bank.

The lucrative careers of these affluent members not only tied them in an interest to sell land but also provided them with the resources to do so, including enough capital to build homes, roads, and bridges. Soon, advertisements marketed Orangevale as a pastoral paradise where one could own a small country plot but still commute to the "big city." One advertisement in the *Sacramento Union* on May 8, 1888, epitomizes their efforts: "No part of California exceeds the localities [the land between Sacramento and Folsom] in picturesqueness of scenery and fertility of soil. They posses every attraction for those who prefer country to city life and have already many of the solid advantages [including schools, churches, and roads] so generally desired."

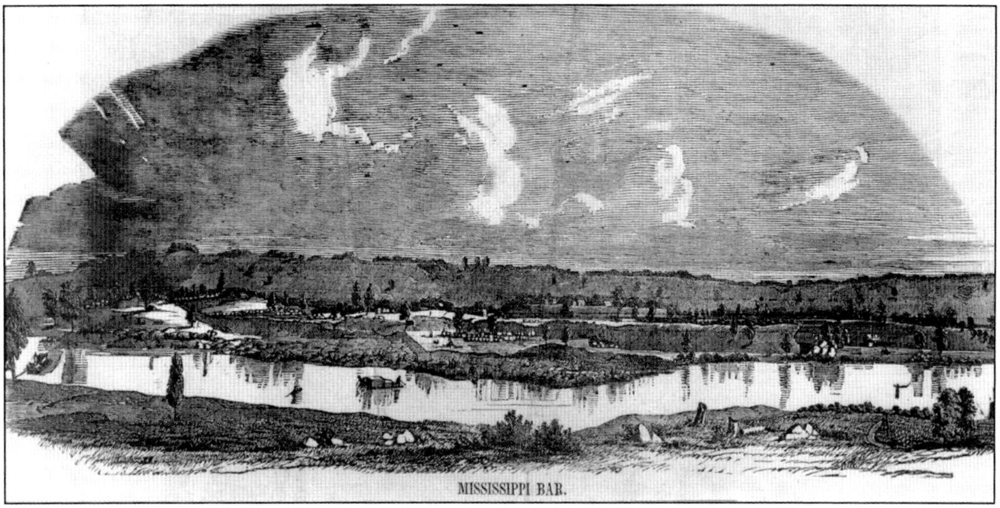

Mississippi Bar, just downstream from Folsom and on the north side of the river by Orangevale, boomed as a mining camp in the 1850s. Portions of it survive today, despite being dredged into huge windrows of tailings. In fact, some residents of Orangevale, once part of the "Mississippi Township," received a Mississippi Township listing in the 1920 federal census as place of residence. (Courtesy SAMCC, No. 80/18/537.)

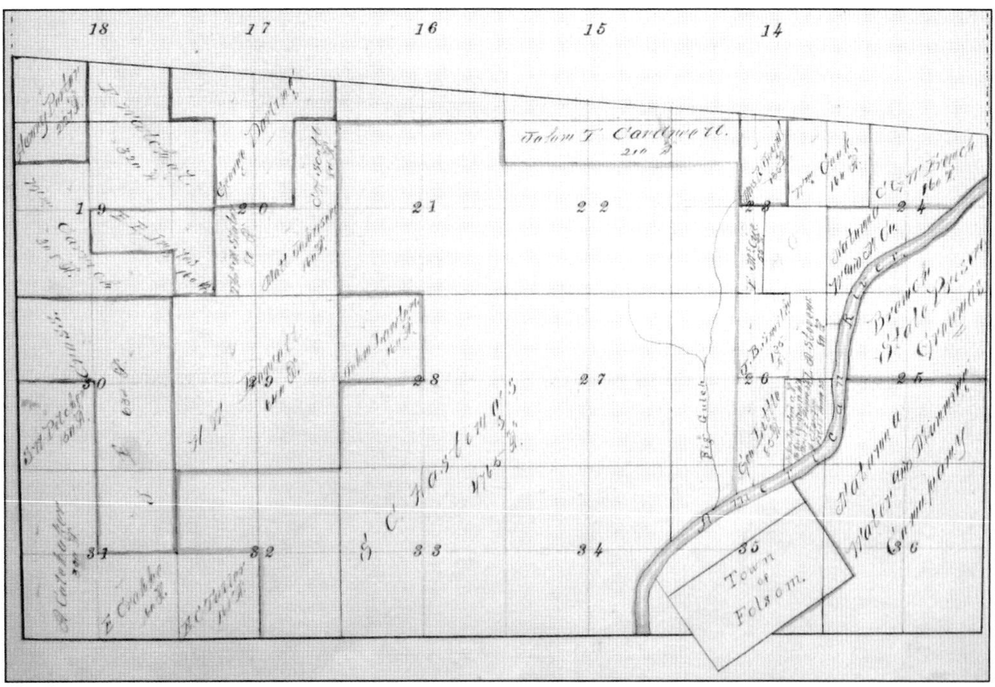

This Sacramento County tax assessor map from 1882 of the San Juan area shows the various landowners of the land grant, including the large tract owned by Serranus Clinton Hastings and John T. Cardwell. Hastings and other landowners sold to Thomas B. Hall and the Orange Vale Colonization Company by 1887, when the colony began. (Courtesy SAMCC.)

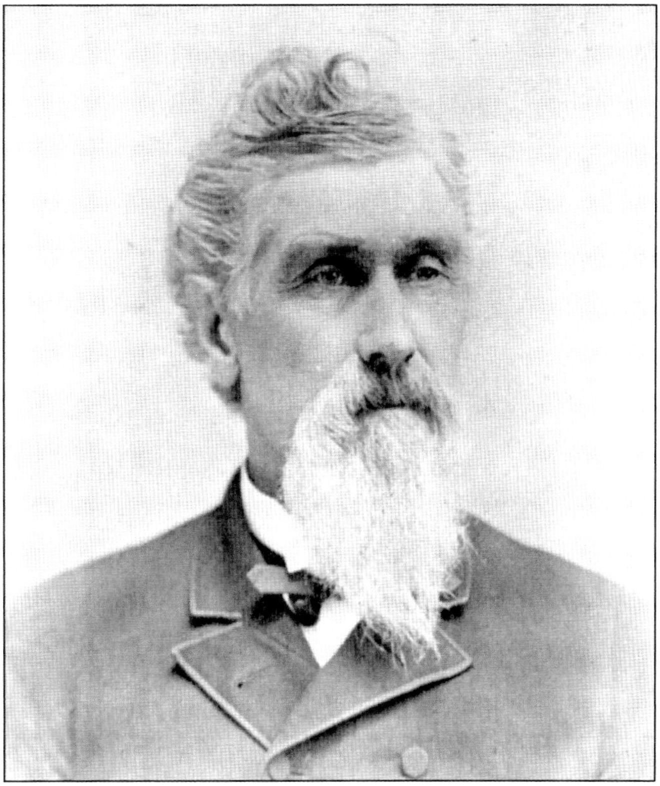

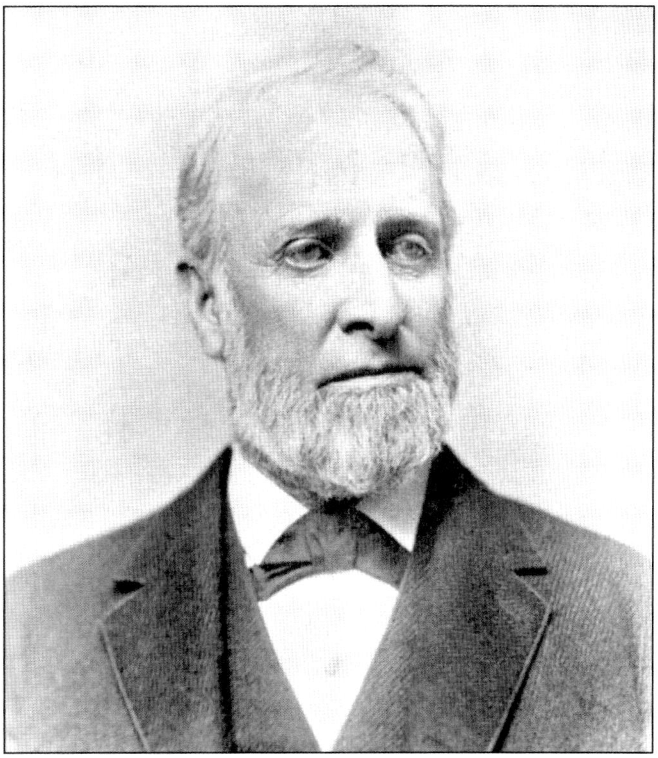

California senator Frederick K. Cox (above) and Crawford W. Clarke (below), pictured here around 1894, owned much of the San Juan grant after 1873. They entered into partnership in 1852, and they soon controlled one of the most extensive cattle ranches on the Pacific coast. In 1888, Clarke and Cox took over the "Eureka Ditch" (which ran from Mississippi Bar along Lake Natoma west to Orangevale) and formed the North Fork Ditch Company, which served Orangevale and eventually Fair Oaks and Citrus Heights. Clarke and Cox sold parts of their land to the Orange Vale Colonization Company by 1887 and later made contract deals with companies that eventually established Fair Oaks and Carmichael. (Source *Sacramento County and its Resources: A Souvenir of the Bee, 1894, Our Capital City, Past and Present*, 160–161.)

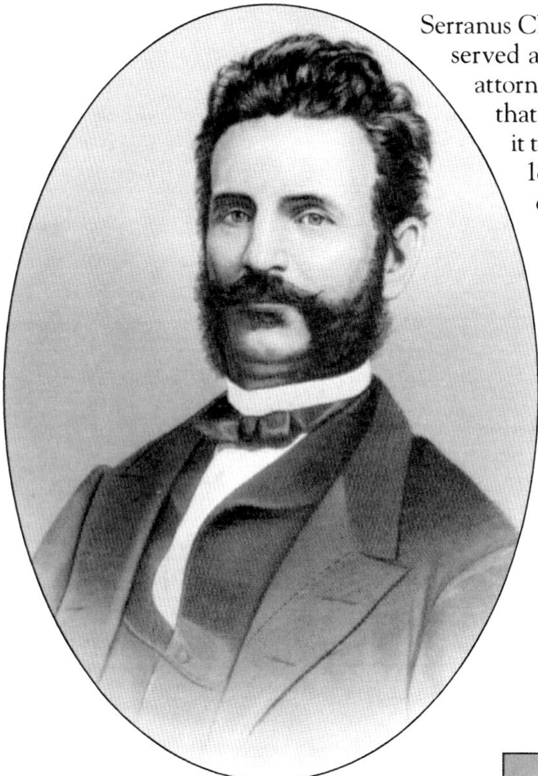

Serranus Clinton Hastings, pictured here around 1870, served as California's first chief justice and third attorney general. Hastings owned most of the land that eventually became Orangevale after he sold it to the Orange Vale Colonization Company in 1887. (Source *Representative and Leading Men of the Pacific*, 432.)

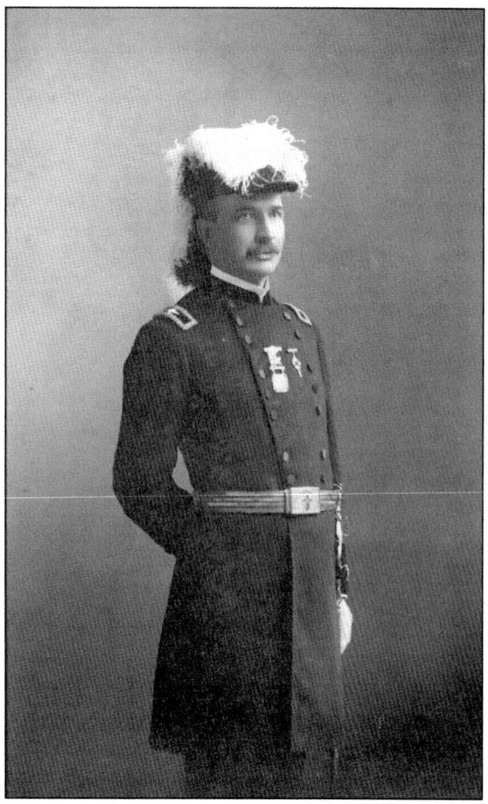

Thomas B. Hall, pictured here in the 1890s, was president of the Orange Vale Colonization Company and served as a captain in the California state militia. He founded the wholesale grocery store Hall, Luhrs, and Company, helped draw up Sacramento's third city charter in 1892, and served on the initial committee to draft bylaws and plan Sacramento's first chamber of commerce in 1895. (Courtesy SAMCC, No. 82/115/13.)

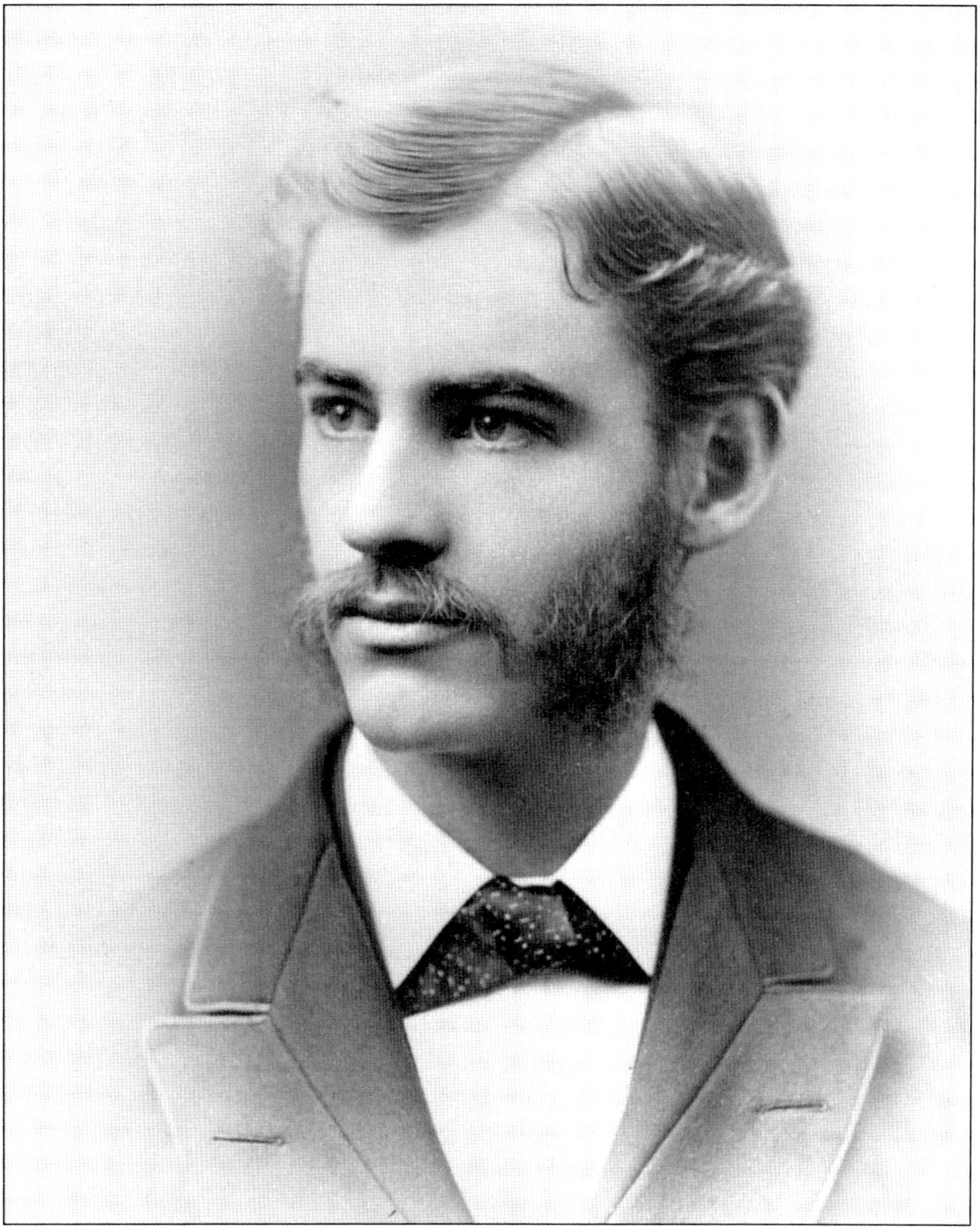

Valentine S. McClatchy, pictured here in the 1880s, served as vice president of the Orange Vale Colonization Company and rode prominently across the Sacramento political and business landscape. Son of James McClatchy, founder of the *Sacramento Bee*, Valentine and his brother Charles (C. K.) became the owners of the newspaper daily in 1884. In addition to his land investments in Orangevale, he bought and sold land throughout the valley and helped establish the Placer County Citrus Colony and the Fair Oaks Development Company. McClatchy also became involved in local politics and helped draft bylaws for the Sacramento Chamber of Commerce. Later he assumed offices for various local and state political organizations, including a stint as president of the California State Reclamation Board. (Courtesy SAMCC, No. 82/05/803.)

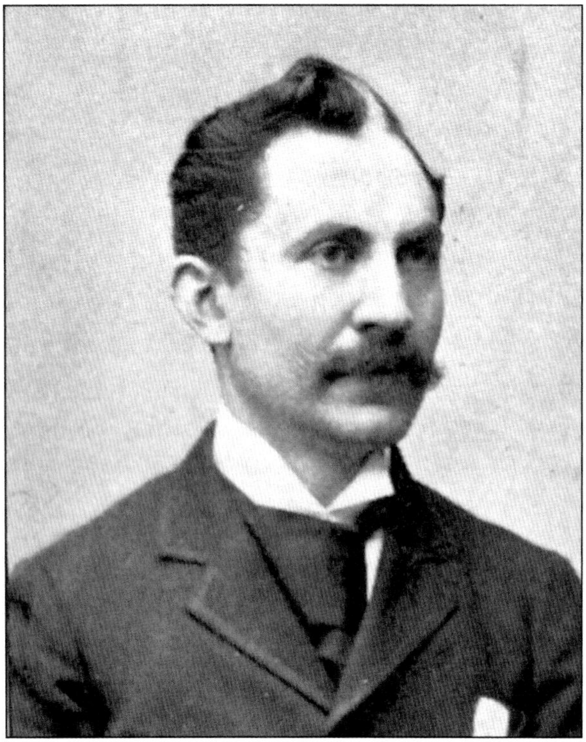

Harris Weinstock, *c.* 1894, a charter member of the Orange Vale Colonization Company, also had a successful business and influential political life, serving on various state and national industrial and agricultural commissions, and helping to frame Sacramento's city charter. Weinstock's influence derived from the success of his department-store chain, Weinstock, Lubin and Company. (Source *Sacramento County and its Resources: A Souvenir of the Bee, 1894, Our Capital City, Past and Present*, 151.)

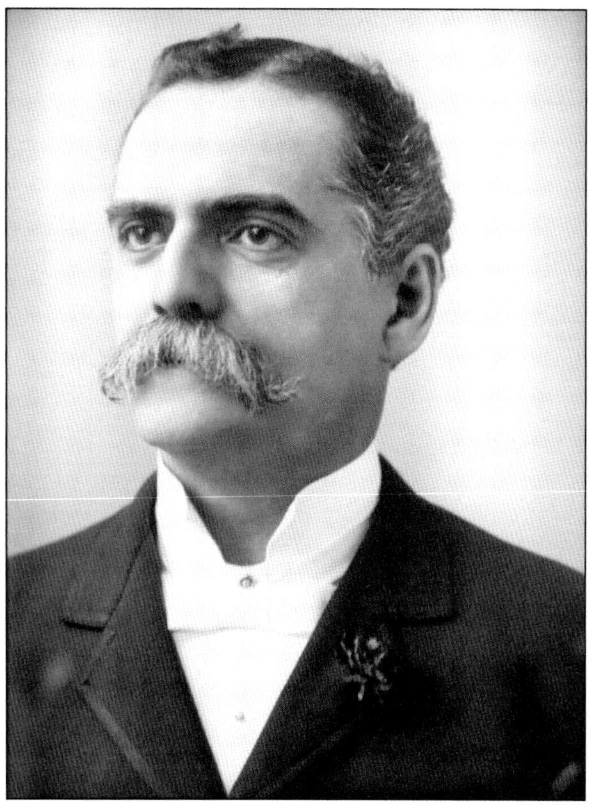

George B. Katzenstein, pictured here *c.* 1896, served as a secretary and manager of the Orange Vale Colonization Company and also had a prominent business career. Most notably, beginning in 1868, he served as a manager of the Earl Fruit Company, the most extensive shippers of deciduous fruits in the state. Katzenstein also rallied for the establishment of the Orange Vale Water Company, which formed in 1896 and still services the community today. (Courtesy Orange Vale Water Company.)

Robert T. Devlin, pictured here *c.* 1894, served as a secretary for the Orange Vale Colonization Company and had a lucrative legal practice, Devlin and Devlin. He served as a member and president of the Board of State Prison Directors, and in 1905, began a seven-year stint as the U.S. district attorney for the northern district of California. (Source *Sacramento County and its Resources: A Souvenir of the Bee, 1894, Our Capital City, Past and Present*, 151.)

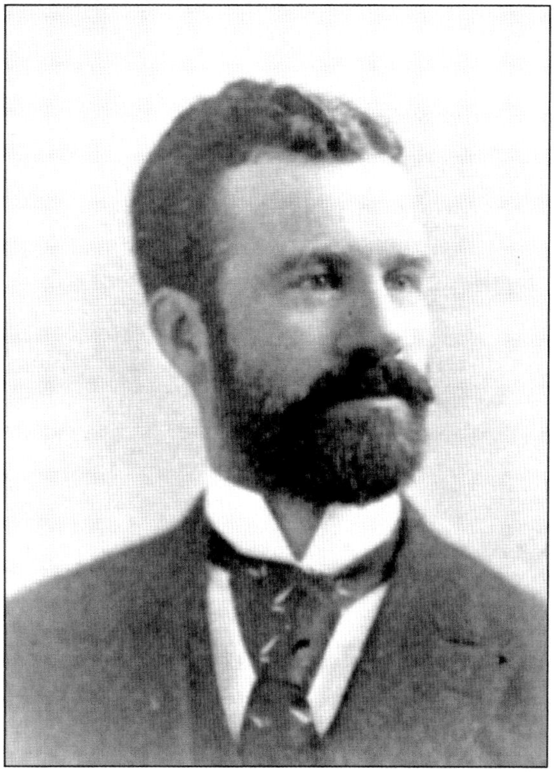

"The Villa," pictured here *c.* 1894, was a stick-style structure built in 1888–1889 that stood along the river bluffs. It was used for entertaining the Orange Vale Colonization Company's investors and clients before it moved to Greenback Lane in 1916 and became, primarily, a private residence. The Villa recently moved again and stands today on Oak Avenue. (Source *Sacramento County and its Resources: A Souvenir of the Bee, 1894, Our Capital City, Past and Present*, 70.)

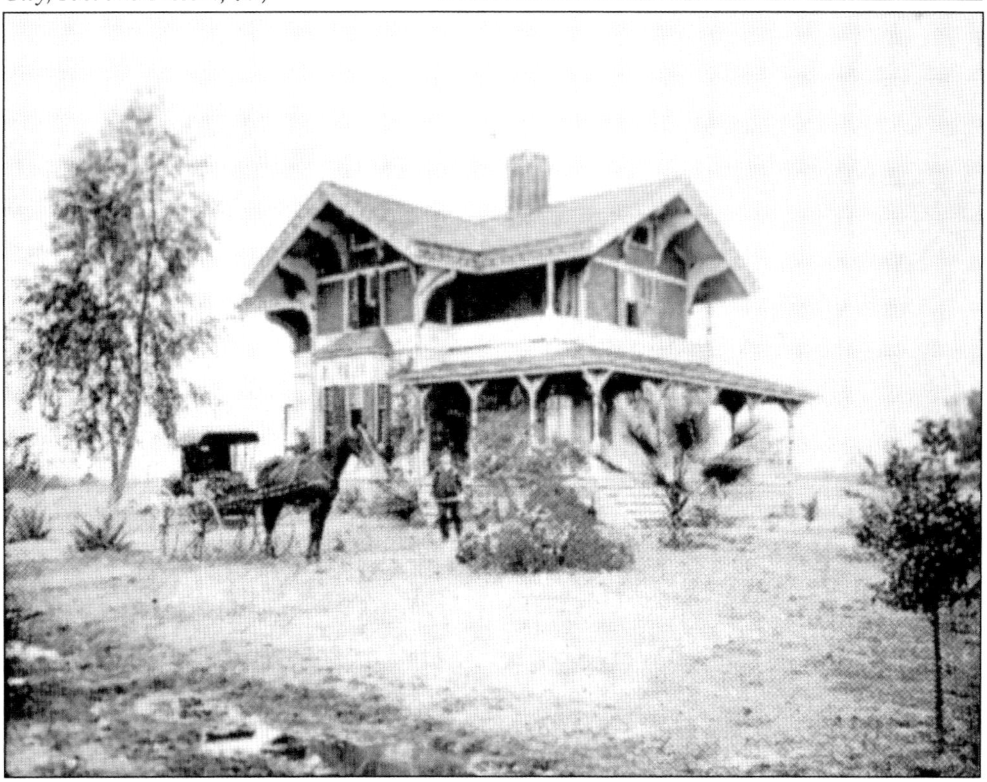

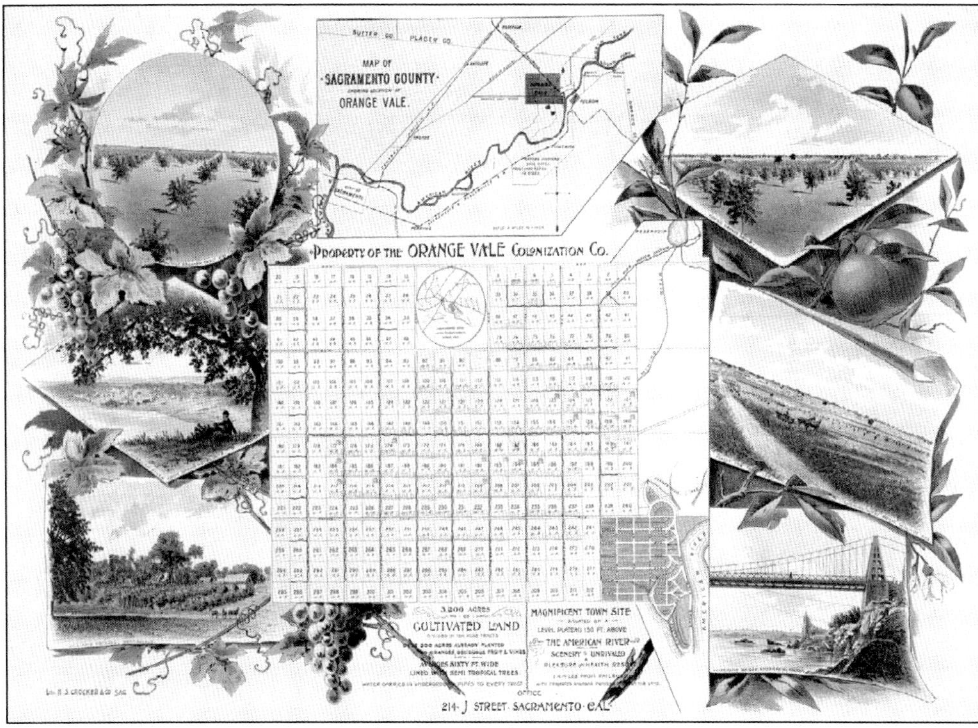

This c. 1892 map of Orange Vale shows not only how the land was originally conceived and developed, but also how Orangevale was advertised as a thriving and growing community with a plethora of streets and roads, diligently planned parcels, lush orchards, and a serviceable bridge across the American River. (Courtesy SAMCC, No. 2002/092/001.)

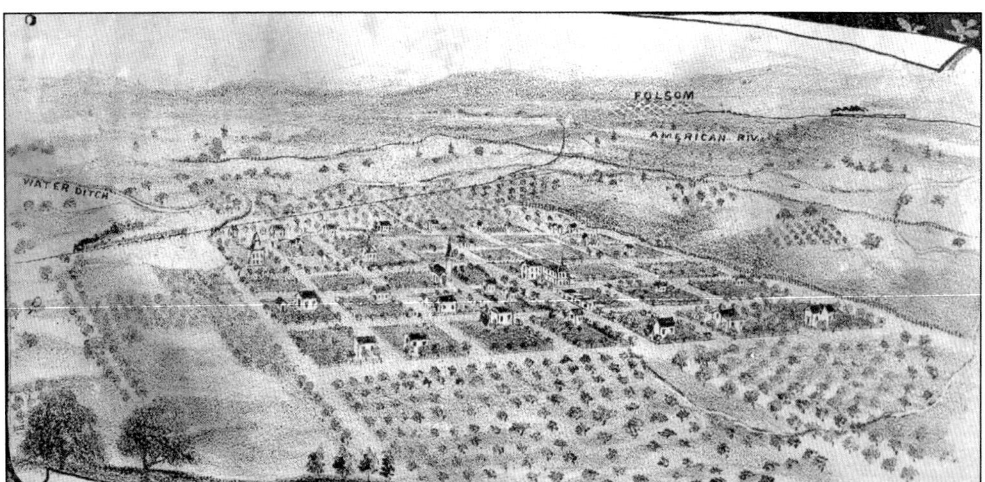

This *Sacramento Union* lithograph, titled *View of Orangevale* and created in 1890, shows the vast amount of acreage that was available to farmers hoping to make a new life and settle in the "Heart of California." (Courtesy SAMCC, No. 68/110/451.)

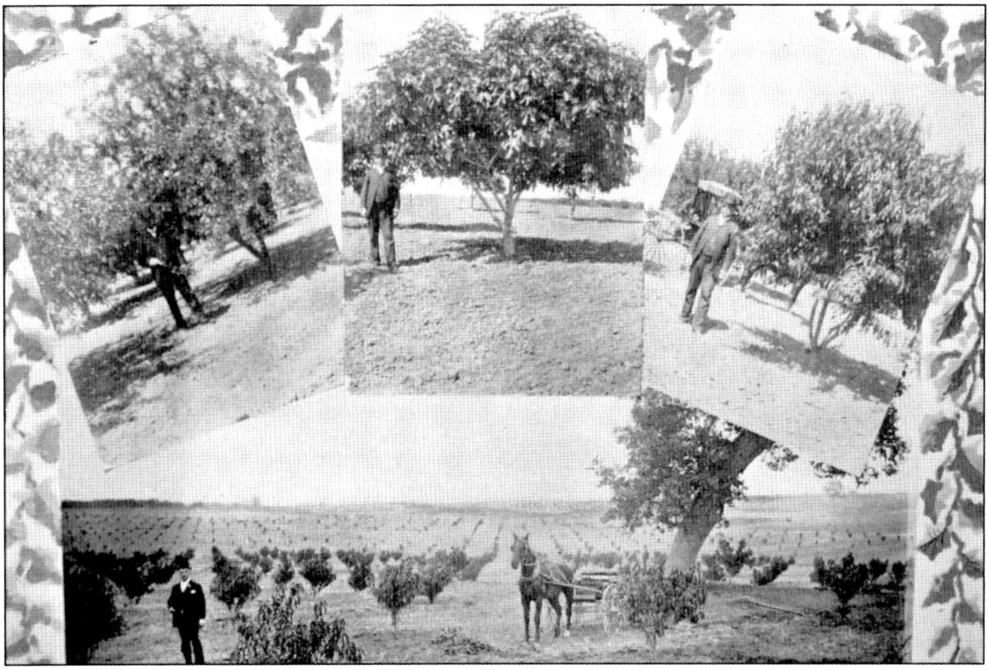

These images, titled "Irrigated and Unirrigated Trees at Orange Vale" (above) and "System of Irrigation at Orange Vale" (below), came from a booster tract by the *Sacramento Bee* in 1894. At the time, because of droughts, irrigation was not only crucial for farming but also for area boosters to advertise. Promoters also touted the success of crops without irrigation. (Source *Sacramento County and its Resources: A Souvenir of the Bee, 1894, Our Capital City, Past and Present*, 28; 29.)

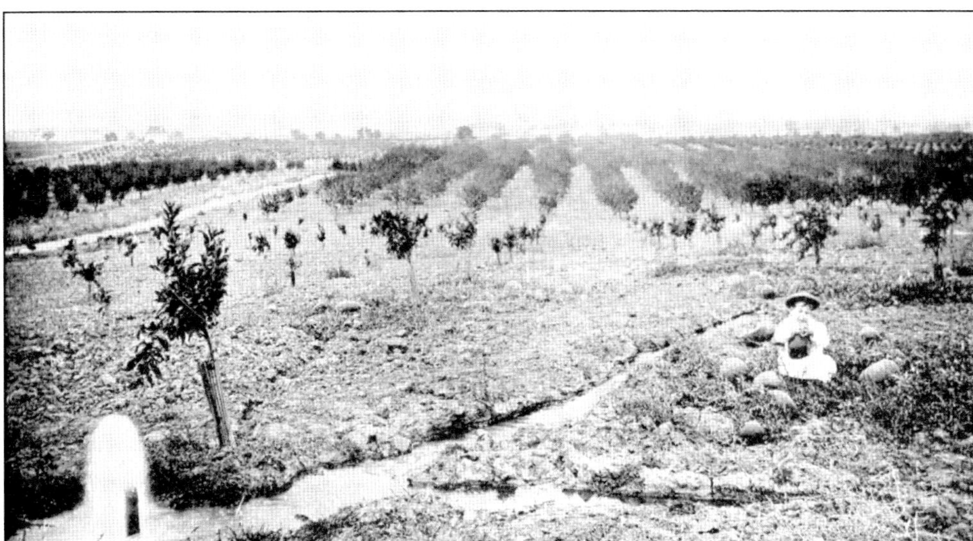

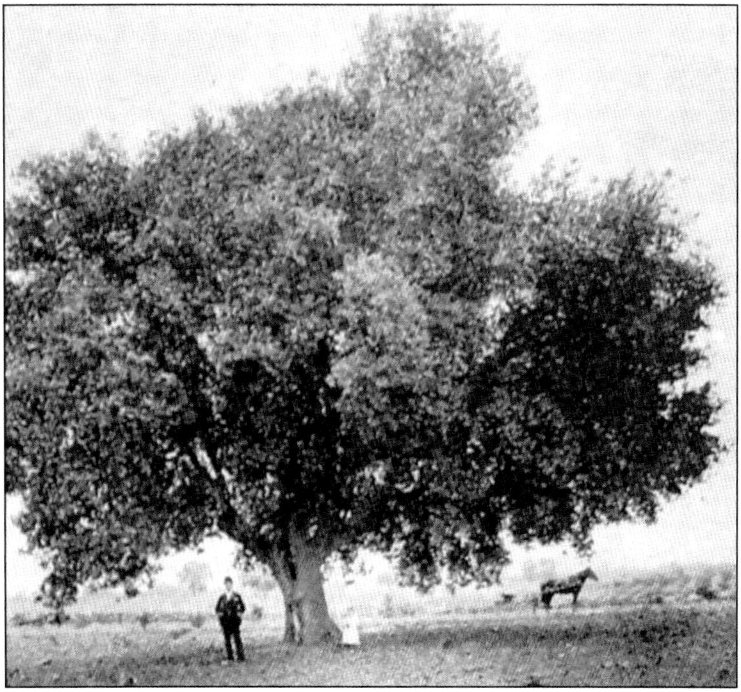

This image, titled "Patriarchal Oak," also came courtesy of the *Sacramento Bee* in 1894. Showing scenes of nature was popular at a time when "back to the land" and "country life" movements swept the nation, promoting the virtues of rural living over the corruption of city life. (Source *Sacramento County and its Resources: A Souvenir of the Bee, 1894, Our Capital City, Past and Present*, 70.)

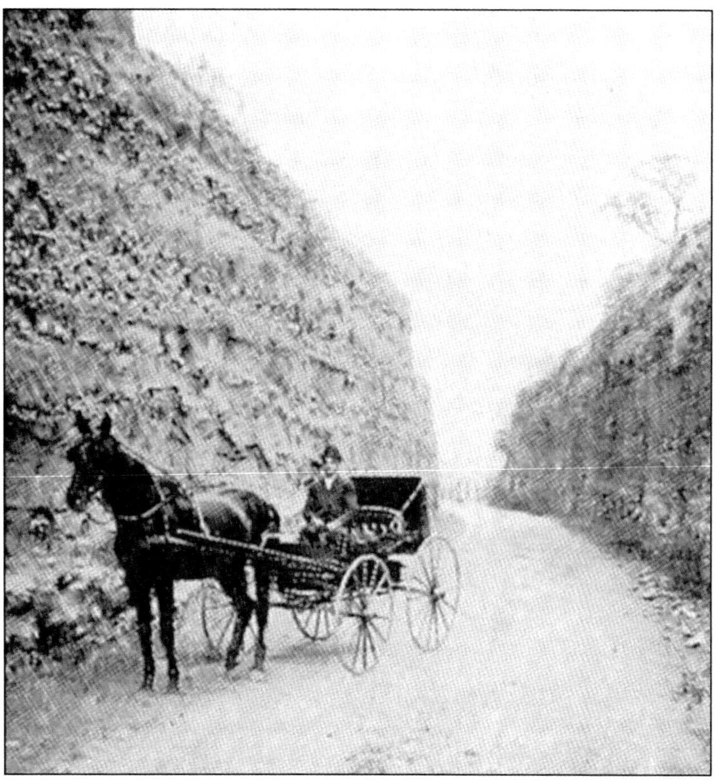

The Lincoln Cut, a cut in the granite of Orangevale's foothills, pictured here c. 1894, served as a route to the Ashland train depot, adjacent to Orangevale. The California Central Railroad, which ran from Ashland to Lincoln, began operation in 1861 and connected to the Sacramento Valley Railroad [Sacramento to Folsom]. After the railroad bridge across the river collapsed in 1867, the line was abandoned. (Source *Sacramento County and its Resources: A Souvenir of the Bee, 1894, Our Capital City, Past and Present*, 70.)

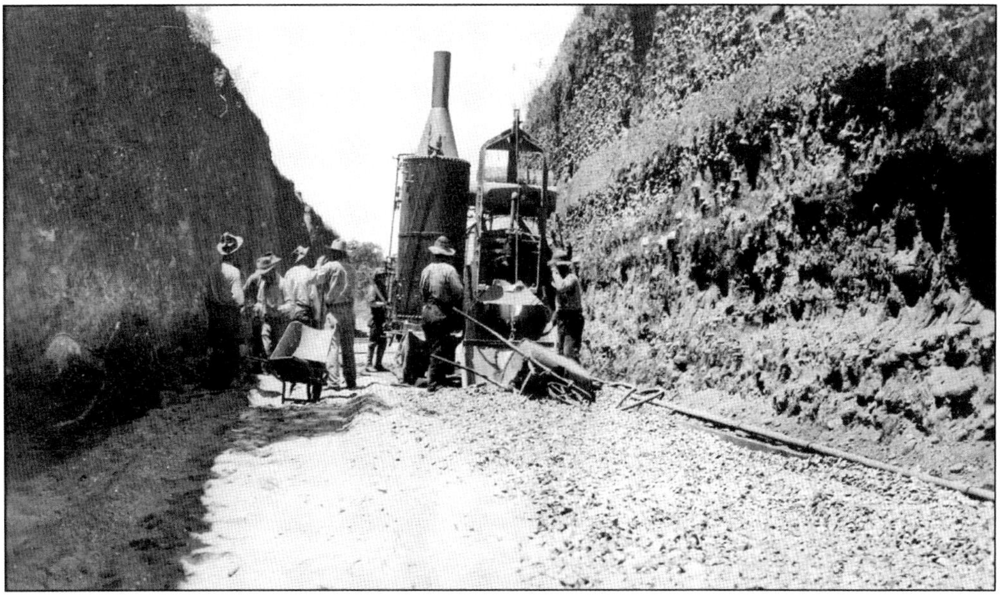

The paving of Greenback Lane, the road along the Lincoln Cut, occurred around 1916. The Lincoln Cut continued to serve the community as it connected Orangevale residents to other bridges over the American River, such as the Rainbow Bridge. Unfortunately, the expansion of Madison Avenue in 1966, which connects with Greenback Lane, destroyed the cut. (Courtesy SAMCC, No. 76/35/279.)

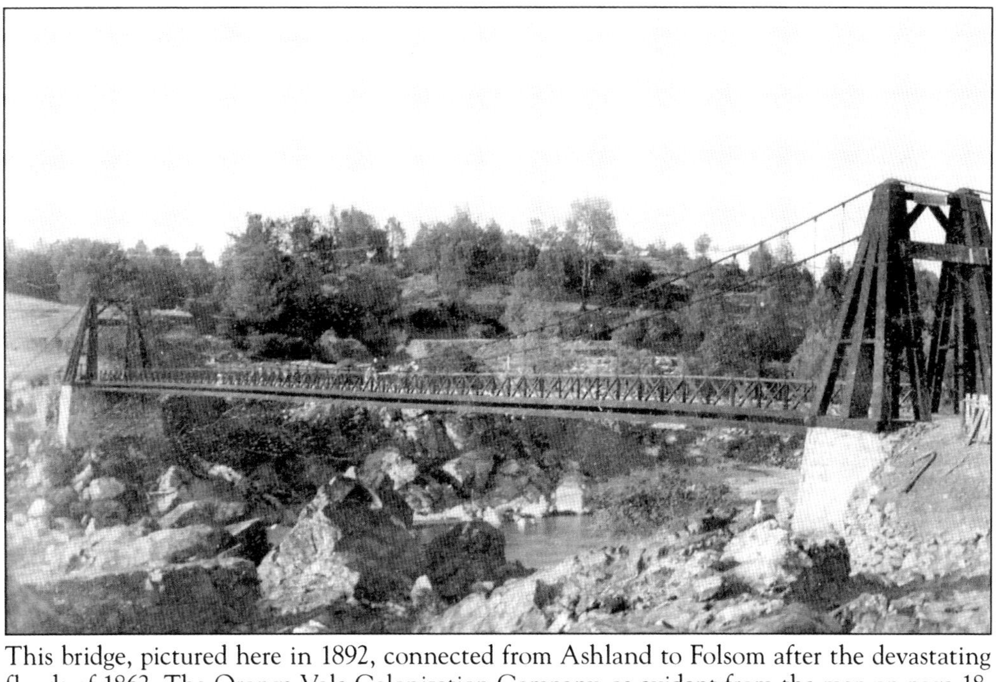

This bridge, pictured here in 1892, connected from Ashland to Folsom after the devastating floods of 1862. The Orange Vale Colonization Company, as evident from the map on page 18, advertised the bridge because it provided access to goods and services in Folsom so desired by early colonists. (Courtesy SAMCC, No. 85/24/5663.)

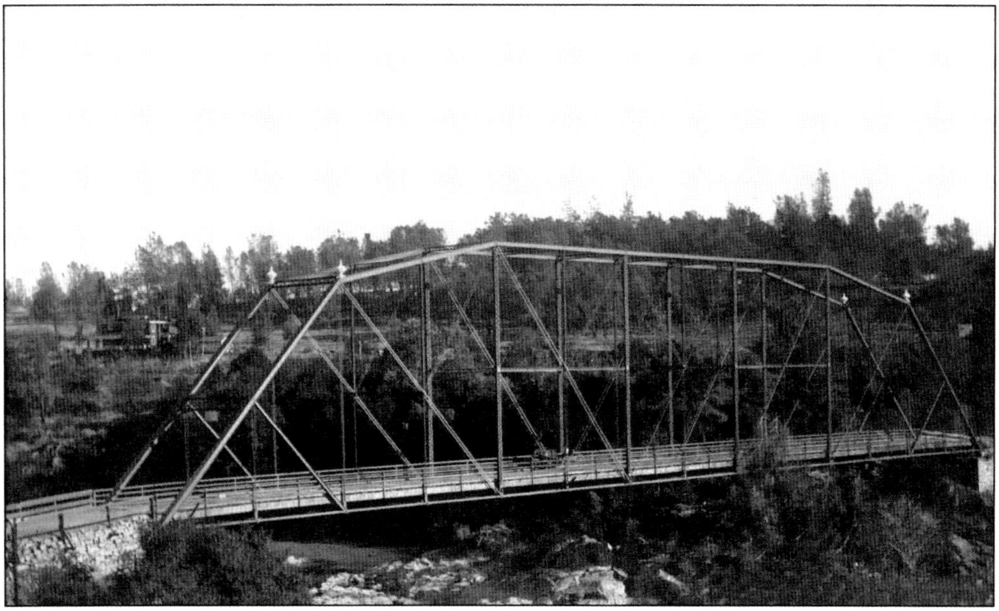

The Orange Vale Colonization Company helped to construct this steel truss bridge across the American River in 1893. The bridge, a Pennsylvania Petit, is the oldest of its type in the state and only one of 10 left. Seen here in 1907, the bridge relocated to Siskiyou County in 1930 after the construction of the Rainbow Bridge and automobile technology bypassed it. The bridge returned home in 1998. (Courtesy Folsom History Museum, No. 2004.05.04.)

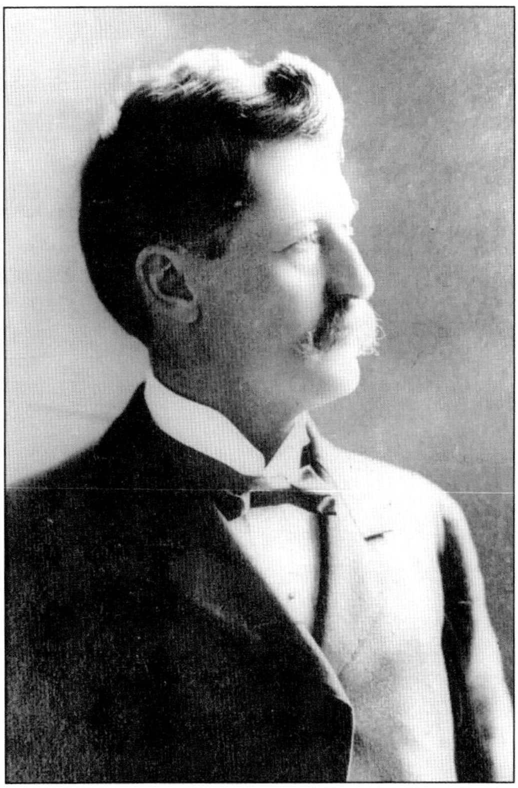

Dr. F. G. Fay, a charter member of the Orangevale Townsite Company, hoped to profit from the sale of land, just as those who ran the Orange Vale Colonization Company had. Formed in 1908, the Townsite company promoted Orangevale with the same vigor and enthusiasm as its predecessor. Unfortunately, because of the prevalent racist attitudes of the time, its advertisement included the claim, "No Japanese. No Chinese." (Courtesy SAMCC, No. 98/12/76.)

Two

TILLING THE SOIL

He intends to plant the entire twenty acres as soon as it can be done, and ultimately to forsake the charms of city life for the more pleasant paths of the successful horticulturist.

—"Orange Vale: Making Rapid Progress," *Folsom Telegraph*, February 18, 1893

Cultivating the land dominated life in Orangevale well before its formal establishment. Numerous small farmers, such as the Heintz family in Fair Oaks and others in modern-day Orangevale, Citrus Heights, and Carmichael, started farms and ranches years before these communities were organized. The Orange Vale Colonization Company used California's agricultural image and the promise of horticultural success to promote the pastoral suburb.

Some of the earliest settlers included the Greenhalgh, Landis, Wahrhaftig, and Wickstrom families. These families often built their own packinghouses, hired local workers—particularly women and Chinese—and sold their produce privately, or contracted with larger companies, such as the Earl Fruit Company. Farmers in Orangevale, like many others throughout the nation, also banded together to form mutual-aid cooperatives that shared labor, equipment, and pooled savings. They formed a grange in 1910 and a fruit-growers exchange in 1914 to aid in the promotion and development of their orchards and crops.

Orangevale had 3,200 acres irrigated by 1913, and by 1915, the community had 2,000 acres in orange trees. Orangevale eventually succeeded in becoming one of the leading producers of oranges, reaching its peak in 1925. Nevertheless, while agricultural production climaxed in Orangevale, other forces began to tear down the community's recently acquired success. A law passed in the 1920s that specified that marketable oranges had to have a six-to-one ratio of solids to acids, a condition Orangevale's produce usually did not reach until mid-December or January, cost growers the high prices of the holiday market and a possible six-week advantage over Southern California. Likewise, by the late 1920s, consumer demand shifted toward orange juice, which placed a greater premium on oranges grown in Southern California and Florida over those cultivated in the Sacramento Valley. As if none of this had been enough, Mother Nature delivered an essentially fatal blow in the Great Depression, when temperatures dropped to around 17 degrees during the winter of 1932, killing most of the trees. Many growers were unenthusiastic about replanting because of the unforgiving economy and fickle consumer tastes. Orangevale's orange acreage, once at 2,000, dropped drastically to 879 in 1935 and then to 473 in 1940.

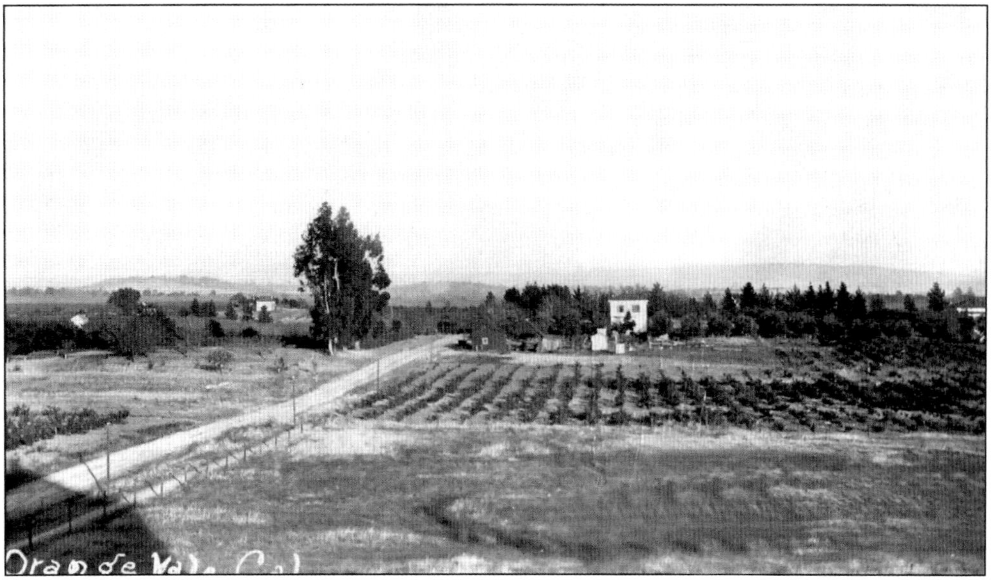

This panorama of Orangevale, taken sometime in the 1890s or early 1900s from the upstairs of the Orangevale School on Filbert Avenue looking east down Central Avenue, shows the vast acres of beautiful orchards in Orangevale at the turn of the 20th century. (Courtesy Tom Tomich.)

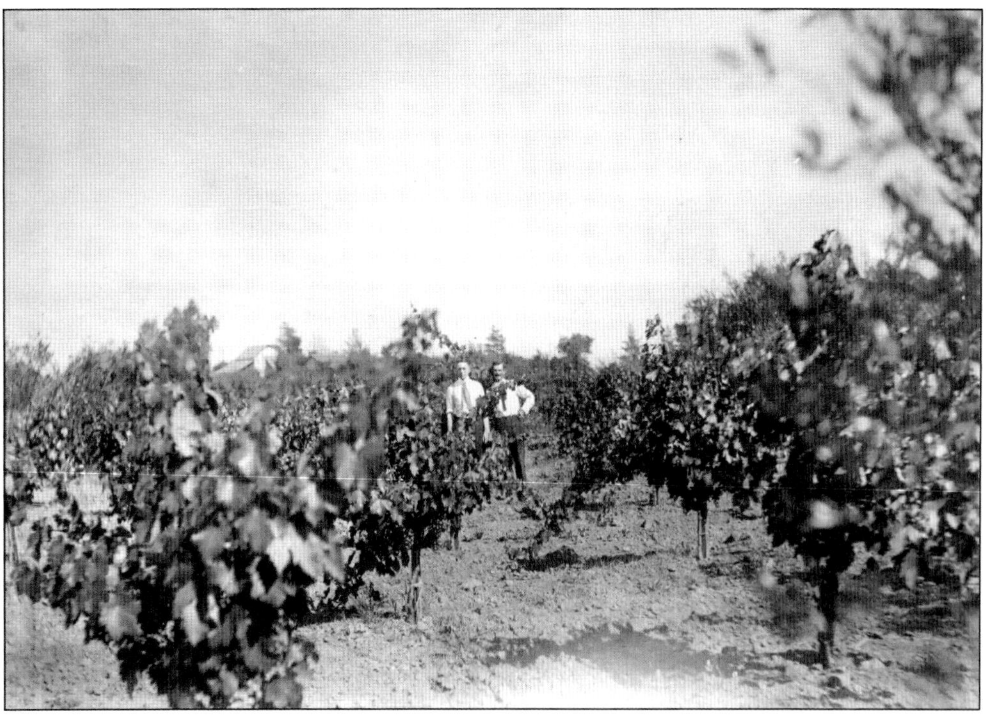

Prosper Tomich (right) is seen here in his vast orchard off Chestnut Avenue around 1915. The Tomich Orchard is still operated by family members after more than 100 years. (Courtesy Fred Tomich.)

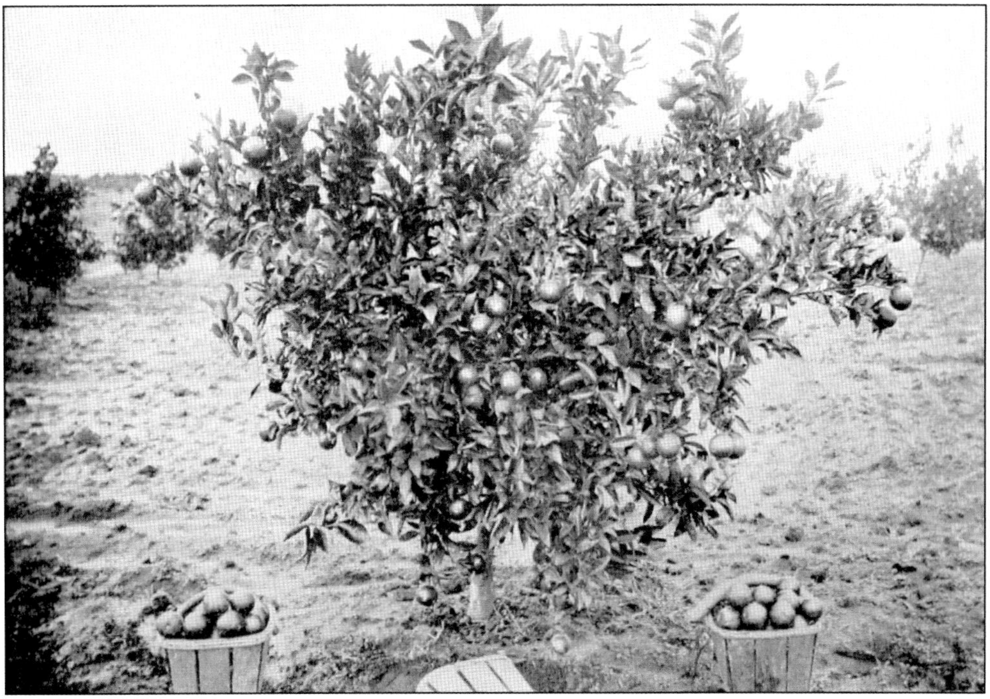

Sacramento County won several prizes for its fruits in 1894, including those produced by this orange tree from Orangevale. Titled, "A Midwinter Fair Prize Winner, Four-year-old Orange Tree—'Hart's Tardiff.'—Orange Vale," this image appeared in an 1894 publication of the *Sacramento Bee* that boasted of the fertile soil in Orangevale. (Source *Sacramento County and its Resources: A Souvenir of the Bee, 1894, Our Capital City, Past and Present*, 24.)

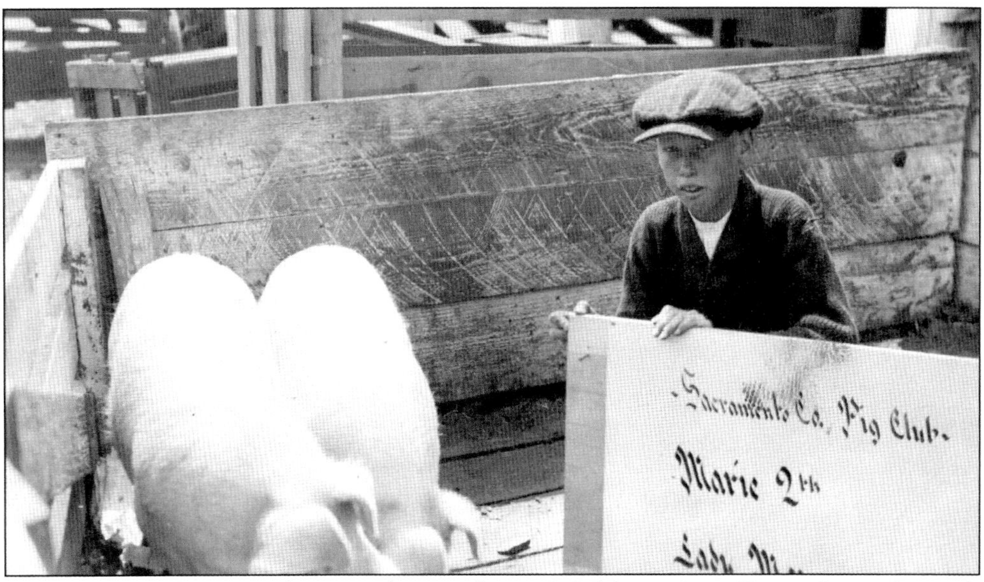

Louie Howard of Orangevale is seen here at the 1920 California State Fair in September with his prize-winning Chester White gilts, "Marie 2th" and "Lady May." (Gilts are young swine.) Ranching, along with farming, was a way of life for many in Orangevale's earlier years. (Courtesy SAMCC, No. 80/02/284a.)

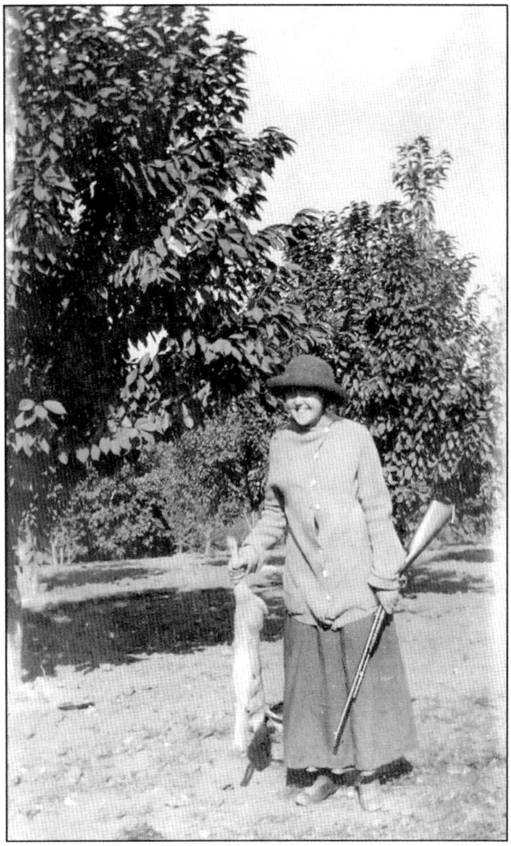

Many Orangevale residents hunted the local wildlife, which included opossums, coyotes, and jackrabbits. Indeed, hunting proved a critical part of protecting crops and livestock. Ellen Wickstrom displays the outcome of her hunt, a jackrabbit, around 1915. (Courtesy Tom Tomich.)

The San Juan High School agricultural class, which included many students from Orangevale, is seen here judging dairy cattle in the 1920s at the University State Farm (later the University of California, Davis), which Orangevale Townsite Company cofounder Peter J. Shields helped establish. (Courtesy SAMCC, No. 80/02/292.)

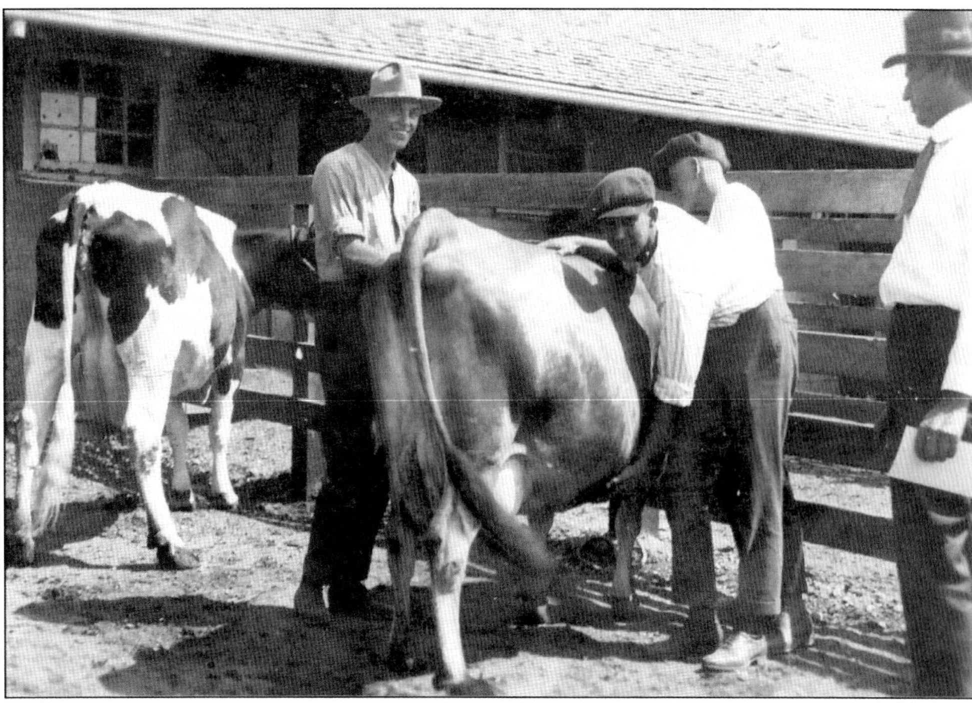

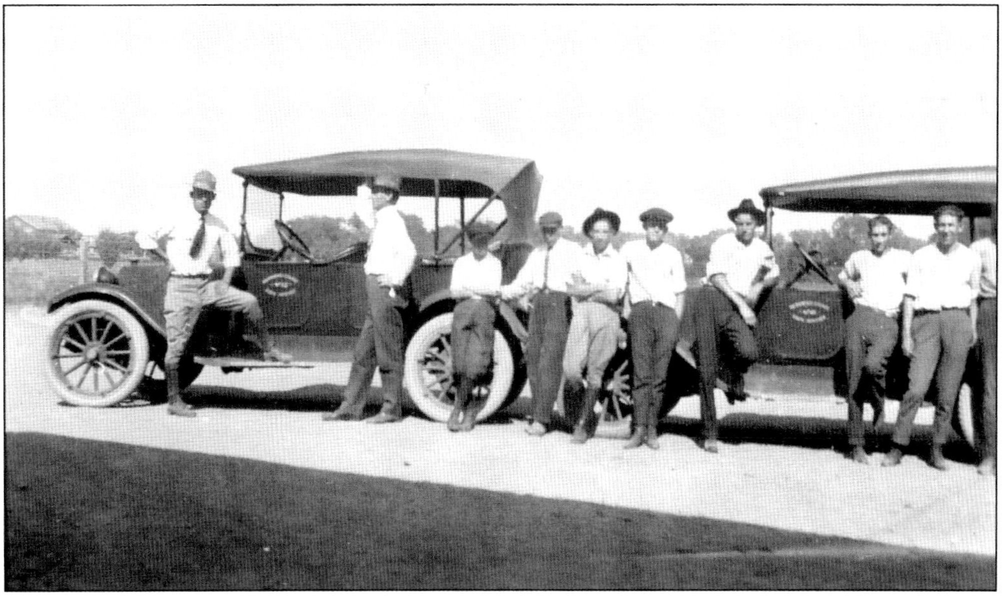

Students from the San Juan High School agricultural class are seen here in the 1920s taking time out from a class at the University State Farm to pose for the camera. (Courtesy SAMCC, No. 80/02/297.)

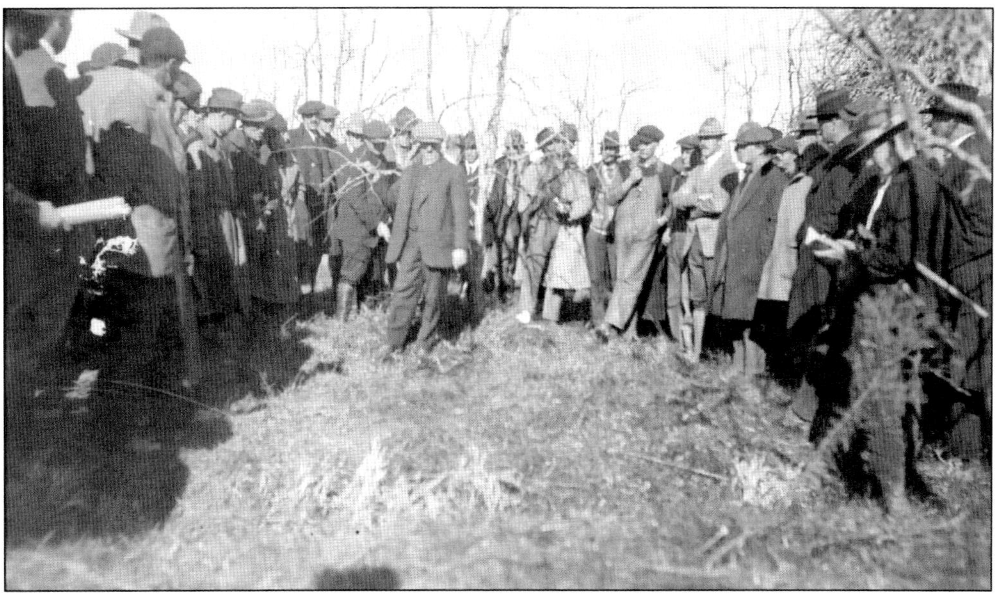

A group of men, pictured here on February 7, 1921, surround a pear tree while members of the Orangevale Farm Bureau discuss methods used in the production of pears. (Courtesy SAMCC, No. 80/02/548.)

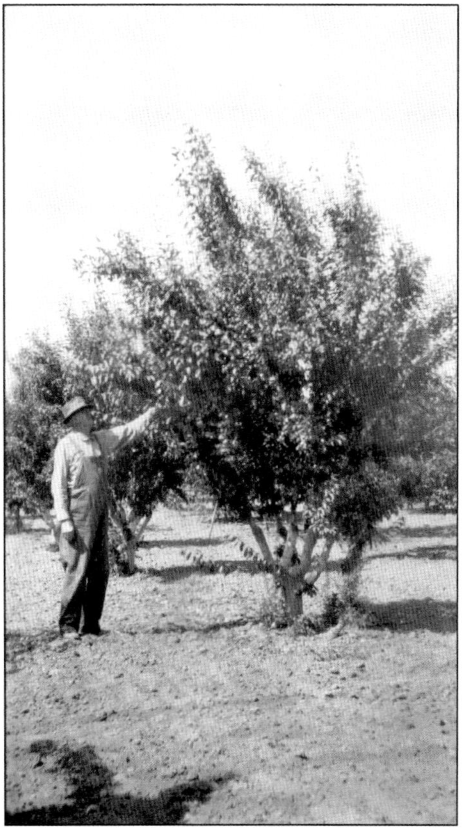

Farmers in Orangevale grew a variety of fruits and nuts (primarily drupes) and not just oranges, as Mr. Thompson of Orangevale, seen here inspecting his plum tree c. 1925, demonstrates. (Courtesy SAMCC, No. 80/02/2247.)

"M. D. Brandon's Hay Bailer" is seen here in Orangevale, as workers loading hay pause to pose for the camera sometime in the 1890s or early 1900s. (Courtesy Folsom History Museum, No. 2004.04.02.)

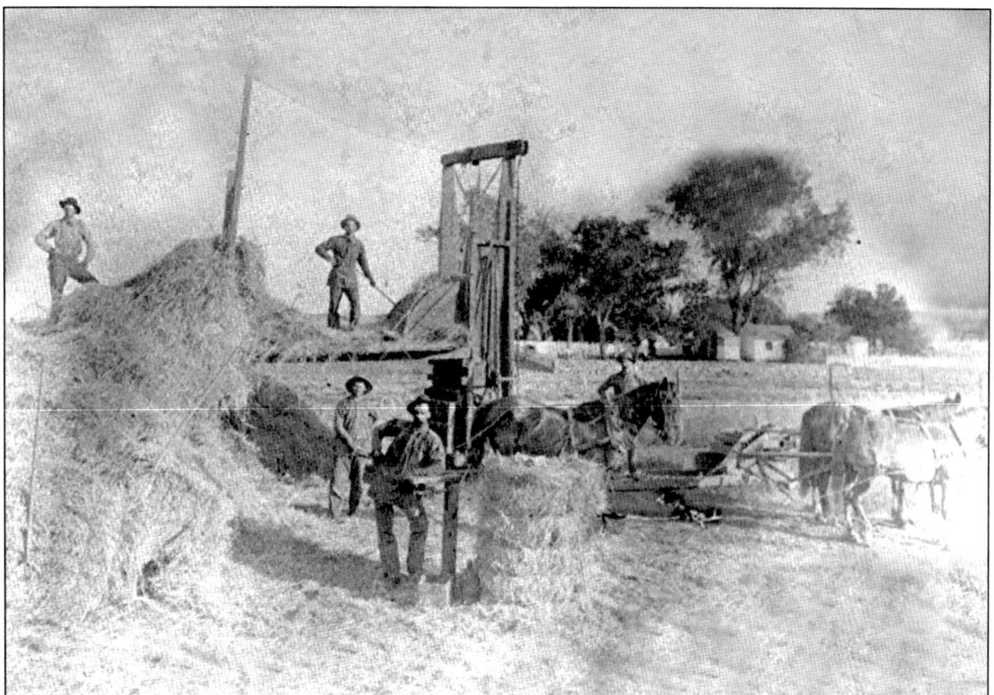

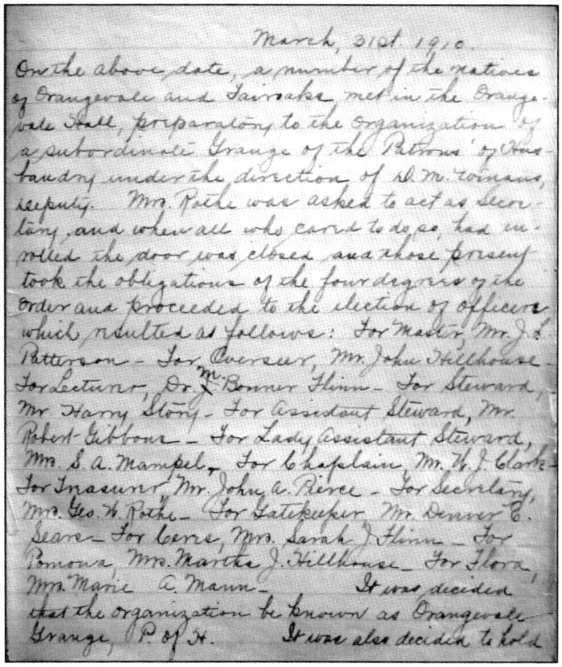
March, 31st. 1910.
On the above date, a number of the natives of Orangevale and Fairoaks met in the Orangevale Hall, preparatory to the organization of a subordinate Grange of the Patrons of Husbandry under the direction of D. M. Romans, deputy. Mrs. Rothe was asked to act as Secretary, and when all who cared to do so, had enrolled the door was closed, and those present took the obligations of the four degrees of the order and proceeded to the election of officers which resulted as follows: For Master, Mr. J. L. Patterson - For Overseer, Mr. John Hillhouse - For Lecturer, Dr. McBonner Flinn - For Steward, Mr. Harry Story - For Assistant Steward, Mr. Robert Gibbons - For Lady Assistant Steward, Mrs. S. A. Mampel, For Chaplain, Mr. W. J. Clark - For Treasurer, Mr. John A. Pierce - For Secretary, Mrs. Geo. W. Rothe - For Gatekeeper, Mr. Denver E. Sears - For Ceres, Mrs. Sarah J. Flinn - For Pomona, Mrs. Martha J. Hillhouse - For Flora, Mrs. Marie A. Mann - It was decided that the organization be known as Orangevale Grange, P. of H. It was also decided to hold

On March 31, 1910, residents from Orangevale and Fair Oaks met for the first time to establish the Orangevale Grange No. 354 and elect officers. The grange movement, which began in 1868, sought to aid agricultural communities with a variety of services. The minutes of the first Orangevale Grange meeting (above) listed the new officers, including J. L. Patterson (below) who served as the first grange master (1910–1911). (Courtesy Orangevale Grange.)

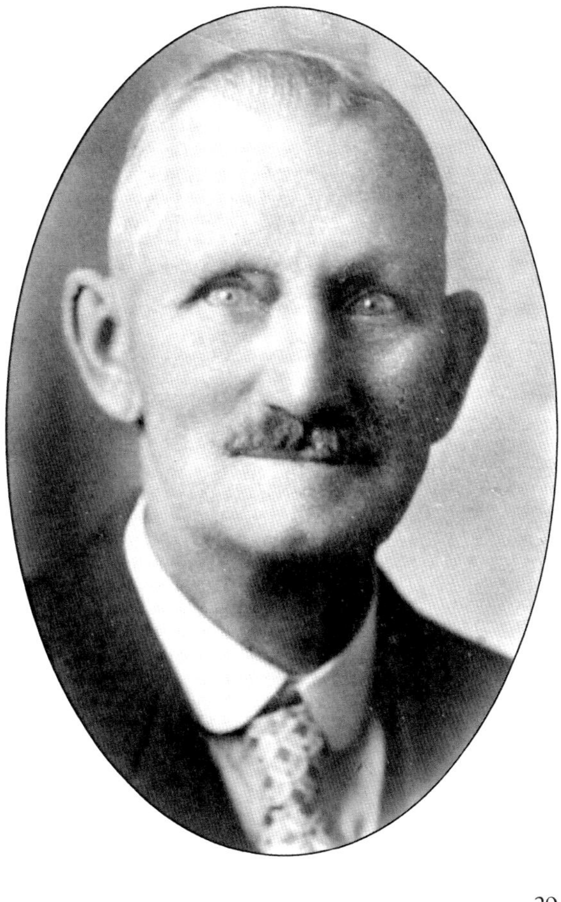

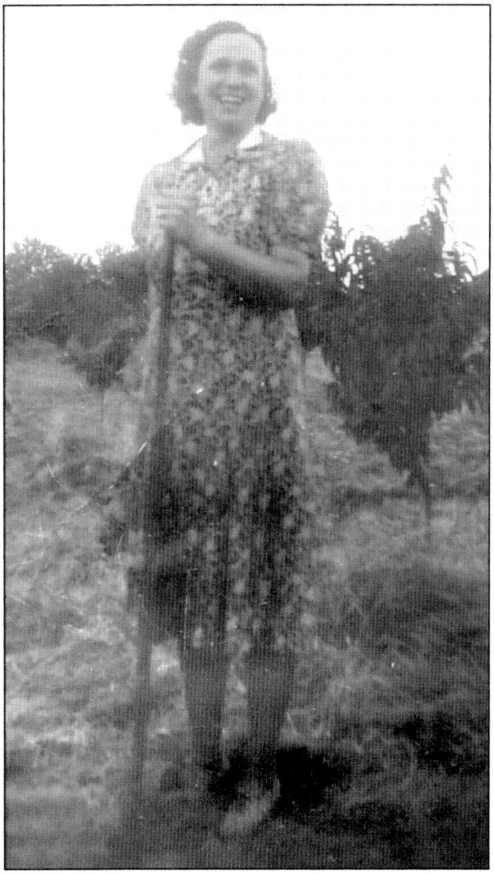

Women have been very active throughout the history of the Orangevale Grange, as Louisa Pippett, a lecturer at the grange, demonstrates in 1945. (Courtesy Orangevale Grange.)

Many women, such as Frances Tomich, pictured here inside the Wickstrom Packing House, worked for packinghouses in and around Orangevale. In addition, Orangevale, for a time, emerged as the leader in Tokay grape production, seen here sometime in the 1920s or 1930s. (Courtesy Fred Tomich.)

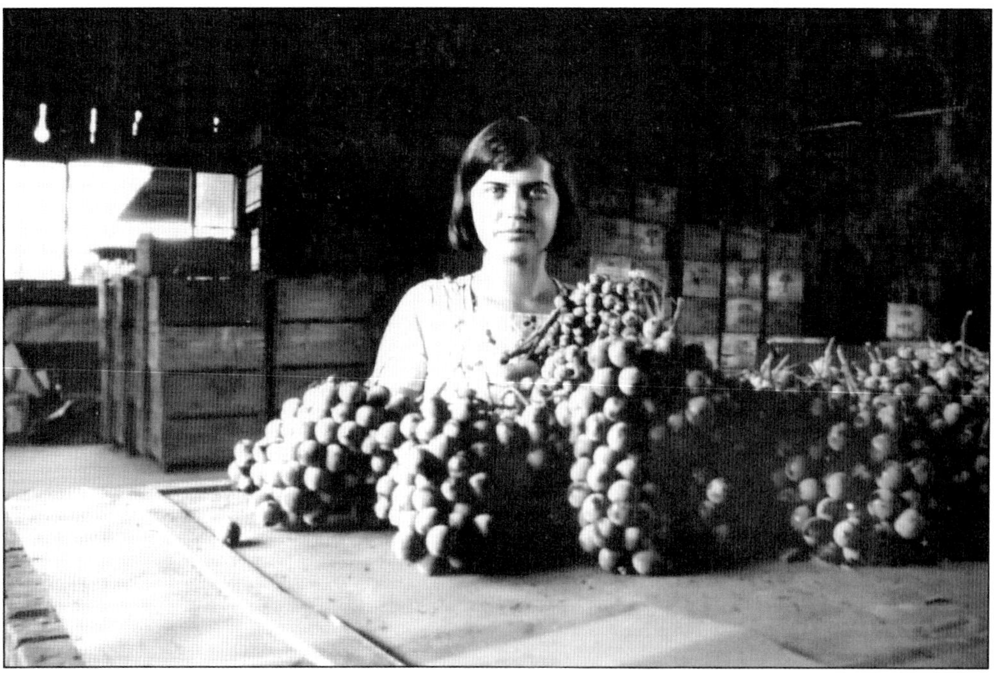

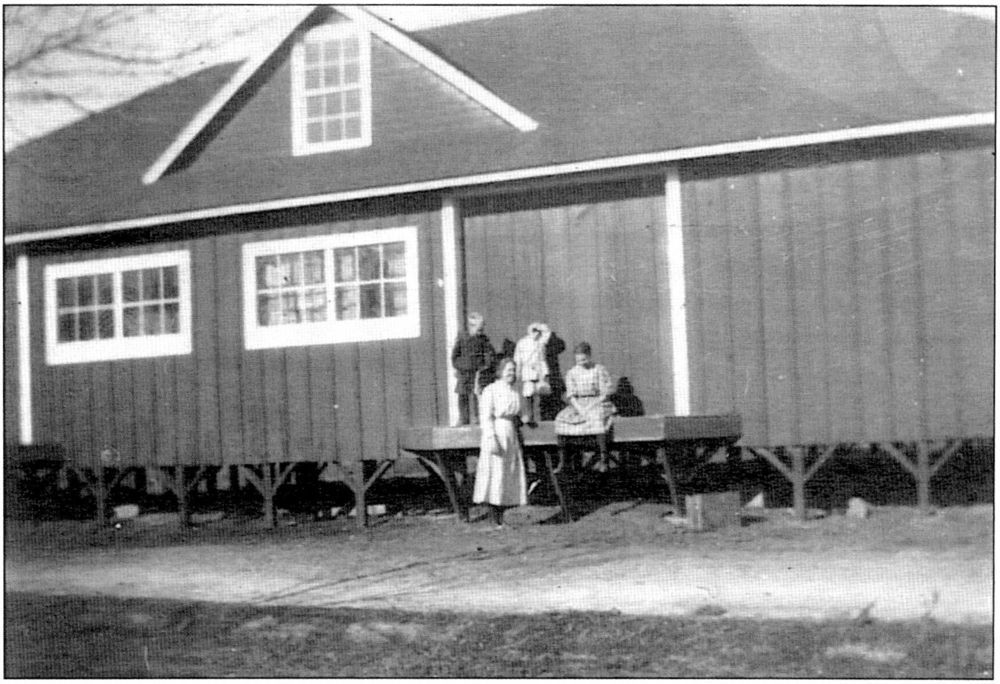

Many families in Orangevale, such as the Wickstrom and Calder families, established their own packinghouses. Hannah Wickstrom and her children (above) are seen here around 1904–1905 outside the family's packinghouse, located 125 yards east of the family's home on Pecan Avenue. Employees or visitors are seen resting in front of Calders Packing House (below) off Greenback Lane sometime in the 1890s or 1900s. (Courtesy Tom Tomich.)

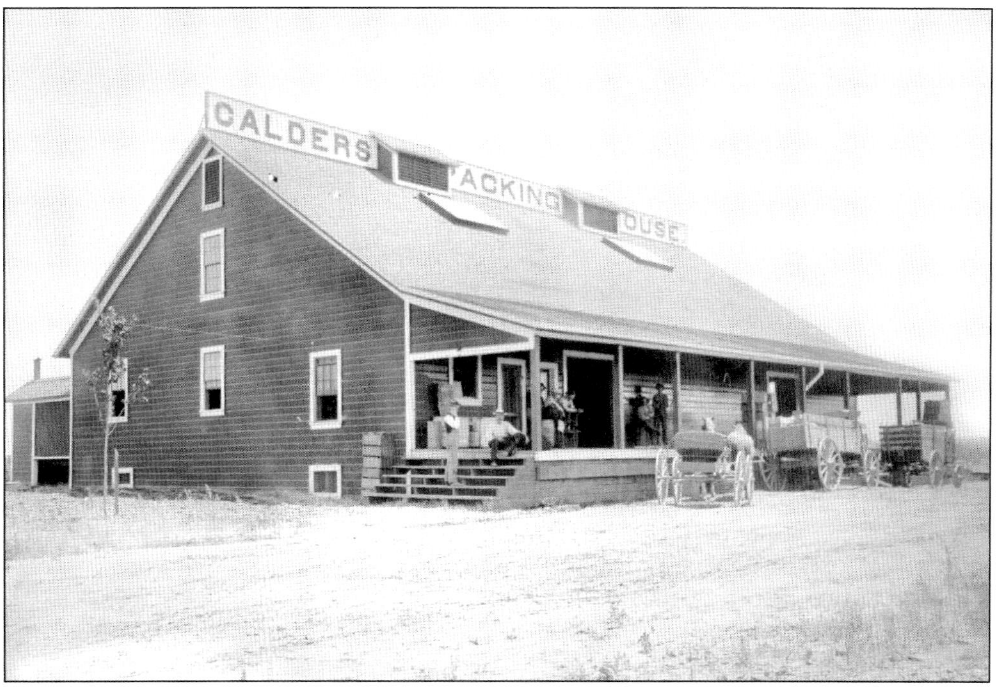

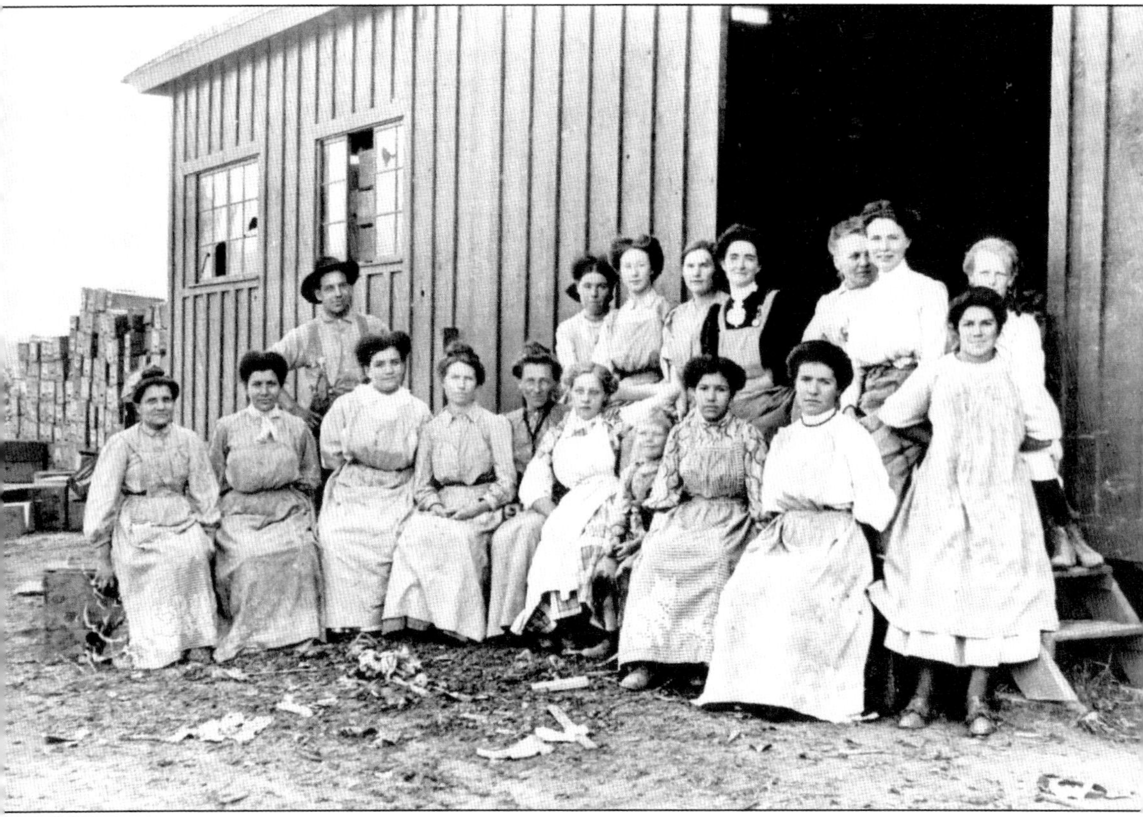

Packinghouse employees in Orangevale were often women from the Sierra foothills. Pictured here *c.* 1915 of those identified on the back of the original photograph (but it does not indicate exactly who is who) include Isabel Relvas, Isabel (Birdie) Brum, Louisa Mendes, and Minnie Relvas. (Courtesy SAMCC, No. 84/181/154.)

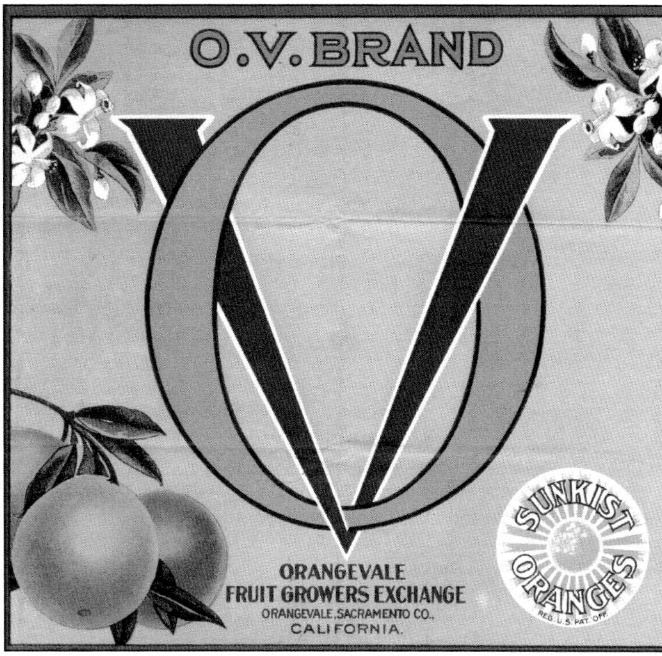

These rare images of Orangevale Fruit Growers Exchange labels show that farmers in Orangevale often contracted with larger corporations, such as Red Ball and Sunkist. The labels are in a starburst pattern, dating them sometime before 1918, and were most likely printed by the Schmidt Lithograph Company in San Francisco. Both labels are stone lithographs, meaning they were printed from big Bavarian limestone blocks. (Orangevale Fruit Growers Exchange, *O.V.*, Box 15:64 (above) and Orangevale Fruit Growers Exchange, *Two Stars*, Box 15:63 (below), in the Lugg Label Collection, 1890-1940, D-211, courtesy of Special Collections, University of California Library, Davis.)

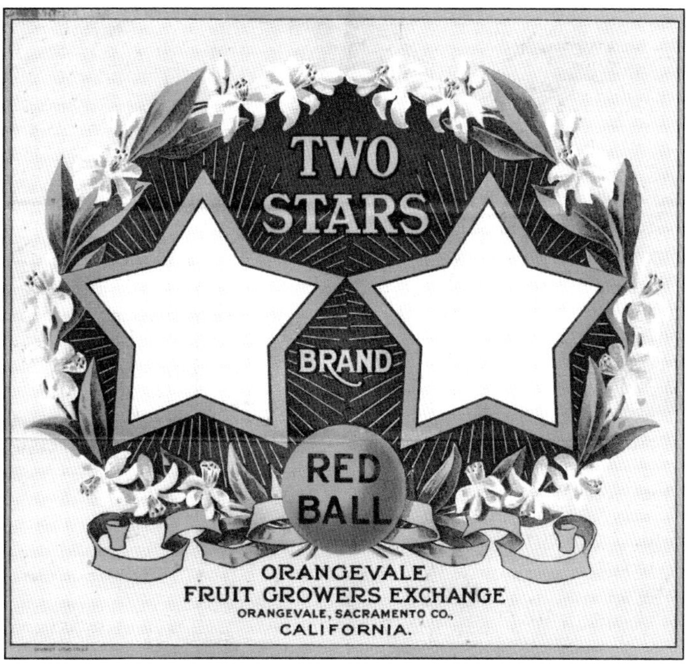

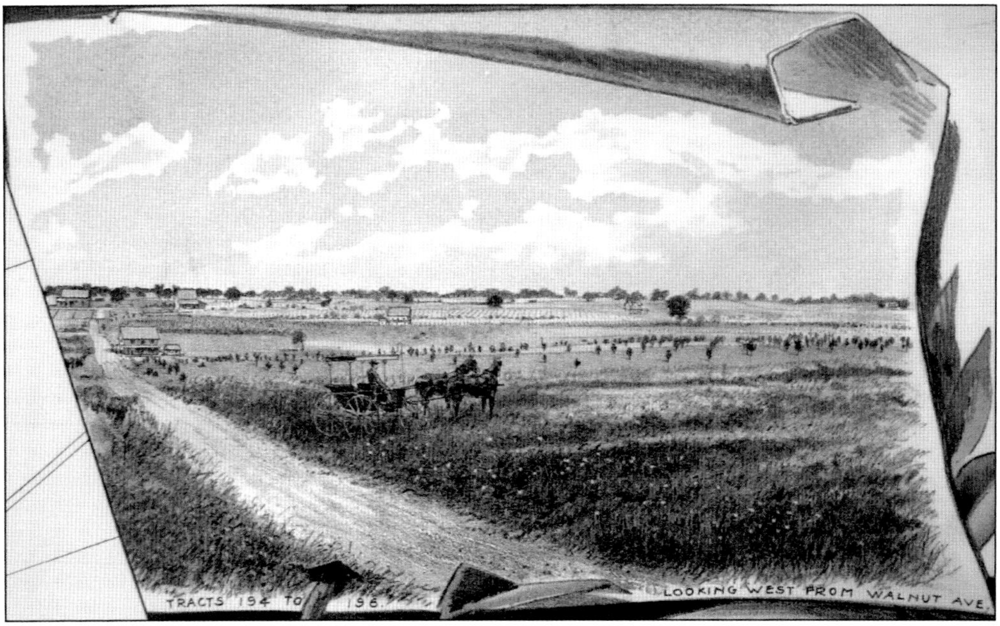

A close-up of a drawing on an 1890s map of Orangevale (above), which shows the dirt road of Walnut Avenue, a horse and buggy, and vast open land, stands in stark contrast to photograph (below) of the paved road of Pardillo Avenue in 1961 as John Lammerding poses next to his car among the large almond trees. (Above courtesy SAMCC, No. 2002/092/00; below courtesy Gerald Lammerding.)

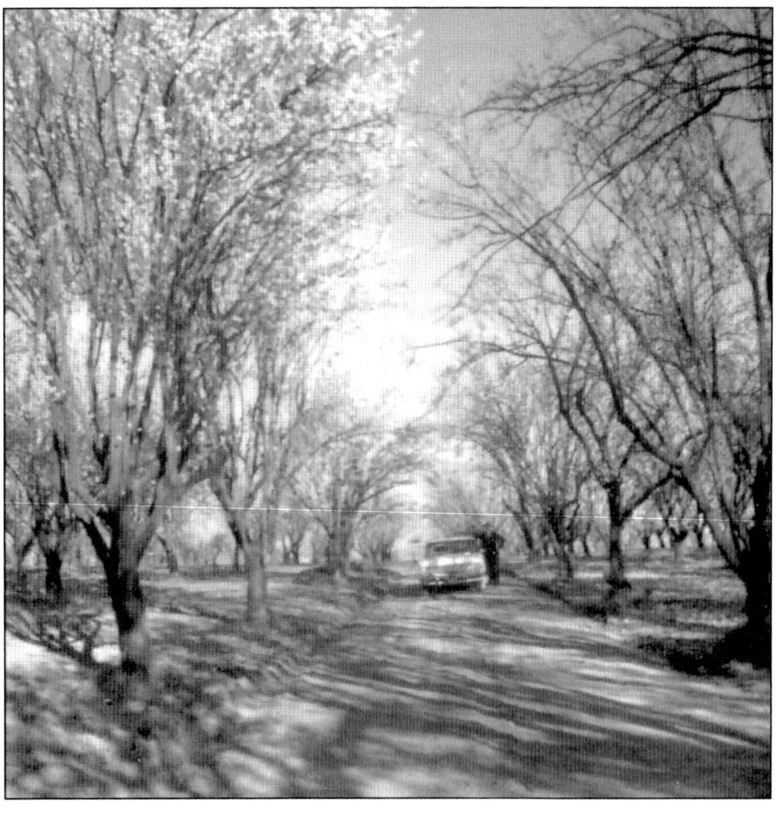

Three

A Place to Hang Your Hat

Be it ever so humble, there's no place like home.

—John Howard Payne, *Clari, the Maid of Milan*, 1823

In the early 20th century, "the single family house," asserts architectural historian Dr. Dennis Doordan, "had become the architectural embodiment of the middle-class ideal for domestic life in Western culture." Architecture is a vehicle through which personal identity is established and fruits of labor are exhibited. Shaped by geographic conditions, social trends, and personal taste, residential architecture defines the various periods of construction style in a community. In Orangevale, early "country" cottages, ranch-style houses typical of the 1950s and 1960s, and modern tract homes dot the area, revealing the community's architectural history.

The *Sacramento Bee*, in their 1894 publication *Sacramento County and its Resources: A Souvenir of the Bee*, described the endeavor of the Orange Vale Colonization Company "as a practical demonstration of the fact that an extensive acreage is no longer necessary to support an average family, and that with the ordinary conveniences provided, and land well selected, a comfortable home and living can be made upon a ten or twenty acre piece of land. . . . The primary object was to prepare the way and provide homes for the better class of colonists, who were invited to build their homes among our people, and thereby add to the material prosperity of the locality." The idea of property ownership and building one's own house were used repeatedly as a selling point throughout Orangevale booster literature. Frequently referring to houses as "cottage homes," "happy homes," or "self-supporting small homes," promoters extended the imagery of successful property ownership to home building. The *Sacramento Bee* stated, "Everything in and around the colony has this end in view: the upbuilding and the prosperity of the small homes."

A dozen houses were erected and occupied in Orangevale in 1894. The Orange Vale Colonization Company's annual report showed that the houses had been built by company contractors by 1899, costing $1,500 each. The Orangevale Townsite Company formed in 1908 after the dissolution of the Orange Vale Colonization Company about a decade earlier. The director, B. F. Hulings, highlighted Orangevale homes in his 1909 booster publication, *Sacramento Valley Sunbeam: Devoted to the Interests of the Ideal Country Homes*, and declared, "Every large American city has a suburb—a place for country homes. We haven't any in Sacramento. . . . We must have a place for country homes, and no more beautiful spot can be found than in Orangevale."

By the year 2000, Orangevale had more than 10,000 housing units. The purpose of these residences remains generally the same: to display property ownership, give shelter, establish identity, and provide a gathering place.

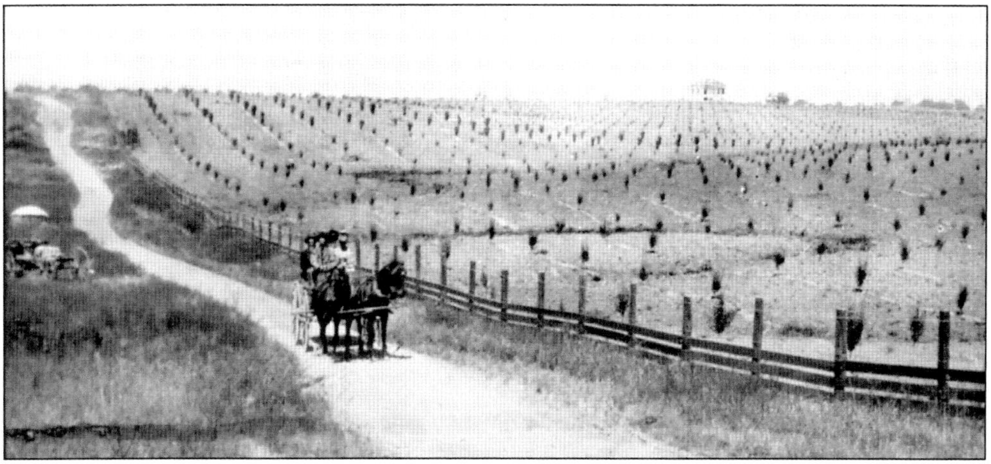

While picturesque scenes, such as this 1885 photograph of a newly planted citrus orchard, have given way to "progress," many farmhouses and cottages still stand throughout Orangevale, reminding all of a bygone era. (Courtesy SAMCC, No. 82/05/5604.)

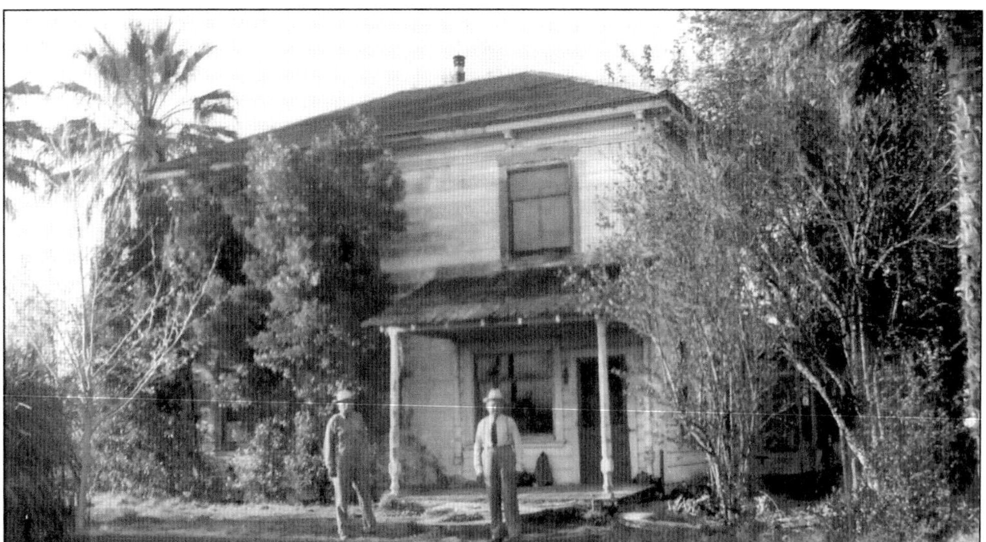

Leonidas H. and Lovicy Landis and family arrived in 1889, when only two other permanent families resided in Orangevale—the Carmichaels and Thompsons. Sons Anthony and Harry Landis are pictured in front of their family home, which no longer stands, at the corner of Central and Pecan in 1941. (Courtesy SAMCCs, No. 85/24/5756.)

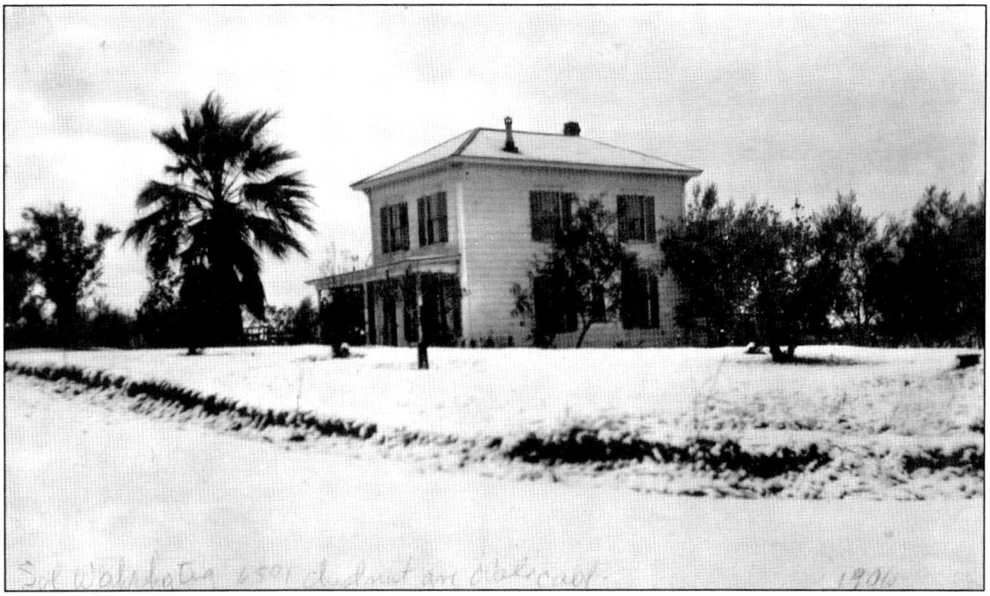

In 1888, the Orange Vale Colonization Company built this house, pictured here in 1906, to serve as the company's headquarters. Peter Wahrhaftig purchased the house in 1896 and moved it across the street to his property at the southwest corner of Central and Chestnut Avenues. (Courtesy Tom Tomich.)

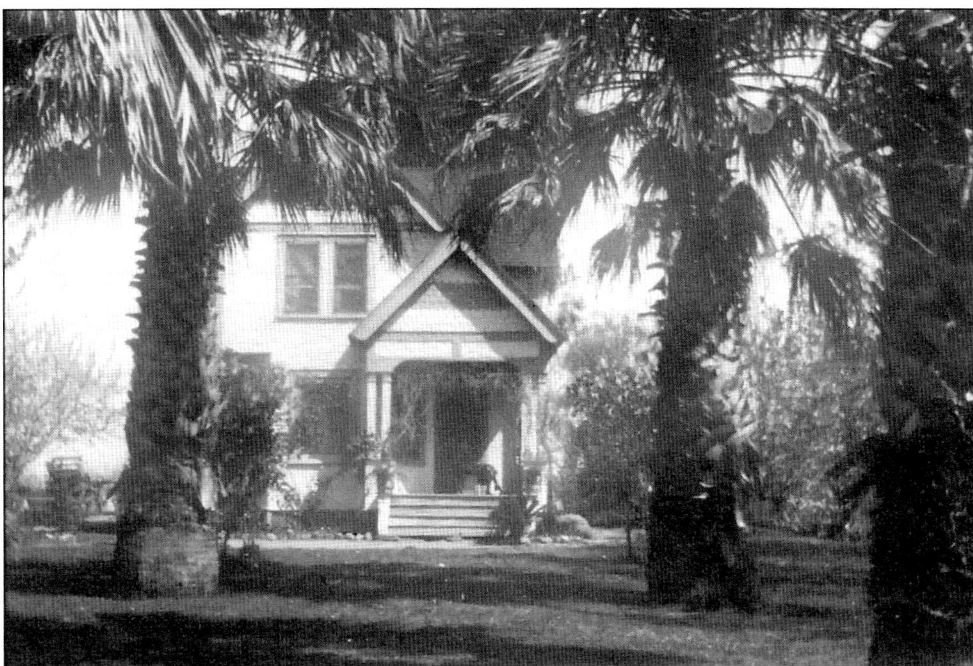

Albert and Hannah Wickstrom built this residence, pictured here in the 1910s, with California Redwood in 1903–1904. The 1910 census shows 11 people living in this household: Albert and Hannah, their children—Eleanor, 20; Ruth, 17; Ellen, 15; Agnes, 13; Aida, 10; Albert, 7; and Arthur, 5—and two laborers. (Courtesy Tom Tomich.)

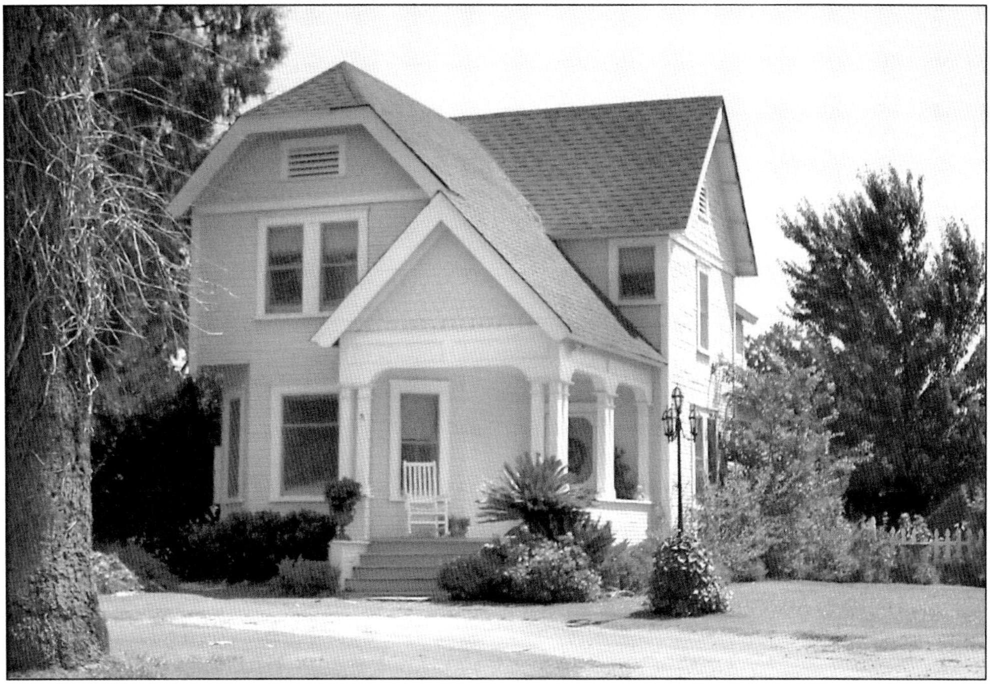

The Wickstrom house still stands on Pecan Avenue near Greenback Lane. Even today, this residence, with simplified form and detailing reminiscent of the Victorian era, is perfectly framed by four grand palm trees. (Courtesy Paul J. P. Sandul.)

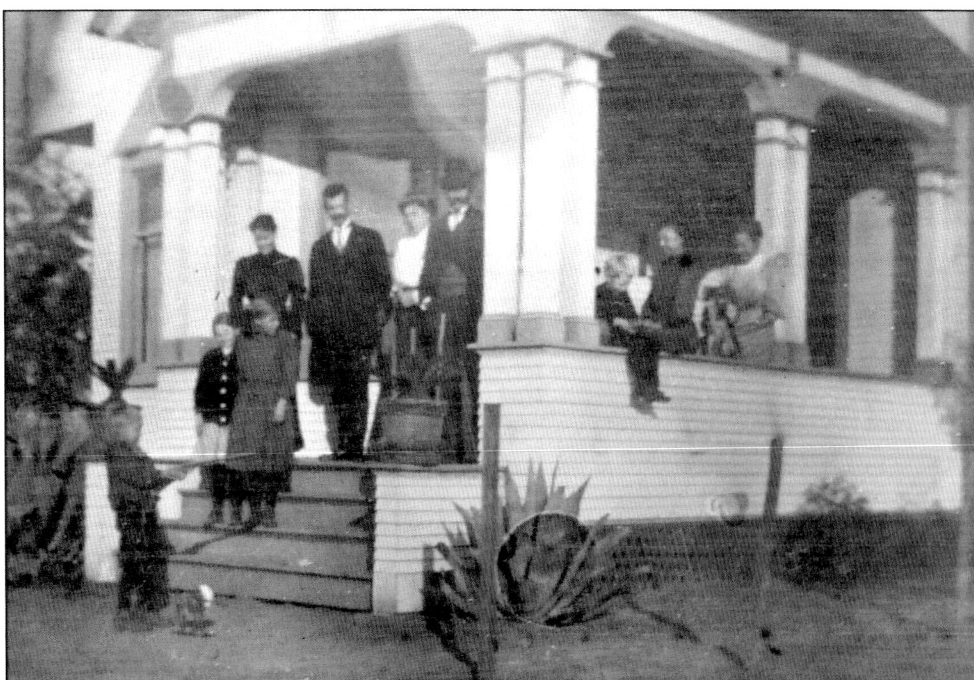

This photograph shows family gathered on the large front porch of the Wickstrom home in the 1910s or early 1920s. (Courtesy Fred Tomich.)

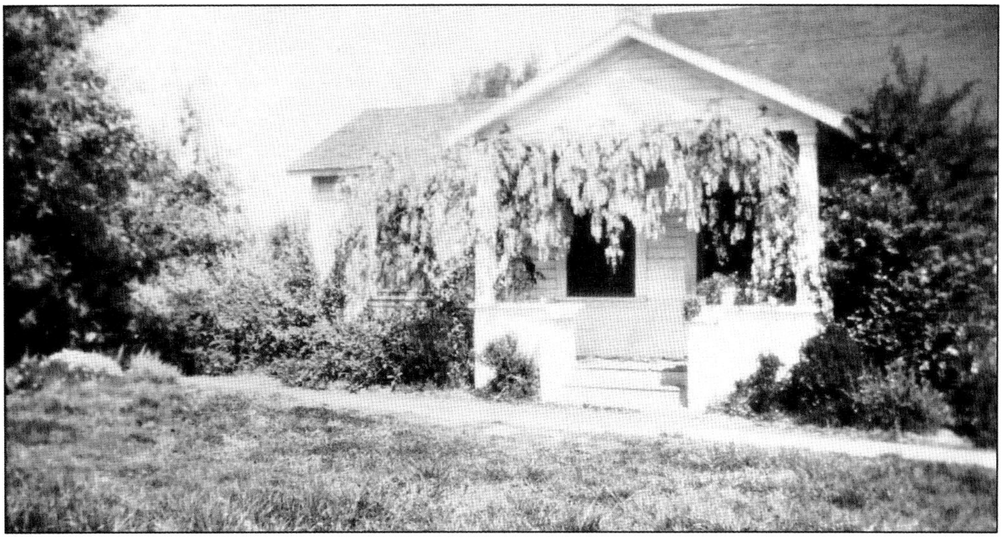

This bungalow, built in 1911 on Chestnut Avenue as the home of Prosper and Eleanor (Wickstrom) Tomich, stands at the entrance to the SilverGreen Farm (originally the Silvergreen Home Dairy). This picture is believed to have been taken in the 1910s or 1920s. Frederick Tomich, born in 1922, chose to remain at his birthplace to run the farm until his passing in the summer of 2006. Tomich served as a board member of the Orange Vale Water Company for 54 years. (Courtesy Fred Tomich.)

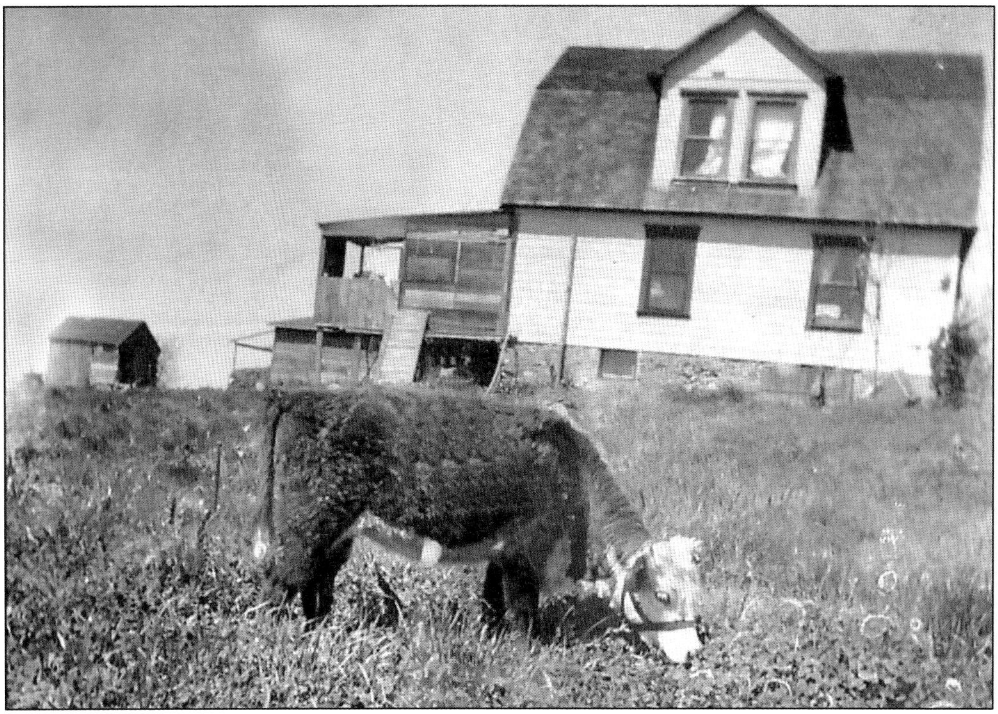

This cow roams freely in front of the farmhouse of John E. (born in Maine) and Resina Johnson (born in Sweden) on Pecan Avenue. The Johnsons, parents of Ida Odlin, moved to Orangevale from Minnesota in 1904. Pecan Park now exists where this house, pictured here in the early 20th century, once stood. (Courtesy Jean Kelly.)

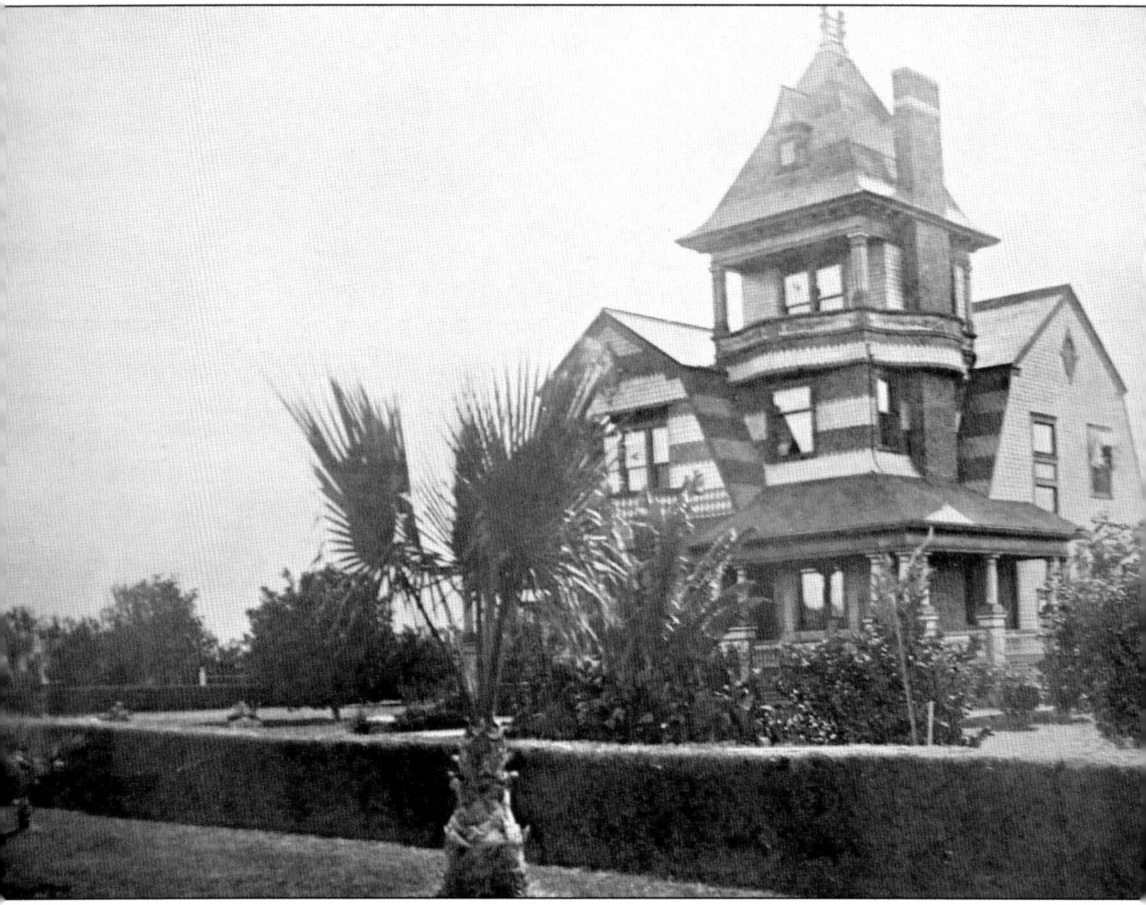

Shakespearean actor William Calder built this impressive Victorian-era house with a prominent three-story Queen Anne tower. Calder began construction on "The Palms" in the 1890s for $37,000. In the 1900 and 1910 U.S. censuses, Calder is listed as an "orchardist" and fruit farmer. The above picture shows the house in 1901. Professional baseball player Earl McNeely resided in this house with his wife, Ethel, from 1928 to 1946. Although details are vague, this residence was torn down sometime between 1946 and 1962. (Source *Sacramento Record-Union*, *Sacramento through the Camera.*)

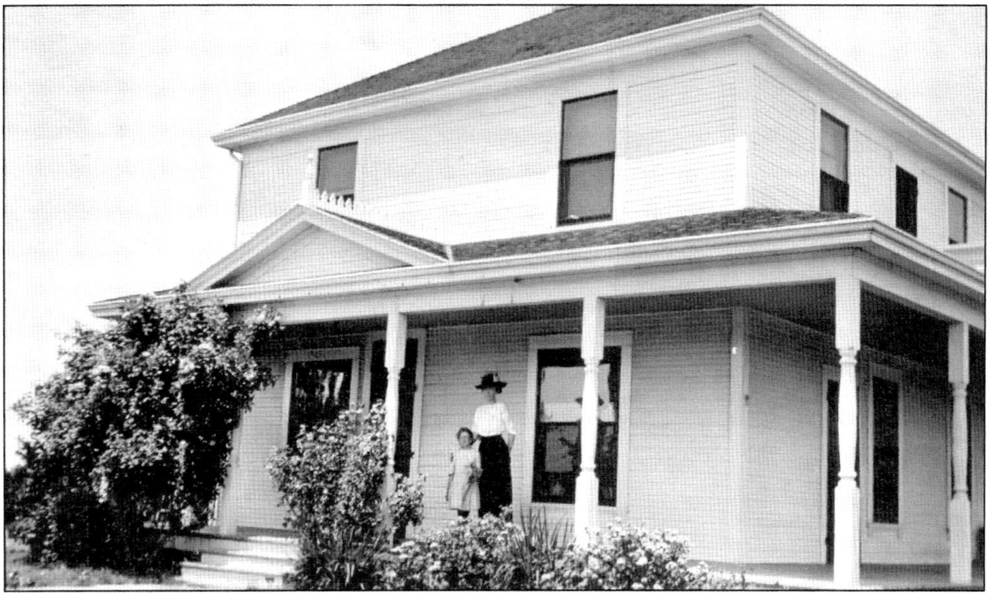

During the 1920s and 1930s, George Van Smith resided in this house, built in the popular American foursquare style, on Central Avenue. Smith, a New York native, worked as a banker and political writer in San Francisco before moving to Orangevale. The U.S. census shows George and Mary Van Smith living in Orangevale in 1920. (Courtesy Marcia Clark.)

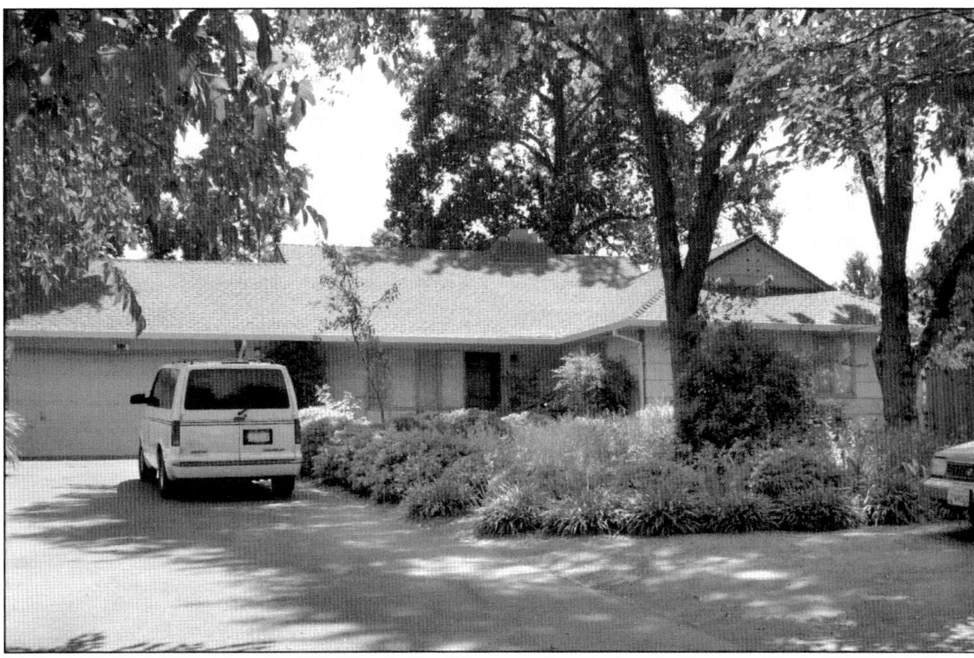

In 1956 and at the age of 63, Ruth Wickstrom Kirsten, daughter of Hannah and Albert Wickstrom, decided to build a new house for herself and her sister Agnes. She enlisted her architect nephew, Nick Tomich, to design the house. Ruth had lived in her parents' home from 1904 to 1956. In 1993, after living in Carmichael for 52 years, Nick returned to Orangevale and moved into this ranch-style house. (Courtesy Paul J. P. Sandul.)

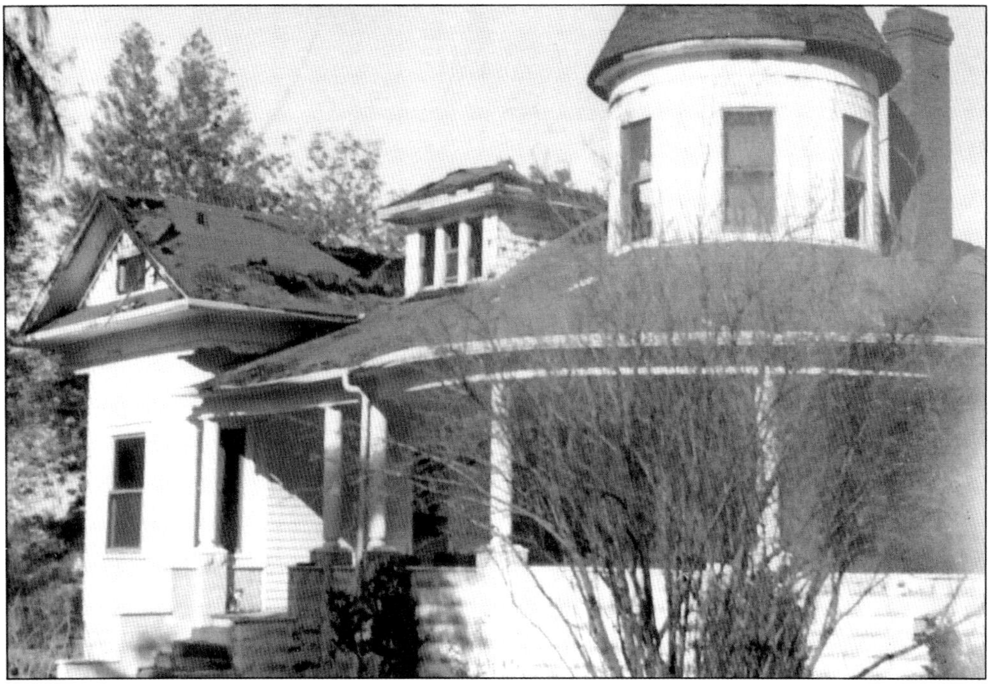

Across from where "The Palms" stood, William Calder built a second and more modest home in 1907. Identified in some sources as Calder's guest house, this property was lined with palm trees on at least the north and east elevations. Damaged by a fire during the 1950s (above), the round tower and other elements were lost and not restored (below, 1958). (Above courtesy Pioneer Mutual Hook and Ladder Society; below courtesy Orange Vale Water Company.)

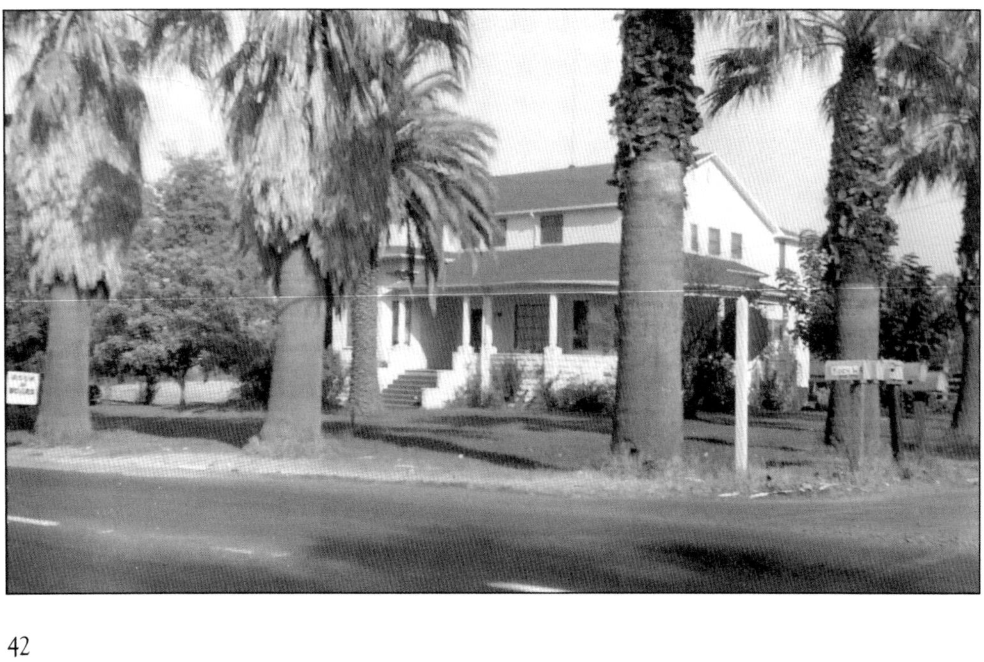

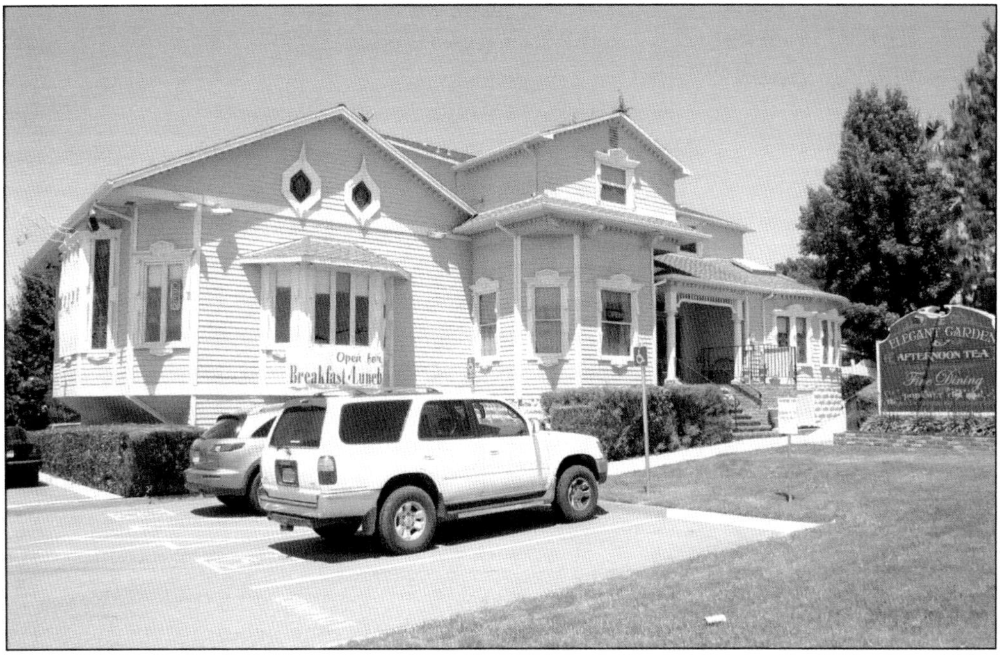

Sometime between 1977 and 1988, when the Calder residence became the restaurant L. W. Calder's, the wrap porch was enclosed, as apparent in this modern photograph dated 2006. Unfortunately, the building has been altered from its original design. Gone is the round tower and the open veranda and added are Italianate features, such as the elaborate window trim. (Courtesy Paul J. P. Sandul.)

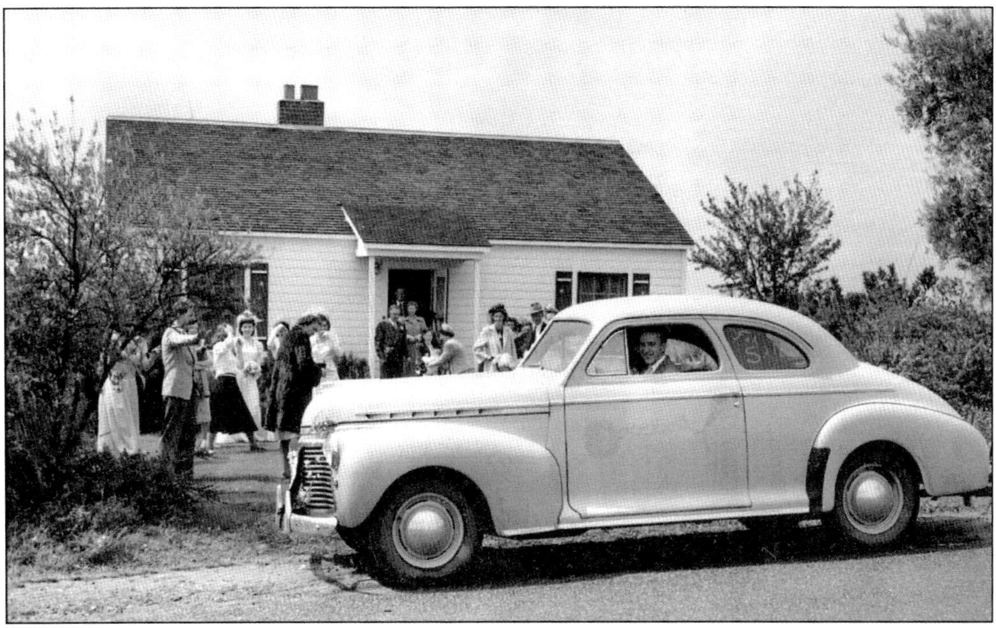

This photograph was taken on the wedding day of Andrew and Naida Effinger on April 3, 1948, in front of the Walnut Avenue home of Effinger's parents, Lottie and James W. Stevenson. The Stevensons moved from north Missouri to Orangevale in 1936. (Courtesy Andrew and Naida Effinger.)

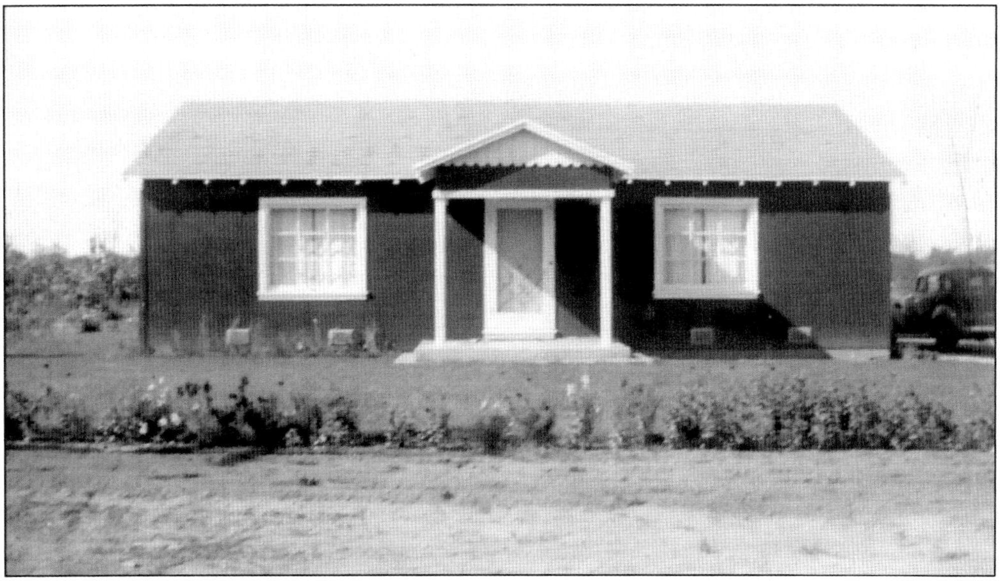

Floyd Field built this house on Naranja Way (now Hazel Avenue) for his family during World War II and, because of war rations, used imitation brick. The Field family moved into the house during the summer of 1948. (Courtesy JoAnn Allred.)

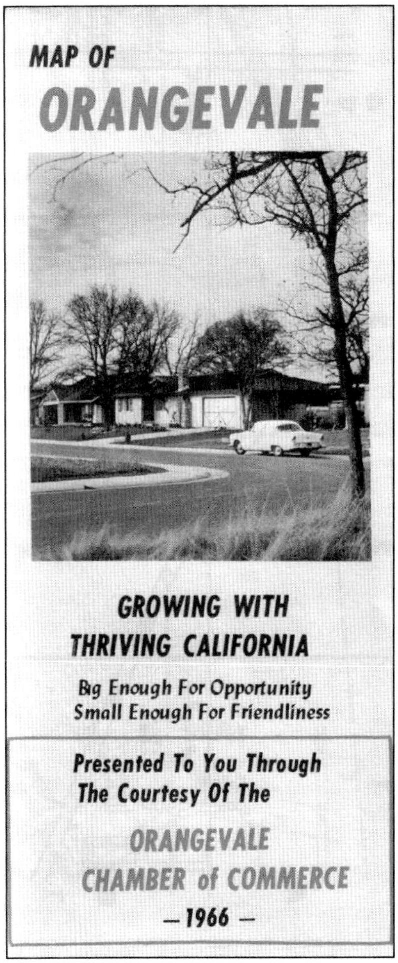

Like many Sacramento suburbs, Orangevale grew during the 1950s and 1960s as a result of the postwar population boom. This cover of a 1966 chamber of commerce map promotes the image of a suburb where convenience and country merge, sentiments similar to those of early boosters. (Courtesy Orangevale Library.)

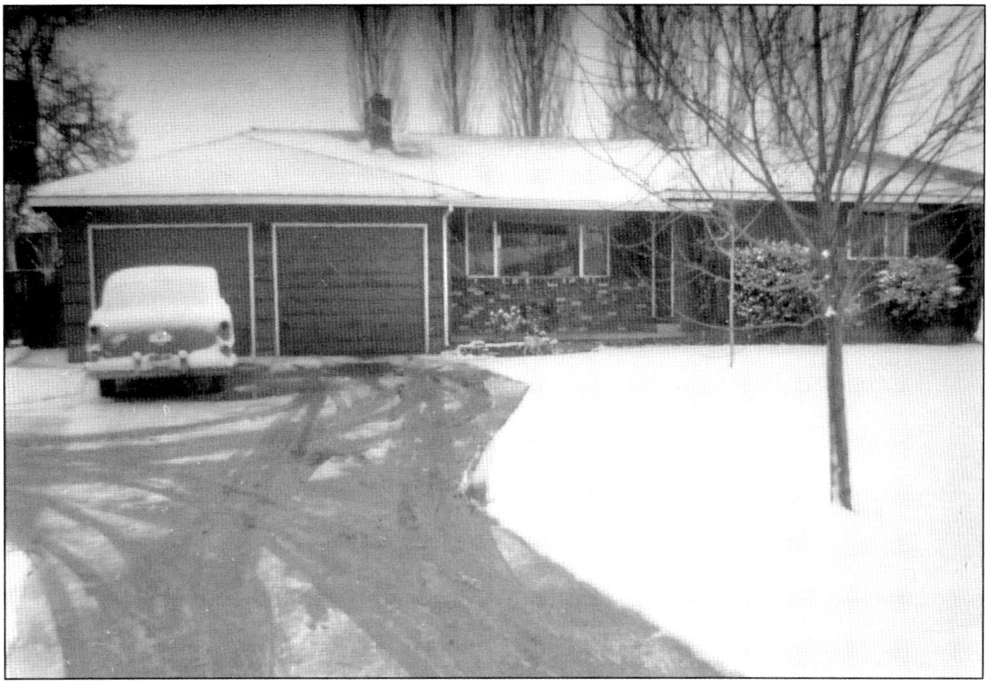

This photograph of Flora Baldwin's home at Greenback Lane and Hazel Avenue, taken in January 1962, captures a rare scene of a blanket of snow. (Courtesy Richard Harke.)

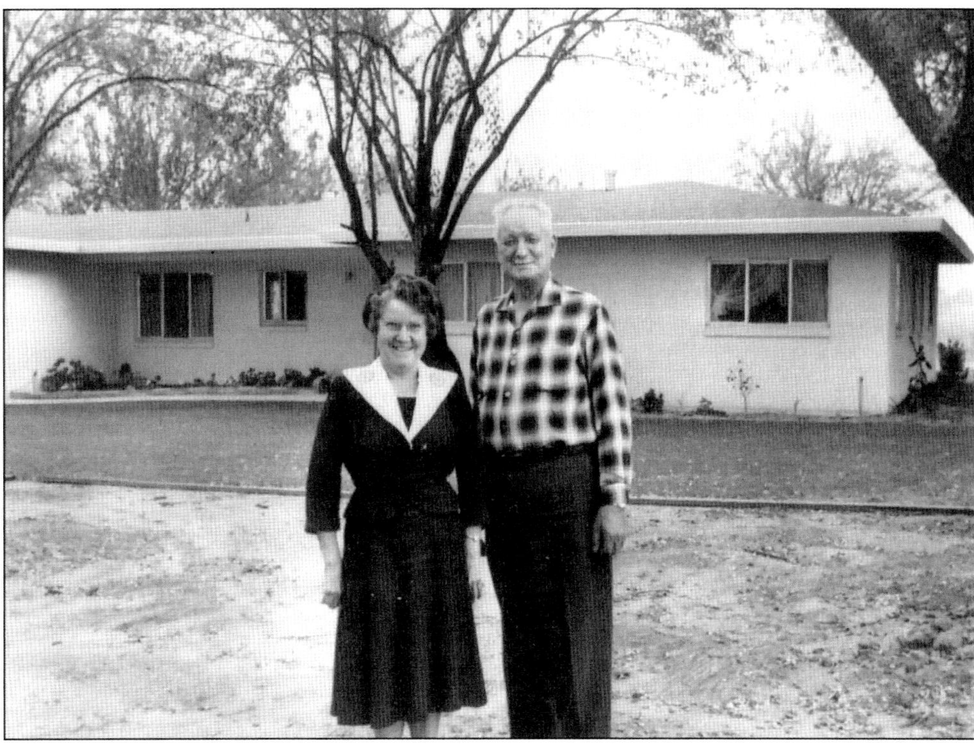

John and Alberta Lammerding stand proudly in front of their home off Pardillo Avenue in the early 1960s. (Courtesy Gerald Lammerding.)

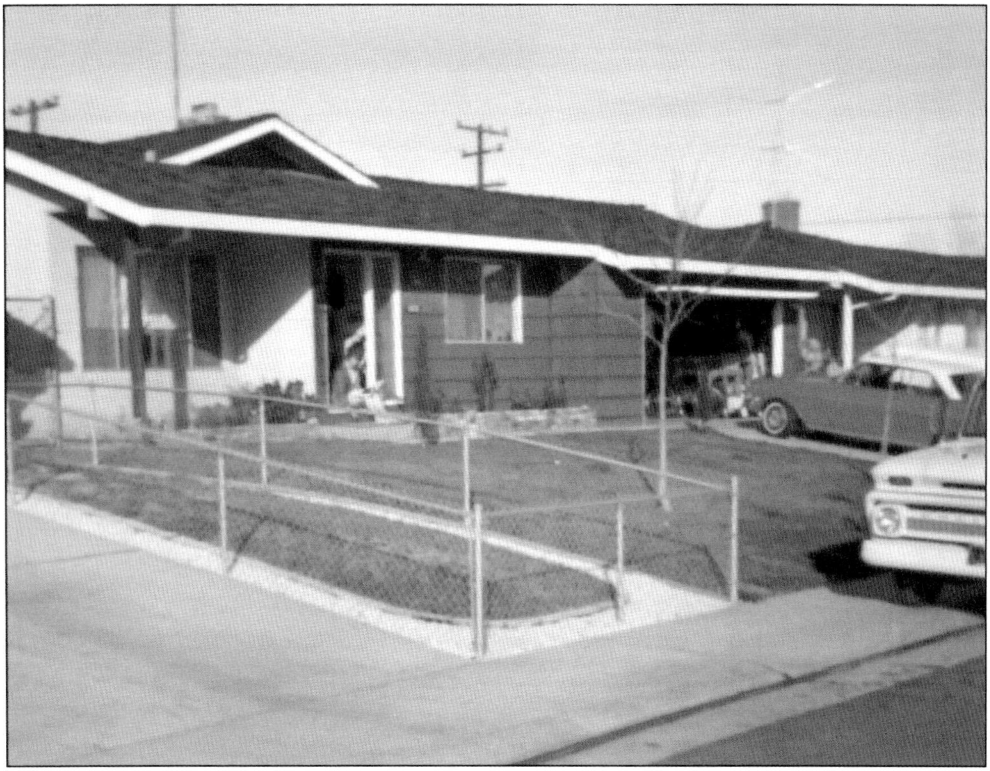

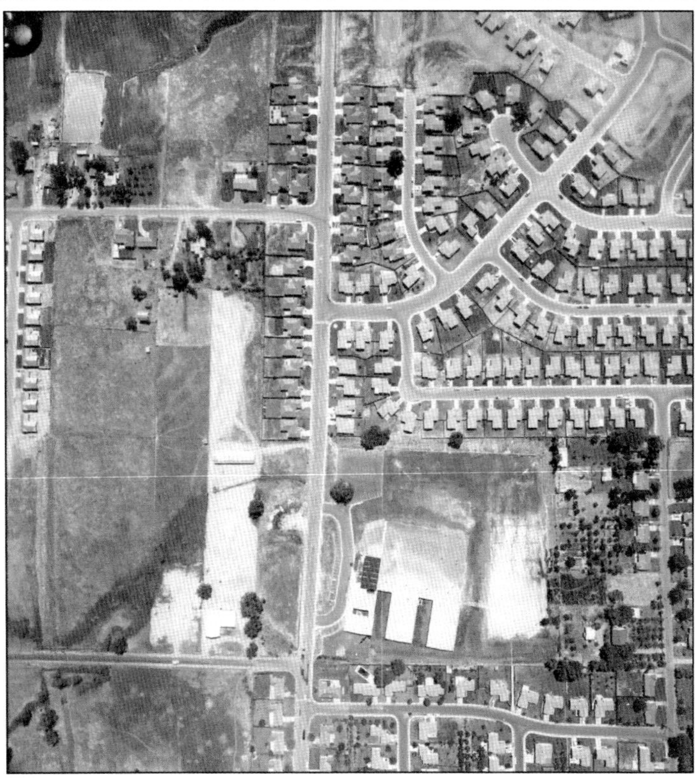

In 1963, Bob and Glenda Lewis purchased this house on Polly Avenue, pictured here in 1972. The street was named by banker Will Wright after his wife, Polly. The Lewis home, one of the first three constructed on this street, served as a model home. (Courtesy Glenda Lewis.)

This aerial photograph, showing Orangevale between Beech and Filbert Streets in 1964, confirms that gone are the spacious 10-acre tracts once promoted. About a dozen houses stood in Orangevale in 1890, but in 2000, that number had grown to 10,098. (Courtesy SAMCC, No. 955/103/153.)

Four

The Fruits of Our Labor

The work goes on, the cause endures, the hope still lives and the dreams shall never die.

—Edward "Ted" Kennedy, U. S. Senator

In the 1902 Sacramento County directory, only the following occupations are listed for Orangevale residents: 1 capitalist, 1 postmaster and agent of Capital Telephone and Telegraph Company, 1 florist, 1 carpenter and contractor, 5 fruit growers, 4 laborers, 1 mail carrier on rural delivery, 2 horticulturists, 1 painter, 1 commercial traveler, 1 orchadist, and 28 farmers. No grocer, restaurateur, or other small-town businessmen are listed. For retail shopping and specialty shops, Orangevale residents went to Folsom and Sacramento. Folsom turned into a successful transportation hub in 1856 with the arrival of the Sacramento Valley Railroad, and Folsom's Sutter Street developed into a thriving business district.

The essential businesses of Orangevale first blossomed in the orchards and family-run packinghouses. As recalled by Sadie Cable in 1958, "Practically all of Orangevale was in orchards and hundreds of boxes of fruit were sent out each day." Still, Orangevale did have other services early on, such as a post office and a telephone service in 1891. According to Sadie Cable, the first store in Orangevale was Linnell's, which stood where Dairy Queen now operates on Walnut Avenue and Greenback Lane.

Until the 1950s, businesses in Orangevale varied little beyond those needed to support farmers and a small community. Concentrated primarily on Hazel and Main Avenues, these businesses included Pop Holmes Market and the Public Market (which opened in 1939), gas stations, a post office, and the Orangevale clubhouse. In 1960, the Woo family opened the Capri Market and introduced automatic conveyors to the area. In 1955, the Orangevale Chamber of Commerce formed and, the following year, Orangevale got its own newspaper, the *Orangevale News*.

During the late 1950s, several husbandry businesses moved to Orangevale. In 1956, Featherland Farm, Inc., started production and supplied eggs to many businesses. In 1958, Ceccardi's Farm Supply arrived, providing Orangevale with seeds, livestock, and pet products, among other items. Guy Ceccardi told the *Sacramento Union* in 1990 that about 55 percent of his customers purchased solely dog-related products, verifying the shift in Orangevale's agrarian groundings.

The business district of Orangevale has extended far past Hazel and Main Avenues, as it has conquered Greenback Lane. Combining the rapid development of housing and businesses alike, many wish for preservation of the agrarian landscape, which is no longer visible from Greenback Lane.

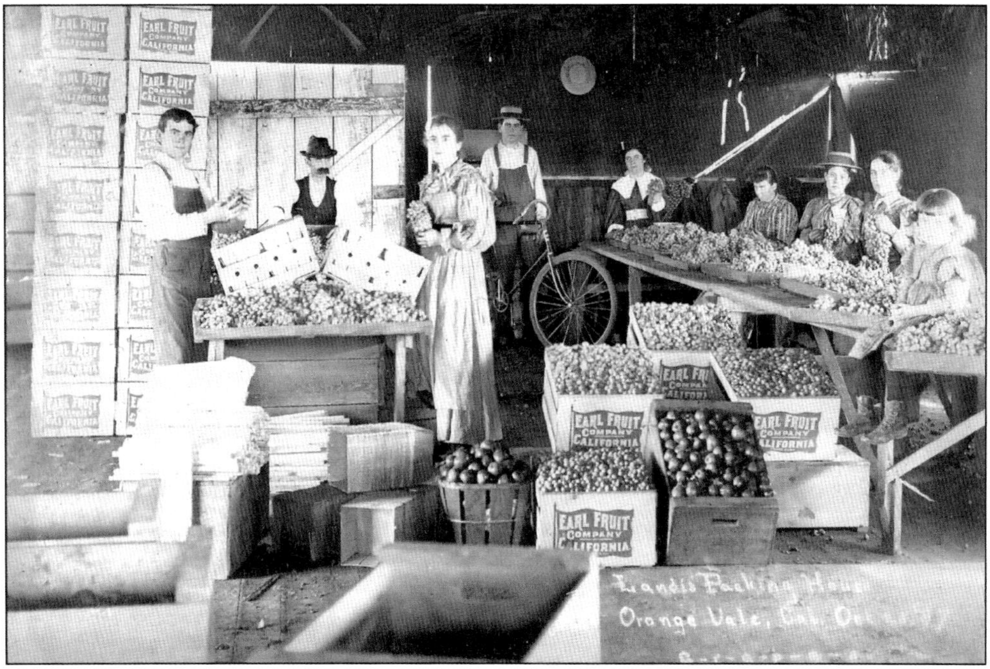

Above is a rare glimpse into the Landis packinghouse in Orangevale around the late 19th century. Often, it took the entire family to prepare fruit, here packed into Earl Fruit Company boxes to be hauled to the railroad depot. George Bloom Katzenstein and others bought the Earl Fruit Company's northern division in 1901, for which he had served as general manager since 1868. Katzenstein, a former Orange Vale Colonization Company director, continued as the fruit company's general manager, which shipped 3,000 carloads of fruit annually to eastern states. The Landis packinghouse was one of many similar operations in Orangevale. Below is the Wahrhaftig packing shed, pictured in 1986. (Above courtesy Tom Tomich; below courtesy Andrew and Naida Effinger.)

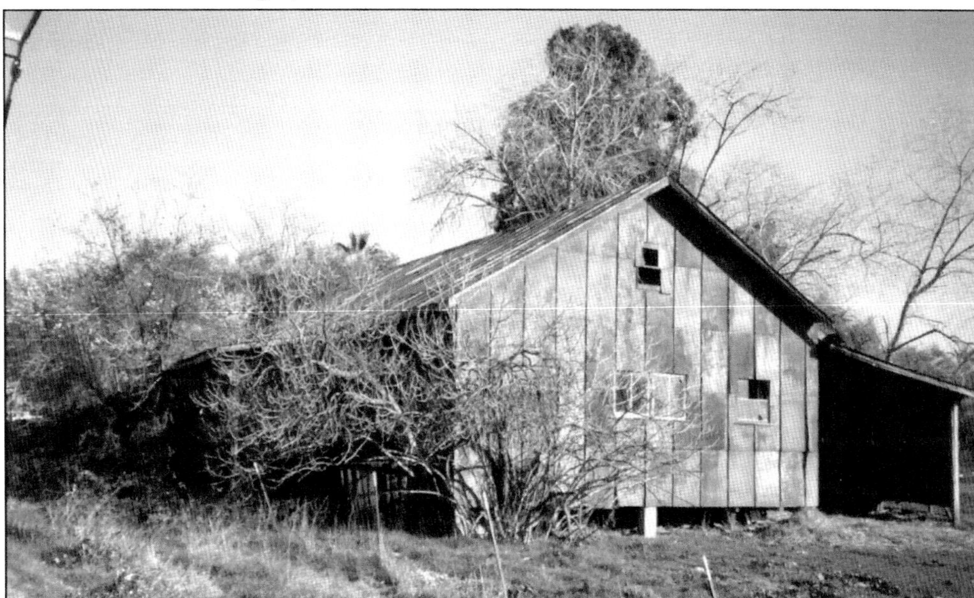

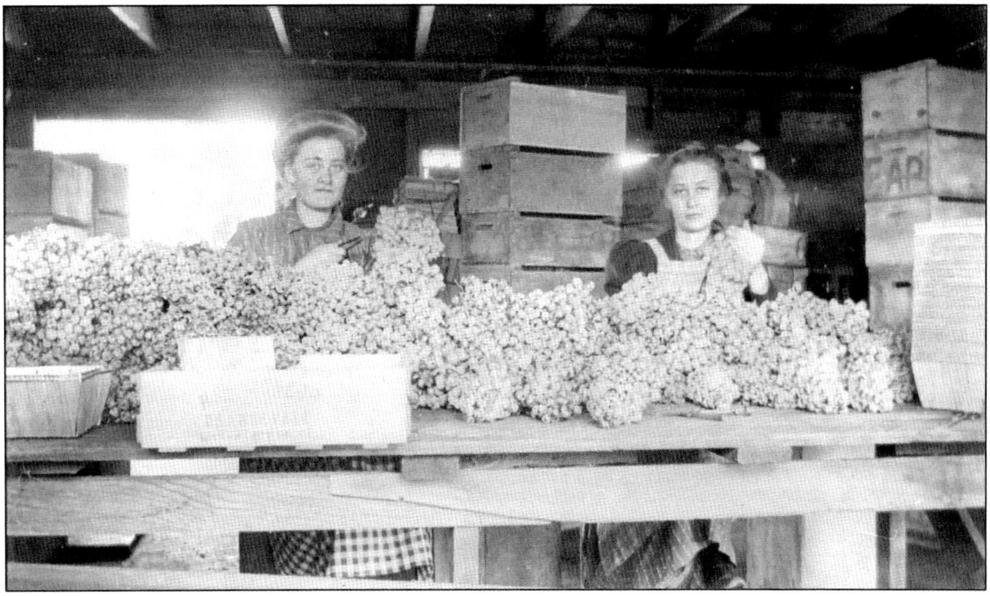

Many women contributed to family earnings by working in the local packing sheds. Taken around 1900, this photograph shows two women at work in a grape-packing shed in Orangevale. (Courtesy SAMCC, No. 81/01/1307.)

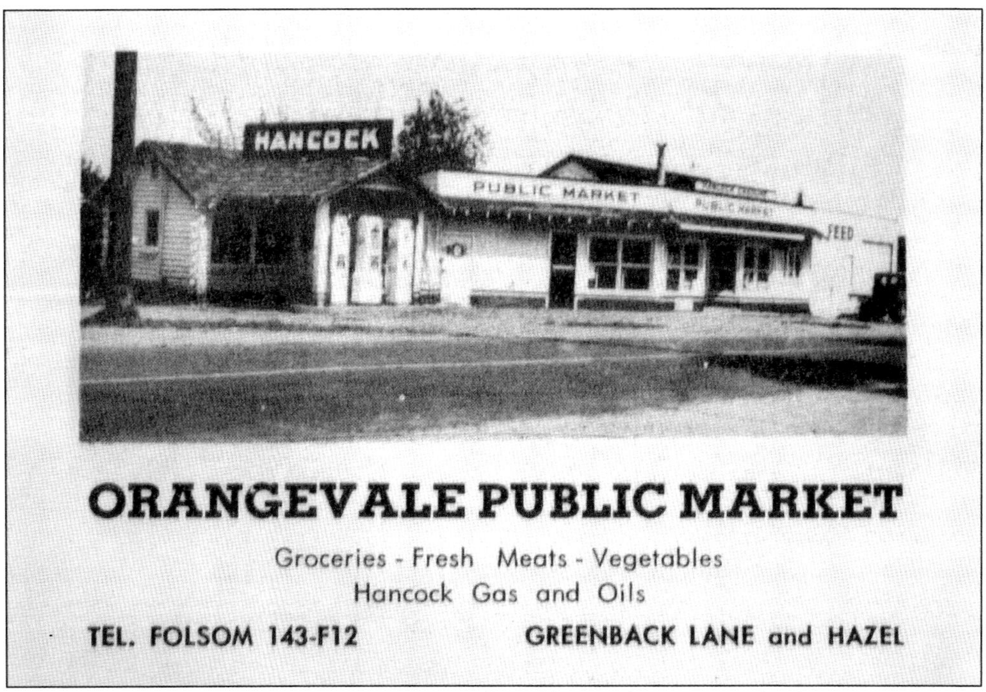

This 1948 advertisement shows the Orangevale Public Market at Greenback Lane and Hazel Avenue. (Courtesy Sacramento Room, Sacramento Public Library.)

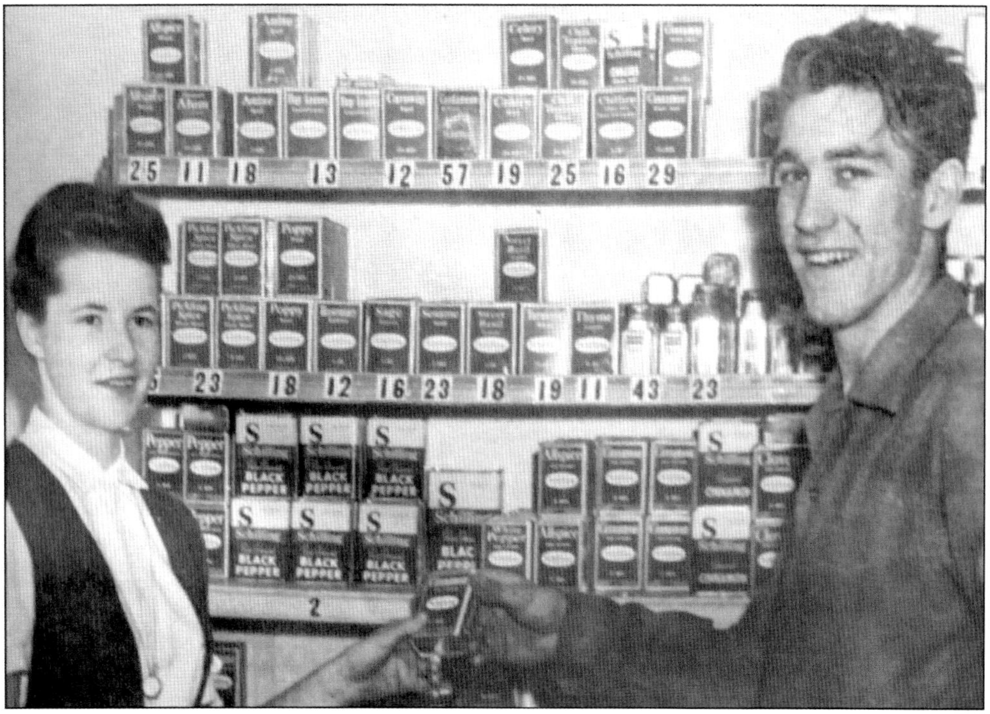

Two students, Carolyn Barnes and Jim Becker, are photographed patronizing the local Jet Market at the corner of Greenback Lane and Main Avenue in 1956. This photograph was included in the 1956 *Greenback Notes*, the yearbook for the San Juan High School. (Courtesy Sacramento Room, Sacramento Public Library.)

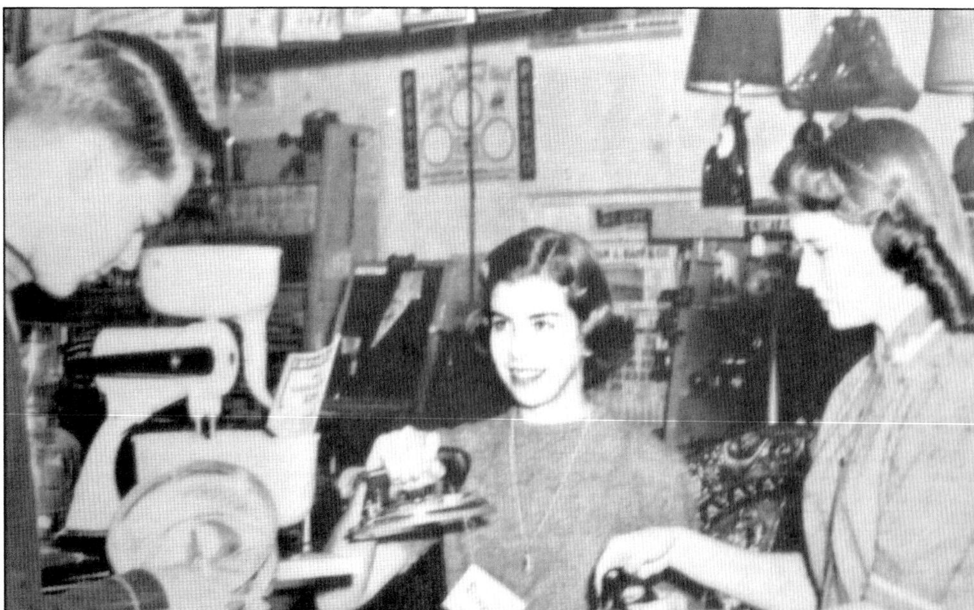

Photographed for the 1956 *Greenback Notes*, students John Haga, Leah Turk, and Gail Davis shop at the Turvan Store, owned by Leah Turk's parents and located at 9198 Greenback Lane. (Courtesy Sacramento Room, Sacramento Public Library.)

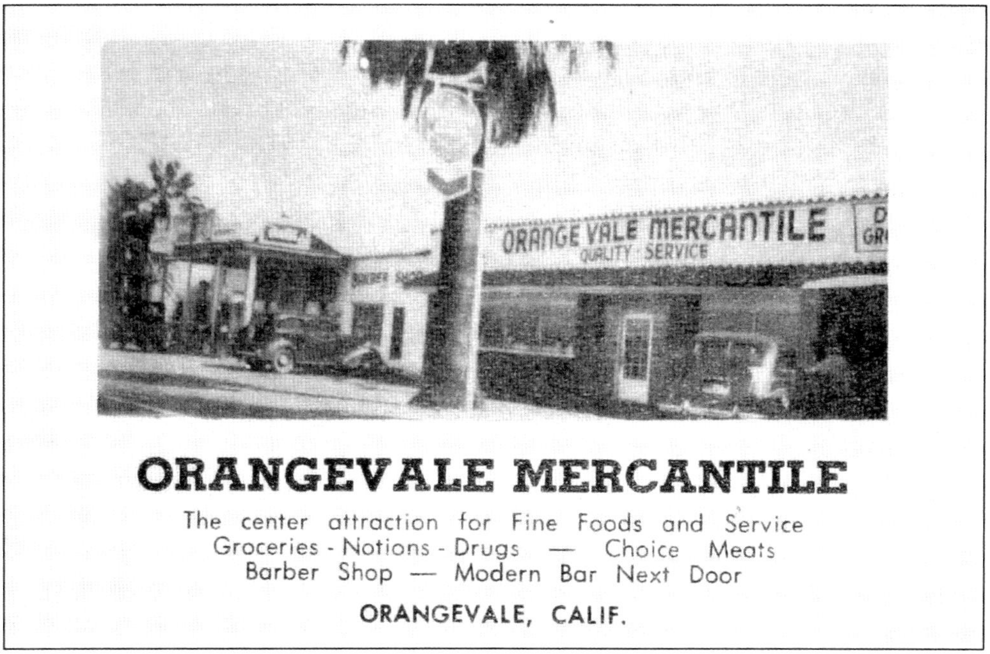

This is a 1948 advertisement for the Orangevale Mercantile where residents could purchase groceries, pick up prescriptions, or visit the local barber. (Courtesy Sacramento Room, Sacramento Public Library.)

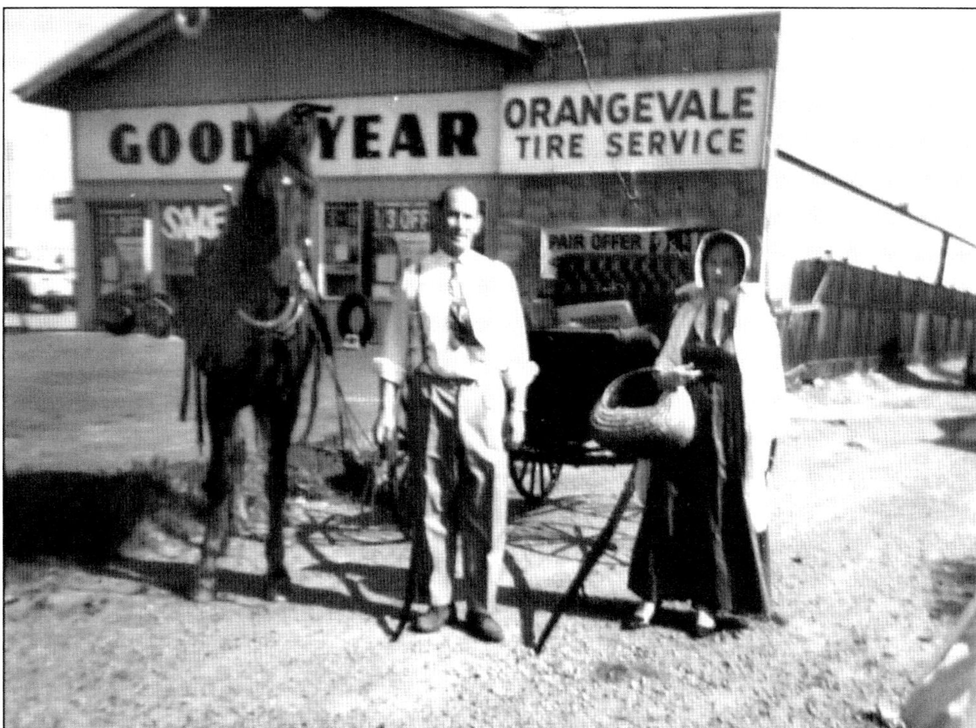

Bert and Gladys ? stand in front of Good Year Orangevale Tire Service in 1966 with their horse and carriage, likely on their way to the Pow Wow Day parade. (Courtesy Orangevale Grange.)

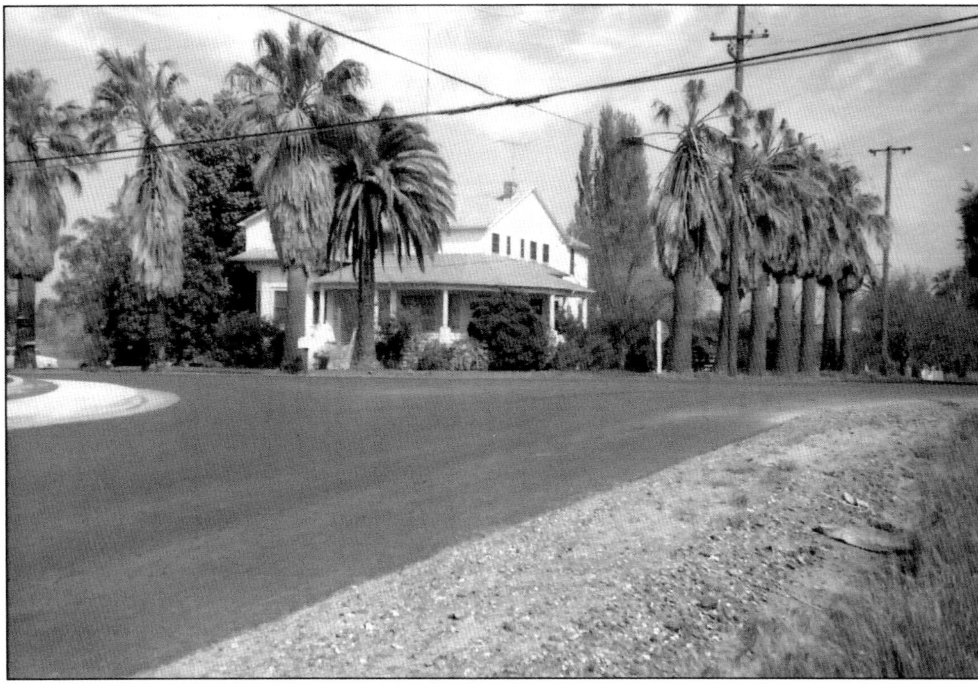

The former residence of William Calder, seen above in 1964, at the northwest corner of Greenback Lane and Pecan Avenue has changed ownership numerous times since its construction in 1907. Various restaurants and an inn have tried their luck in putting the old-fashioned feel of Calder's residence to good use, including the White House Inn, L. W. Calder's, the Ambassador, and, currently, the Elegant Garden and Afternoon Tea. (Courtesy Orange Vale Water Company.)

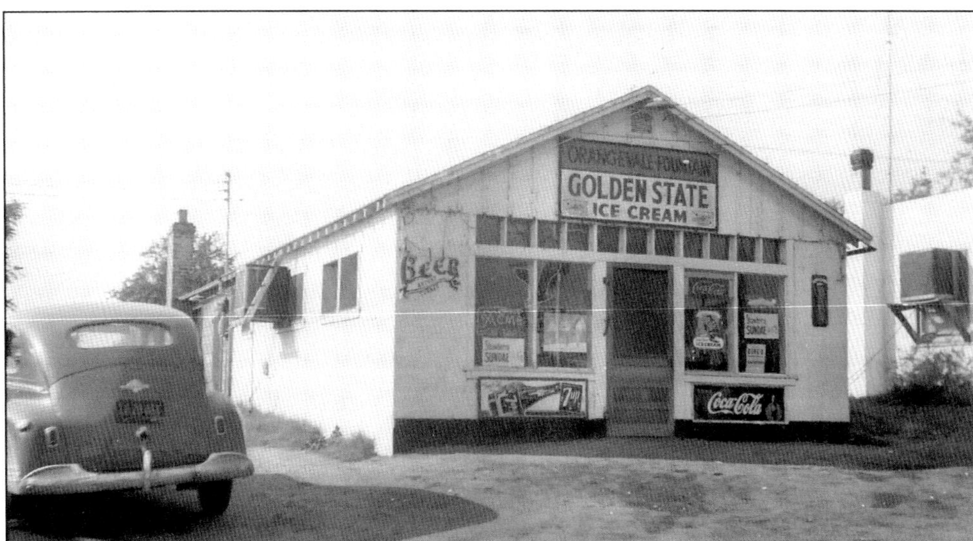

Pictured here in 1958, Golden State Ice Cream sat on the south side of Greenback Lane near Hazel Avenue. (Courtesy Orange Vale Water Company.)

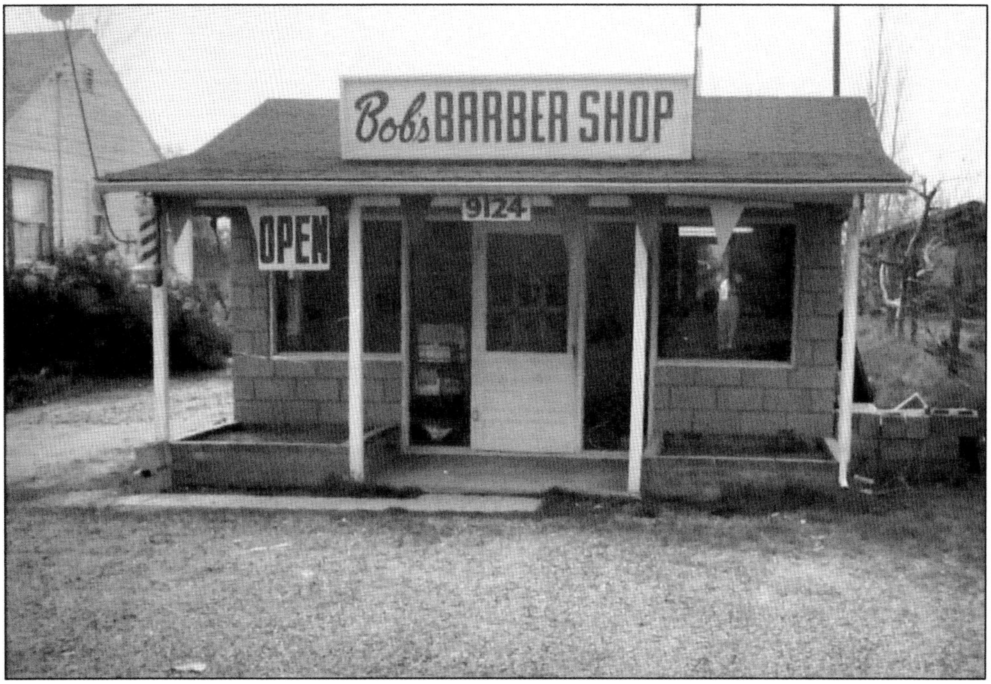

In 1962, Bob Lewis opened this blue barbershop on Greenback Lane. (Courtesy Glenda Lewis.)

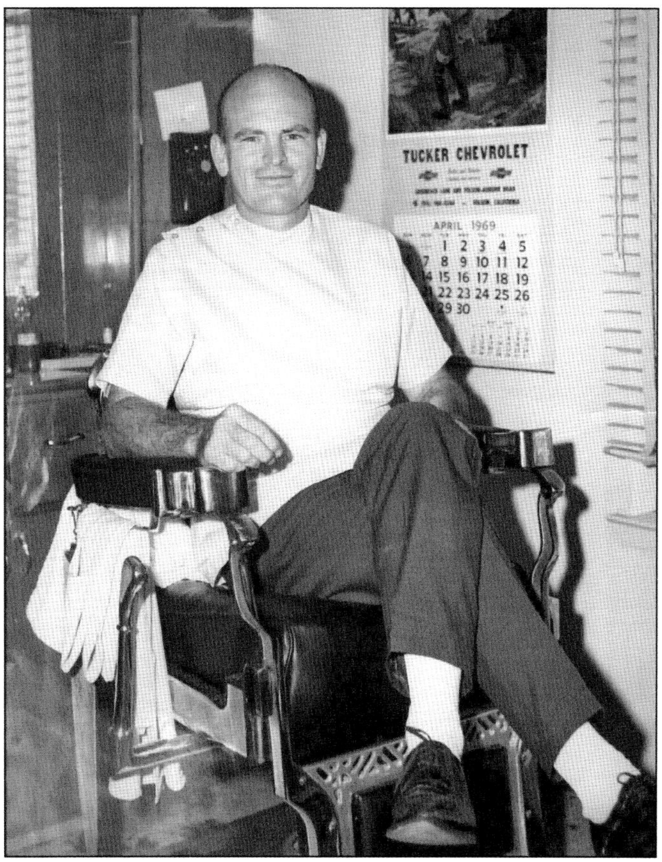

About 1963, Bob Lewis relocated his barbershop farther east on Greenback Lane to where he thought more traffic and space would improve business. This 1969 photograph shows Bob sitting in one of his barber chairs at the new location. He stayed there until 1980, when he entered the construction business. (Courtesy Glenda Lewis.)

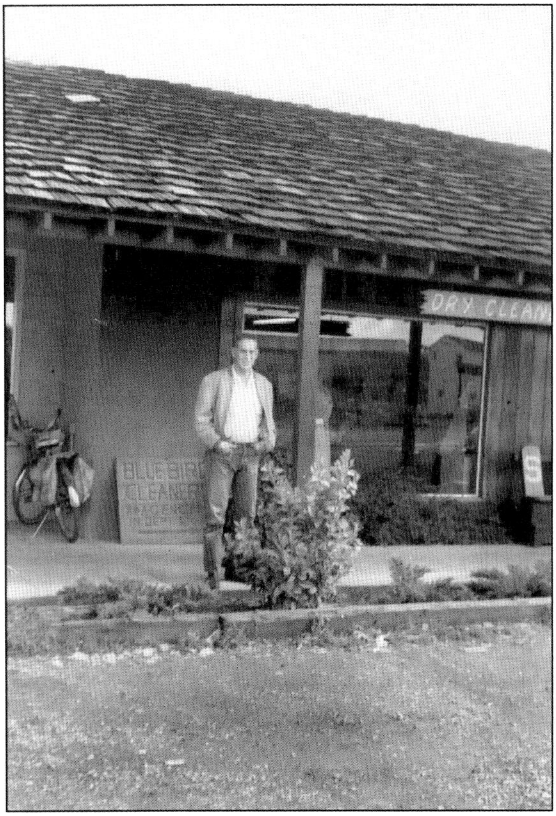

This photograph of Vern Allred was taken in May 1957 as he stands in front of the Blue Bird Cleaners, where the current Orangevale post office now stands. Vernon Cable's office was also on this strip off Greenback Lane. (Courtesy JoAnn Allred.)

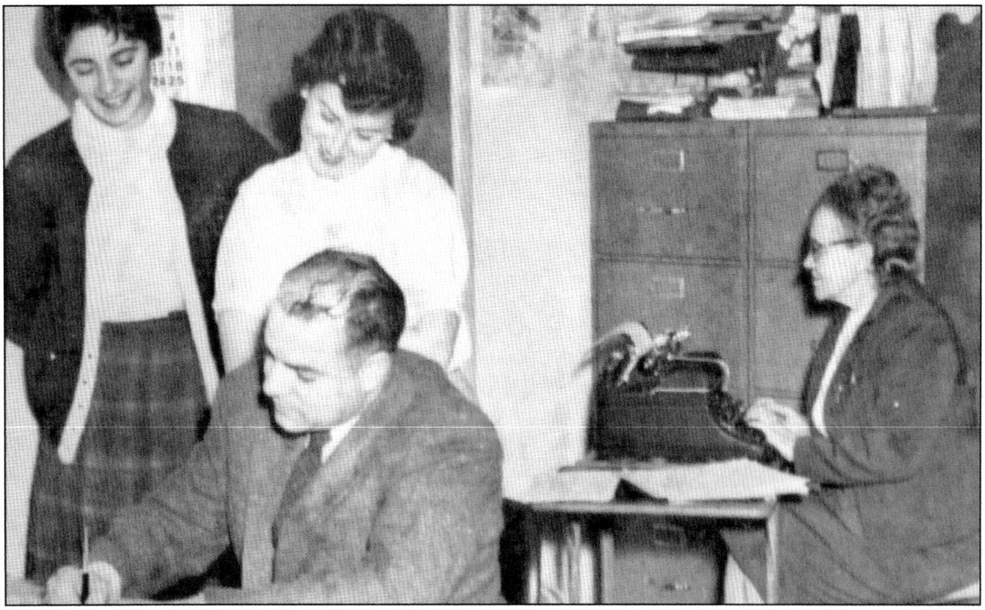

This interior shot of the Vernon A. Cable Insurance office at 8885 Greenback Lane in the 1956 San Juan High School yearbook shows Emile Mitchell (left) and Charlene Greenhalgh looking over Vernon Cable's shoulder. Vernon was the son of Sadie Cable and owned the Cable Shopping Center. (Courtesy Sacramento Room, Sacramento Public Library.)

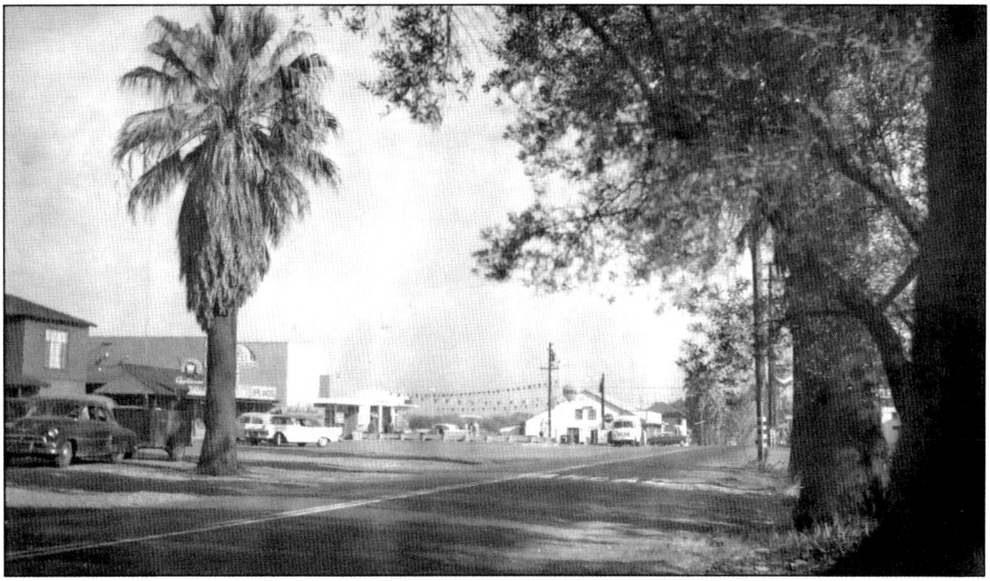

In the late 1950s, Hazel Avenue and Greenback Lane were not the congested thoroughfares they are today. This photograph captures the quiet intersection (north side) of Greenback Lane and Hazel Avenue in 1958. (Courtesy Orange Vale Water Company.)

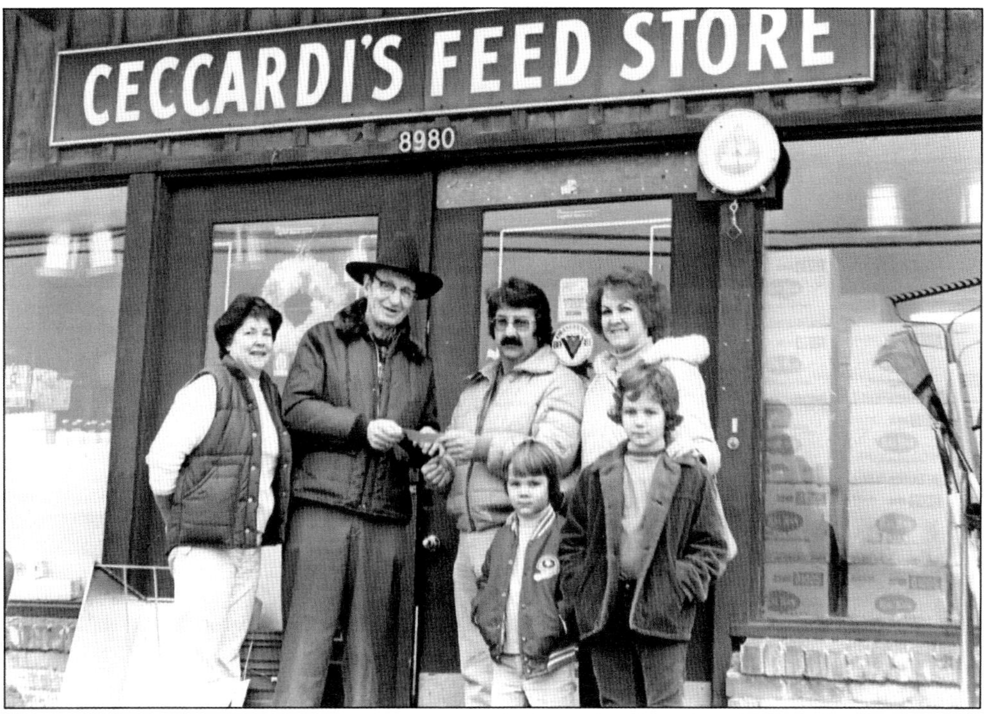

Guido "Guy" Ceccardi, an Italian native, opened Ceccardi's Farm Supply in 1958. In 1960, the store moved across the street to 8980 Greenback Lane, and by 1978, it had been renamed Ceccardi's Feed Store (pictured above in 1981). In 1978, the *Orangevale News* recognized Ceccardi's as "one of those businesses which hold the community together." In 1998, Ceccardi's was sold and became Western Feed and Pet Supply. (Courtesy Orange Vale Water Company.)

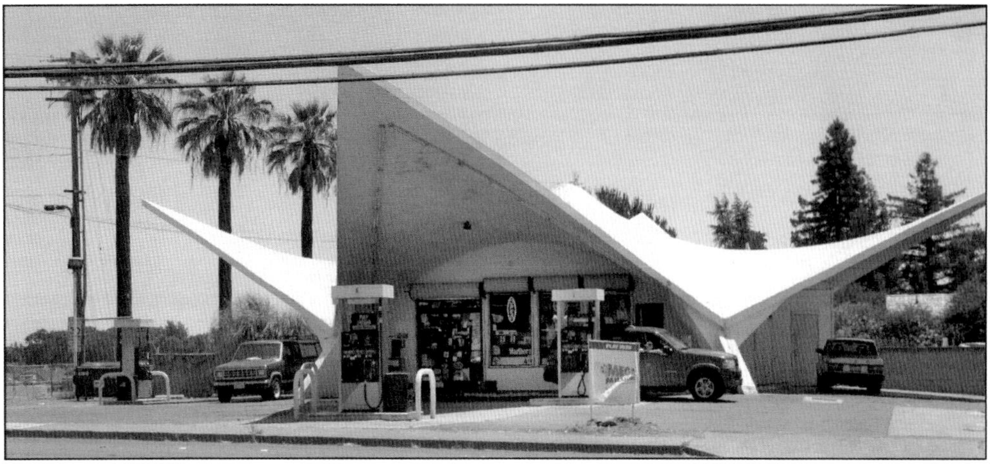

Pictured above in 2006, the Orangevale Orbit Gas Station was built in 1963. Designed in an aircraft style during an era when space travel was new and exciting, the gas station provided a compelling and recognizable architectural design to capture the attention of busy passerbyers and shade those filling up. Pictured below in 1964, the Orangevale Orbit Gas Station looks even more like a spaceship from this aerial view. Across from the Orbit stands William Calder's 1907 residence. The openness of Greenback Lane and Pecan Avenue seen here is now a remnant of the past, especially with the impending residential development at this intersection. (Above courtesy Paul J. P. Sandul; below courtesy SAMCC, No. 955/103/138.)

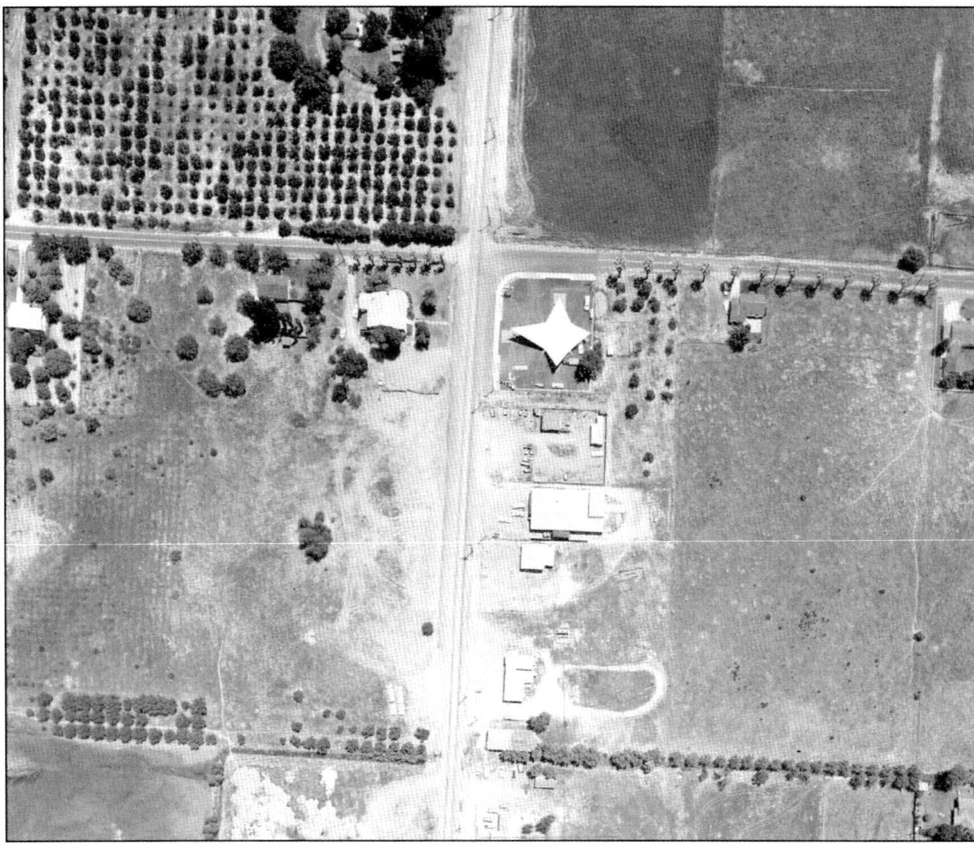

Five

A Common Cause

The American city should be a collection of communities where every member has a right to belong. . . . It should be a place where each of us can find the satisfaction and warmth, which comes from being a member of the community of man.

—Lyndon B. Johnson, 1965

In 1968, historian Constance McLaughlin Green identified three major subjects from which a community history can be drawn: people, the physical environment, and the institutions within a community:

> To state it simply are the institutions that arise in a community, some the result of environment, but more of them a result of the attitudes and the pressures of the people living there, their neighbors, the State, and the nation at large. Institutions, I think, can be treated as the outgrowth of people's wishes and efforts, modified at best by the natural circumstances, forces of nature under which they have to live.

From the available records, it appears that the Orangevale Grange, Orangevale Woman's Club, and Orangevale Civic Improvement Club were among the first established institutions in the community. Each organization focused on community progress and self improvement. For example, the Orangevale Woman's Club began because a female member of the community believed that individual talents could be used beyond the domestic sphere.

Organizations that formed in the mid- to late 20th century carried on the tradition of service and sense of belonging. The Orangevale Youth Center Board formed in 1948, after the need for youth to have a center was identified. The Orangevale Lions Club formed in 1953 and has taken an interest in contributing both time and money to the community through sponsoring local events and supporting drug-abuse programs in schools. Veterans and their families can receive support from the local chapter of Veterans of Foreign Wars of the United States. In 1975, after recognizing the needs of the elderly in the Orangevale area, Serve Our Seniors, Inc., was created.

All institutions, whether they are churches, schools, businesses, or clubs, contribute to the success of the community, as can traditions. One local fondly remembers the yearly clean-up day during her childhood, when the men went out to clean the ditches, roadways, and signs while the women prepared a big meal at the clubhouse. "It was a community thing," added Naida Effinger, "It was like family."

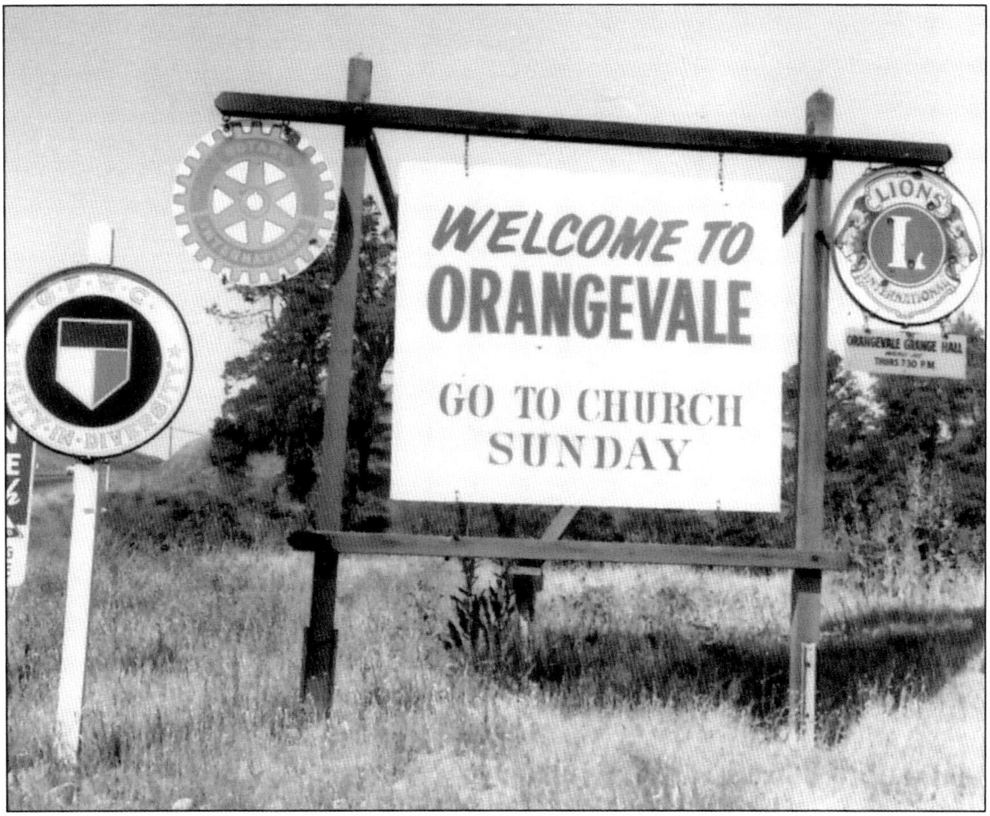

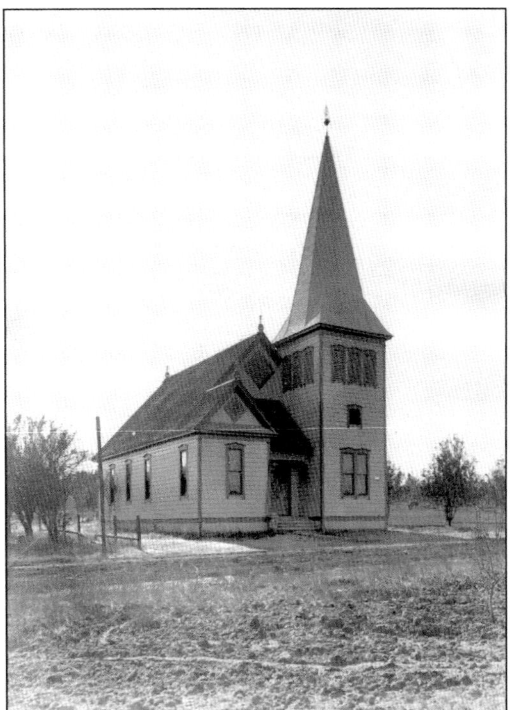

This sign reflects the sense of religion that has existed in Orangevale, although no date or location is provided. The first worship service was held on July 5, 1890, at the schoolhouse. The Orangevale Methodist Church may have organized first, but worship in Orangevale has grown to include at least 15 religions of various denominations. (Courtesy Orange Vale Water Company.)

The first church building constructed in Orangevale, according to cultural resource expert Catherine Heck, was the Presbyterian church that arose on Central Avenue between Hazel and Pecan Avenues. The Sacramento Presbytery organized the Presbyterian church on June 5, 1895, and completion of the building occurred sometime between 1895 and 1905. It is pictured here, possibly, sometime in the early 20th century. This church building no longer stands. (Courtesy Orange Vale Water Company.)

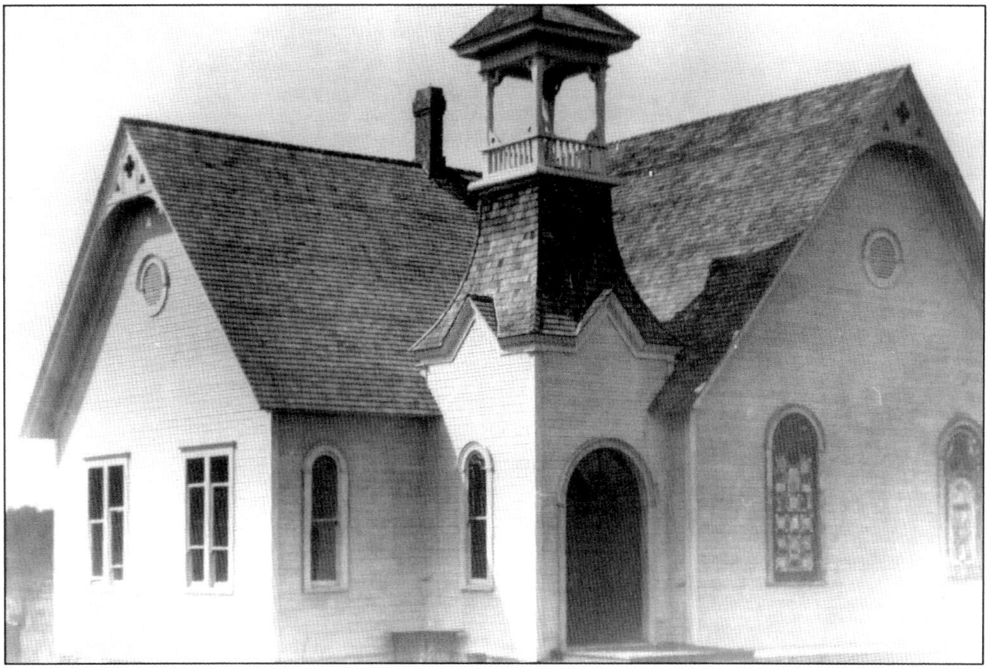

Methodists were the first to organize in Orangevale and met at the schoolhouse on July 5, 1890. The first Methodist church (above) was built on Central Avenue between Pecan and Filbert Avenues. Completed in 1906, the building, pictured here in the early 20th century, was sold to another denomination in the 1950s, and in 1958, a Methodist church was built across the street. Below, a modern photograph (2006) of the original building shows its subtle transformation into a residence. (Above courtesy Orange Vale Water Company; below courtesy Paul J. P. Sandul.)

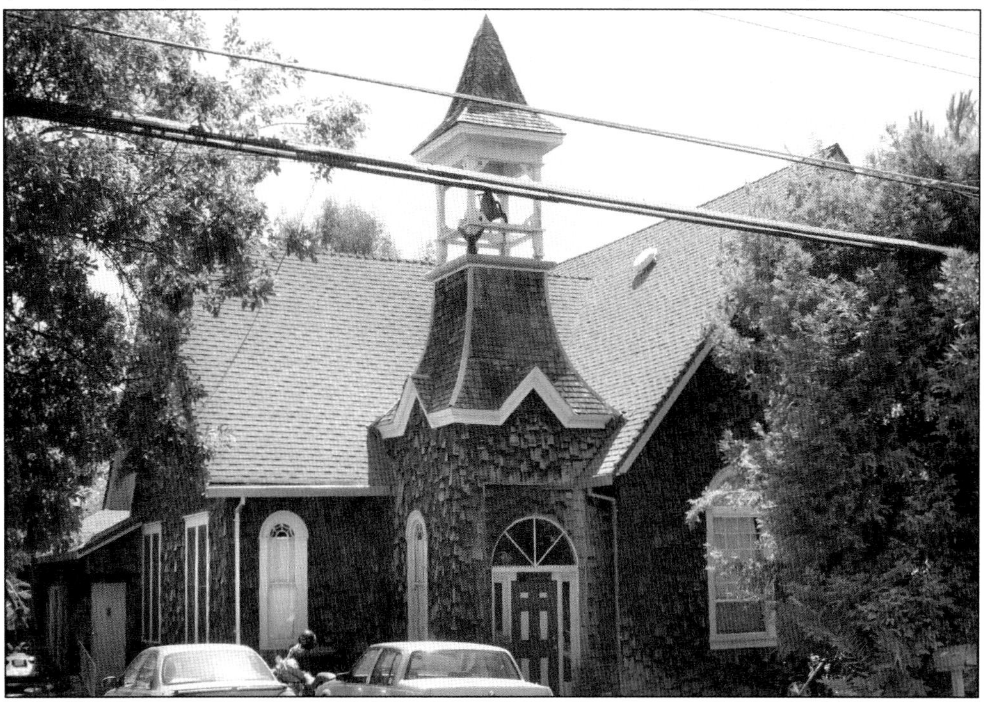

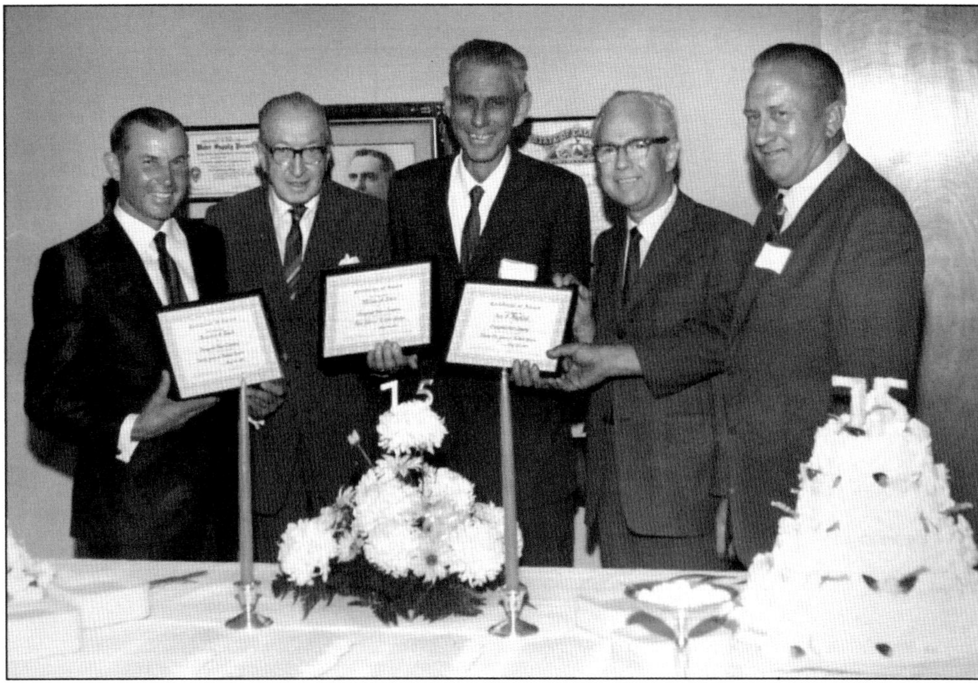

The Orange Vale Water Company formed on June 11, 1896, and purchased water rights and a pipe system from the Orange Vale Colonization Company. Seventy-five years after its formation, the Orange Vale Water Company celebrated on Central Avenue. Above are, from left to right, Frederick Tomich (director), William Sitton (attorney), Iven Mayfield (superintendent), Leroy Greene (senator), and Richard Bacon (director). (Courtesy Orange Vale Water Company.)

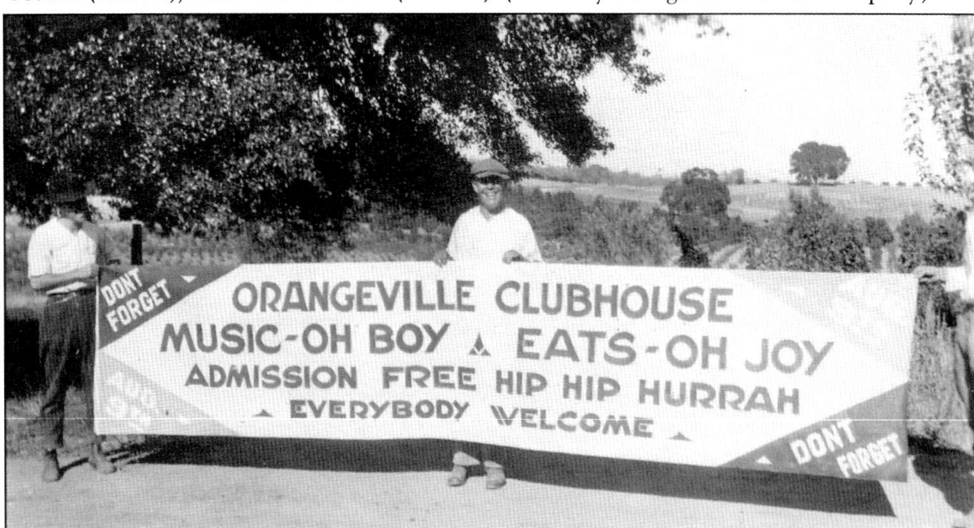

This photograph, likely taken in 1916, shows the excitement for the newly built Orangevale clubhouse at Hazel Avenue and Greenback Lane. Various institutions and organizations, such as the Orange Vale Water Company, county library, and Orangevale Grange used the clubhouse. In many regards, the building served as a community center, making its destruction in 1953 by an act of arson especially devastating. (Courtesy SAMCC, Sacramento County Agriculture Extension 80/02/868.)

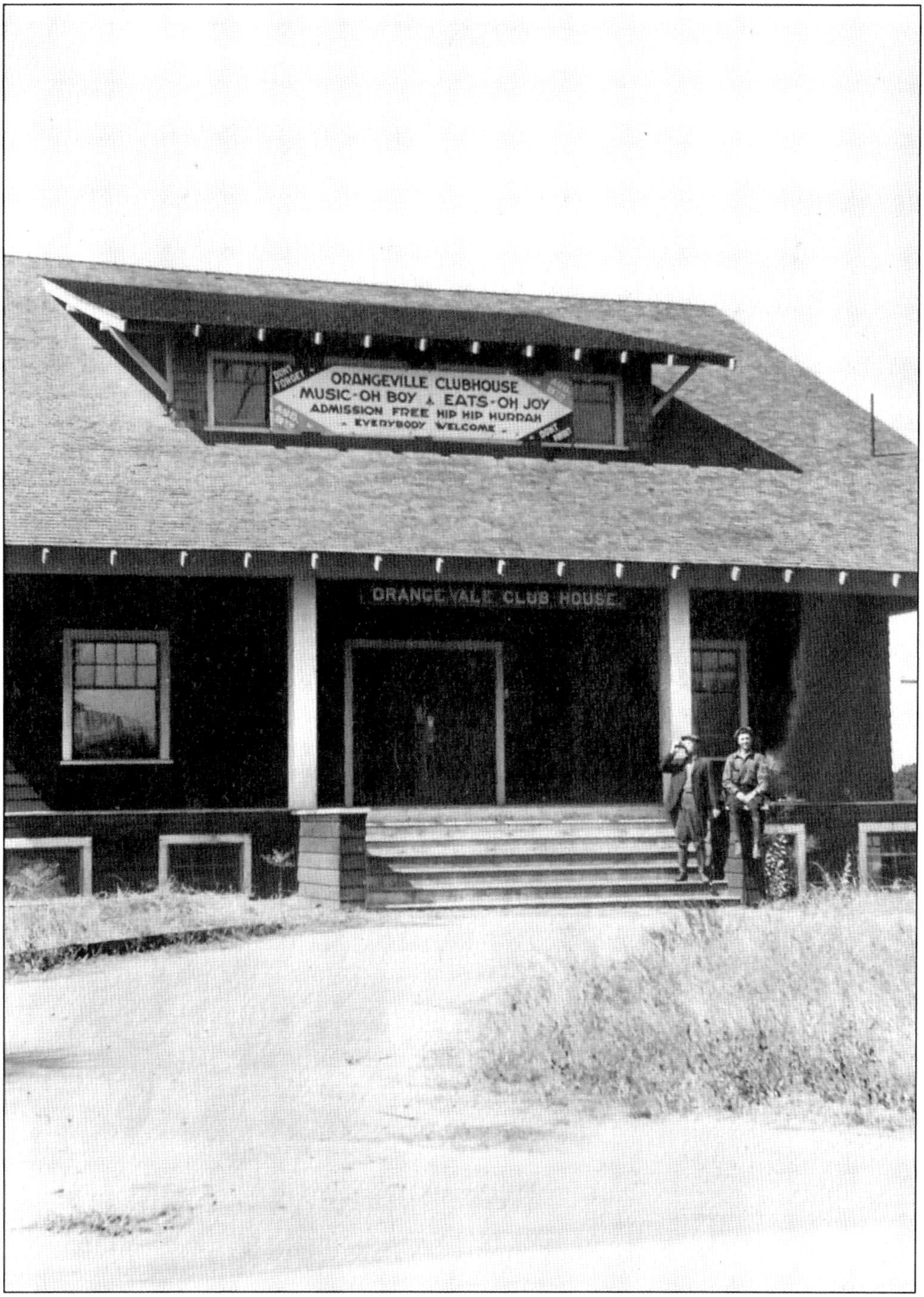

This bungalow-style clubhouse opened in 1916 on the northwest corner of Hazel Avenue and Greenback Lane. In 1953, the clubhouse was damaged by a fire set by a young, 17-year-old local volunteer firefighter who started approximately 50 fires in the Orangevale area with friends for "the excitement of fighting them." He also destroyed the old Roberts School. (Courtesy SAMCC, Sacramento County Agriculture Extension No. 80/02/840.)

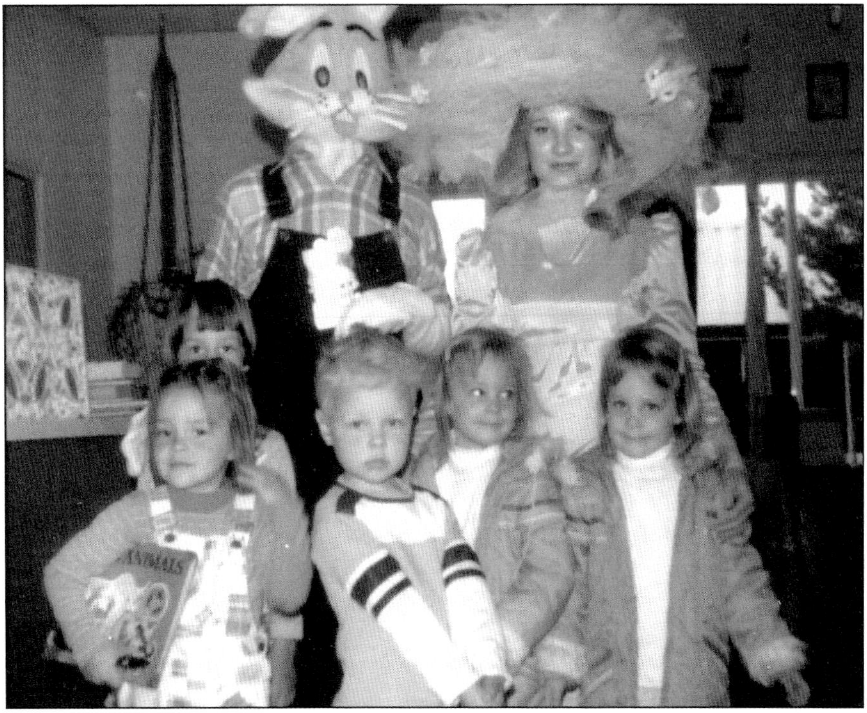

The Orangevale Library has supported local events and programs for children. Whether it is the summer-readers program, Delilah the "storytelling" dog, or special visitors like those pictured above, the gracious and efficient librarians work to do more than just house books for the public; they also provide a place of learning. The group photograph above was taken in 1980 at the Orangevale/Casa Roble Community Library. Pictured below, Orangevale children gather to hear a story in 1980. (Courtesy Orangevale Library.)

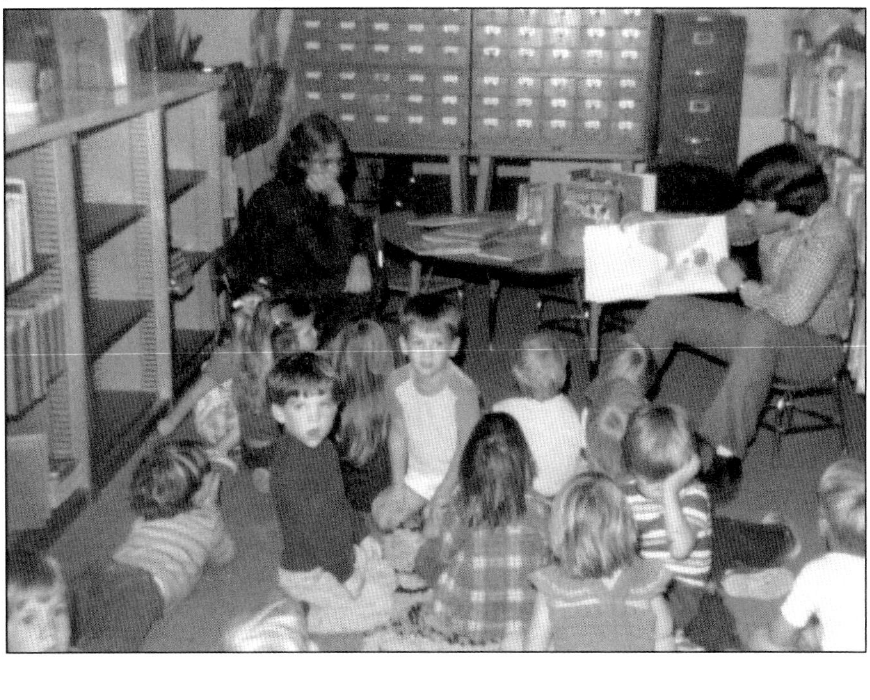

After many moves since its establishment in 1912, the Orangevale Library opened at its present site on January 25, 1984 (right). Volunteers ran it until a full-time paid staff was employed in March 1984, consisting of Dorothy Kilgore, library supervisor; Ann Bratt, library assistant; and Silvia Smiley, library clerk. (Courtesy Orangevale Library.)

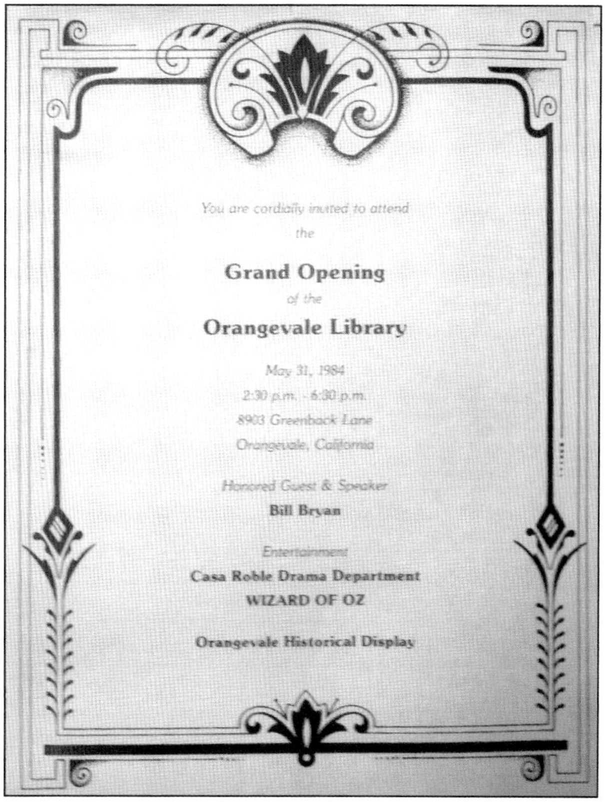

You are cordially invited to attend
the
Grand Opening
of the
Orangevale Library

May 31, 1984
2:30 p.m. - 6:30 p.m.
8903 Greenback Lane
Orangevale, California

Honored Guest & Speaker
Bill Bryan

Entertainment
Casa Roble Drama Department
WIZARD OF OZ

Orangevale Historical Display

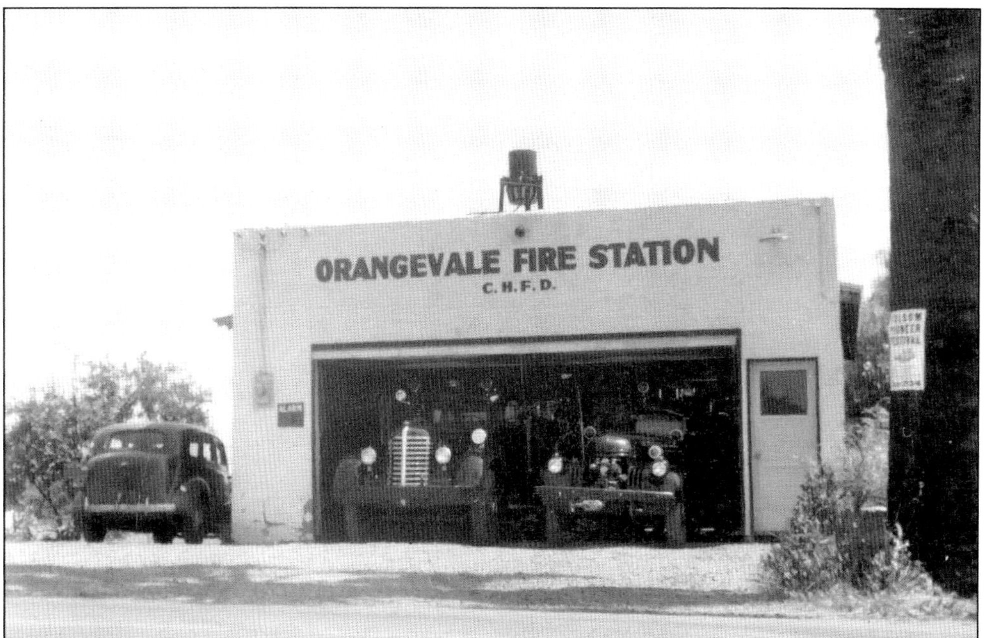

Pictured above sometime in the 1960s is the one of the Orangevale fire stations. The Orangevale Volunteer Fire Department was founded in 1933. Howard Greenhalgh served as the first fire chief and Lloyd Greenhalgh as first assistant. (Courtesy Pioneer Mutual Hook and Ladder Society.)

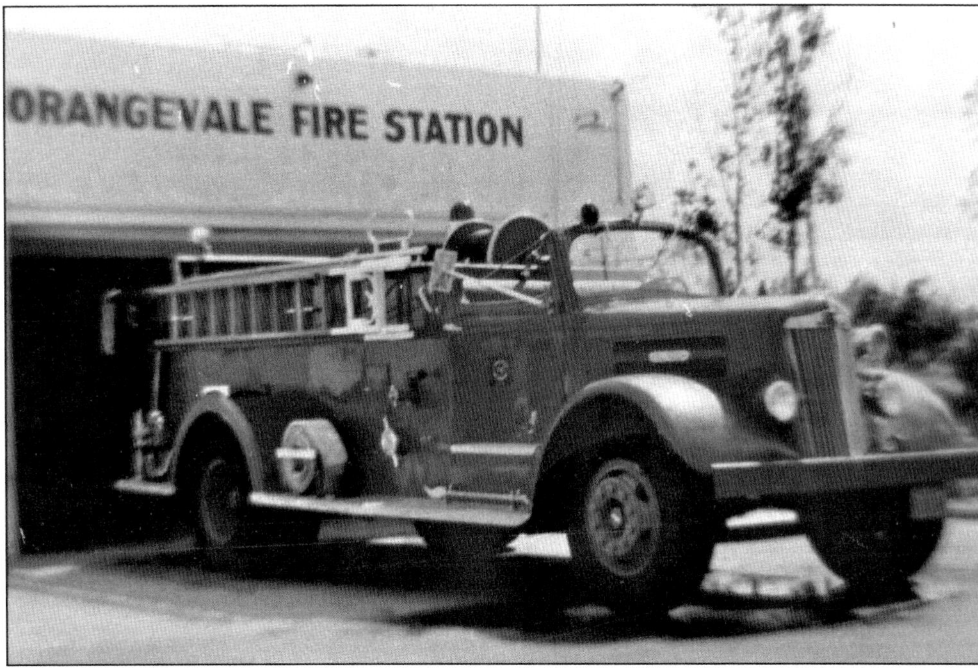

Pictured above sometime in the 1960s is one of the Citrus Heights Fire District/Orangevale fire stations. After the first Orangevale volunteer fire station was built in 1933, the Orangevale volunteer firefighters merged with the Citrus Heights Fire District around 1945. A new station replaced the original one on Greenback Lane and Pecan Avenue in 1953, and new stations were built at Hickory and Blythe Avenues in 1964 and at Chestnut Avenue, just north of Greenback Lane. Pictured below sometime in the 1960s is a view of the fire station built in 1953 by the Citrus Heights Fire District. (Courtesy Pioneer Mutual Hook and Ladder Society.)

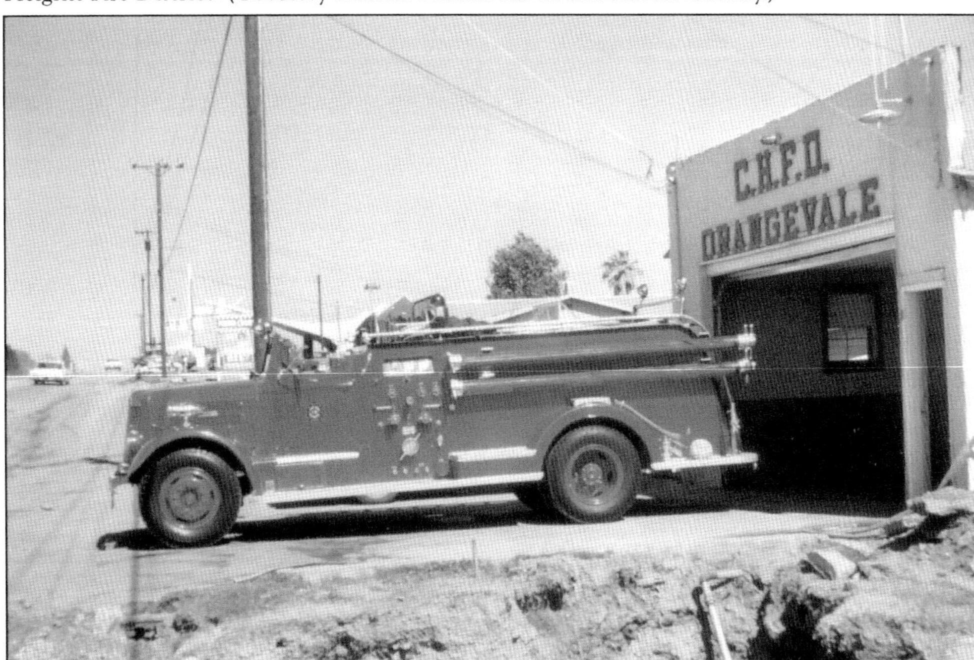

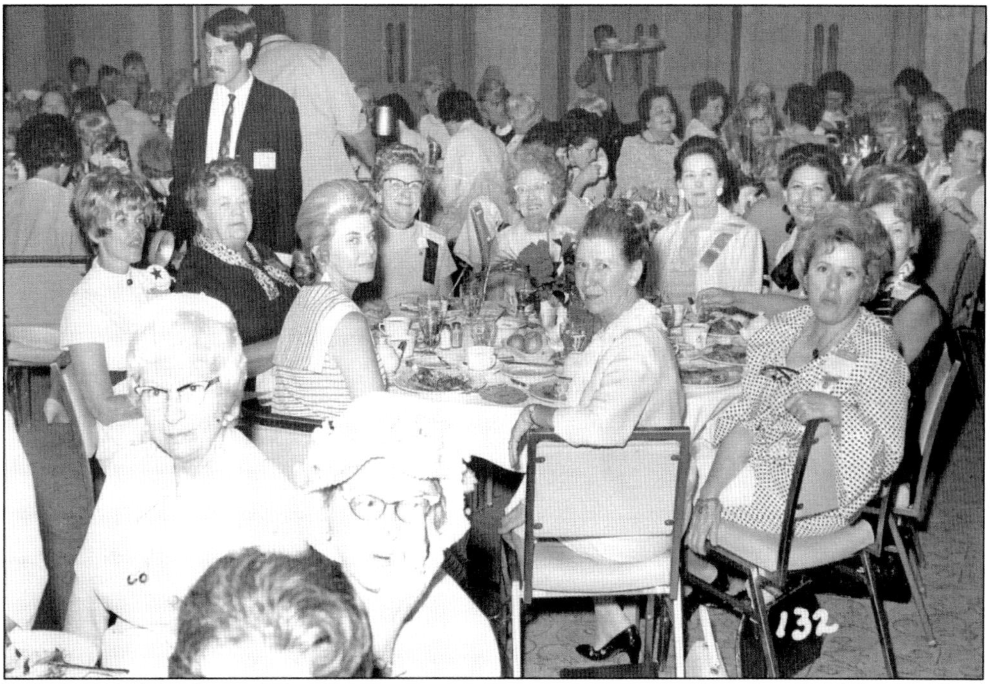

Pictured above in 1969, the Orangevale Woman's Club gathers for a social event. Below, the Orangevale Woman's Club float makes its way down Greenback Lane in the 1966 Pow Wow Days Parade. Mary Alice Calder invited a group of women to her home in 1913 to discuss the formation of a club that put their talents toward building the community and taking part in world affairs. This meeting resulted in the formation of the Orangevale Woman's Club, which has stayed true to its founding principals. "If a woman is looking for prestige," wrote Gertrude Greenhalgh in 1973, "she can find it in the Woman's Club which embodies this quality; if she is seeking friendship, the members have much of it to give; if she cares to be involved in the service to fellow men, then this club needs and appreciates her." (Courtesy Marcia Clark.)

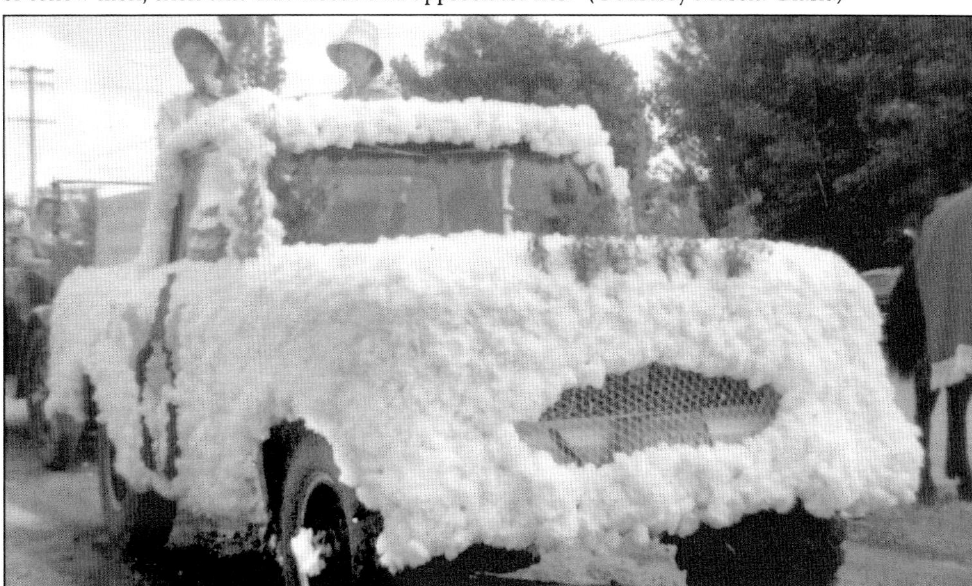

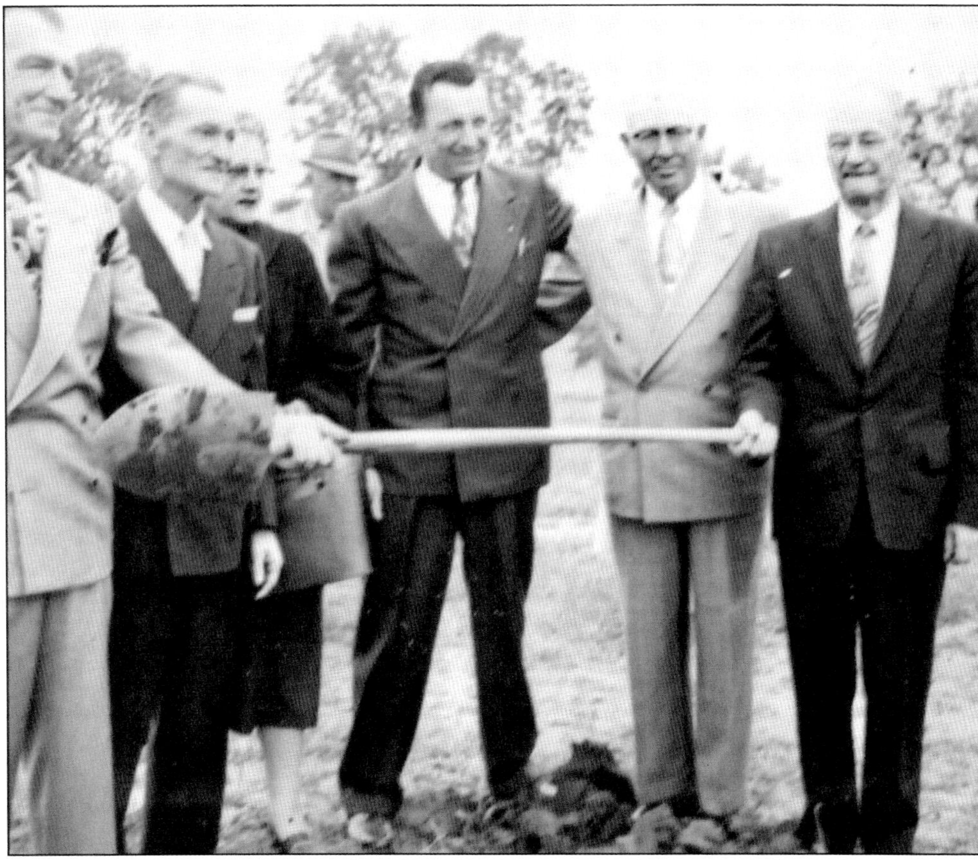

Pictured above in 1956 is groundbreaking for the Orangevale Grange hall. In the foreground stand, from left to right, Jack Cuthbertson, W. H. Pope, Kay White, James A. Wagner, Alton O. Healy, and Rev. D. G. Decherd. The Orangevale Grange organized in 1910 and held their first meeting in the hall above the Carson and Castleman store at the corner of Walnut Avenue and Greenback Lane. The grange also assisted in raising funds to help maintain the clubhouse and held meetings there. Yet, because of an act of arson, the building was severely damaged and lost. In 1955, the grange purchased a 10-acre lot on Walnut Avenue and broke ground in 1956. Below, Alton Healy works the shovel at the groundbreaking. (Courtesy Orangevale Grange.)

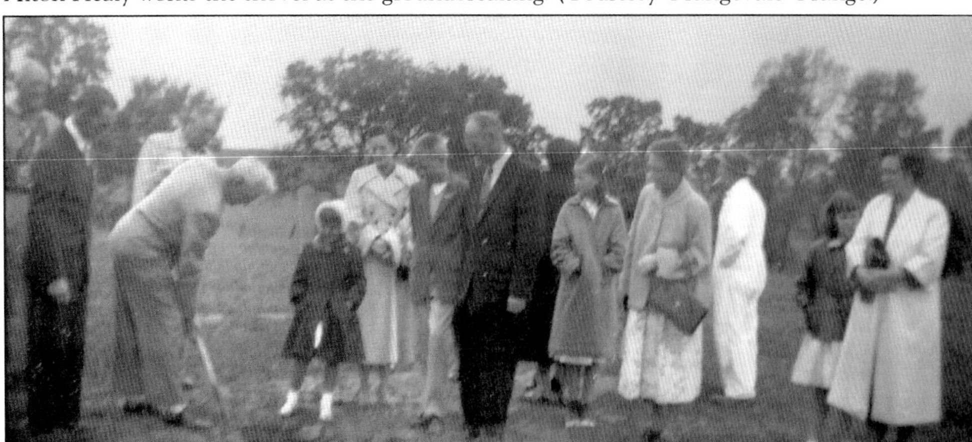

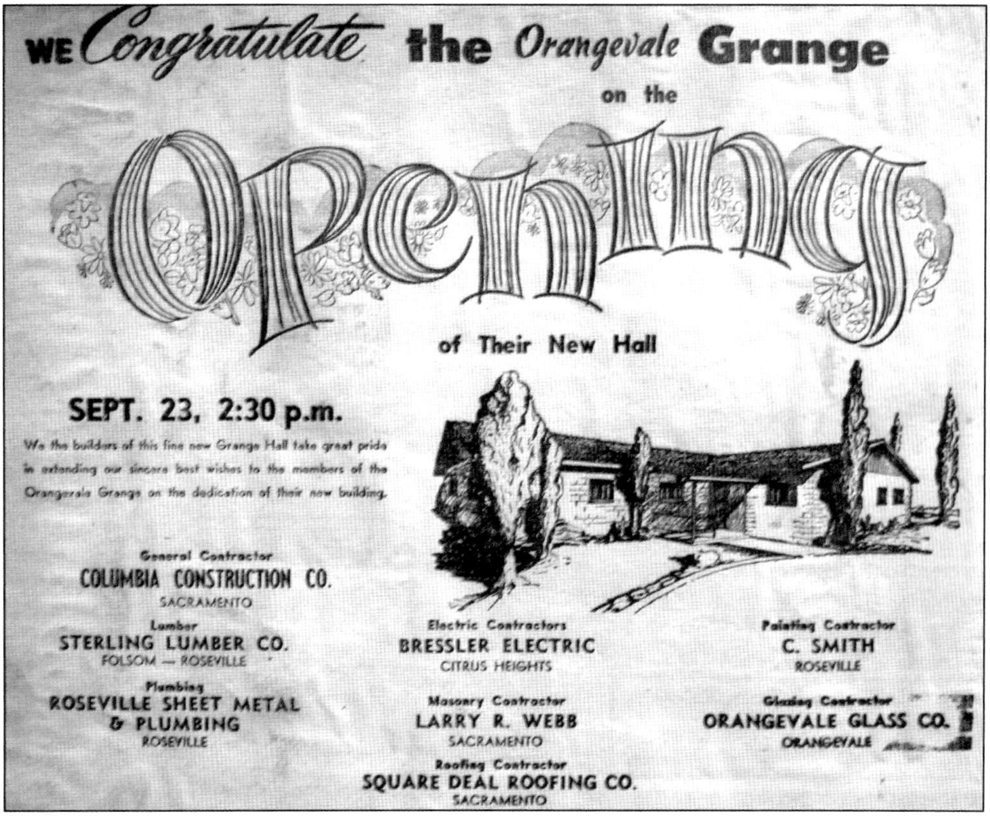

On September 23, 1956, the completed Orangevale Grange hall on Walnut Avenue was dedicated. Below, this photograph of the Orangevale Grange shows it sometime during the 1960s or 1970s. The Orangevale Grange has been indispensable in the development of the community. The grange is credited with bringing electricity to Orangevale, assisting in bringing a library to Orangevale, supporting and sponsoring local youth groups, such as the Boy Scouts, helping Orangevale become part of the Citrus Heights Fire District, supporting the construction of the Orangevale Youth Center, awarding scholarships to local students, and sponsoring local events. (Courtesy Orangevale Grange).

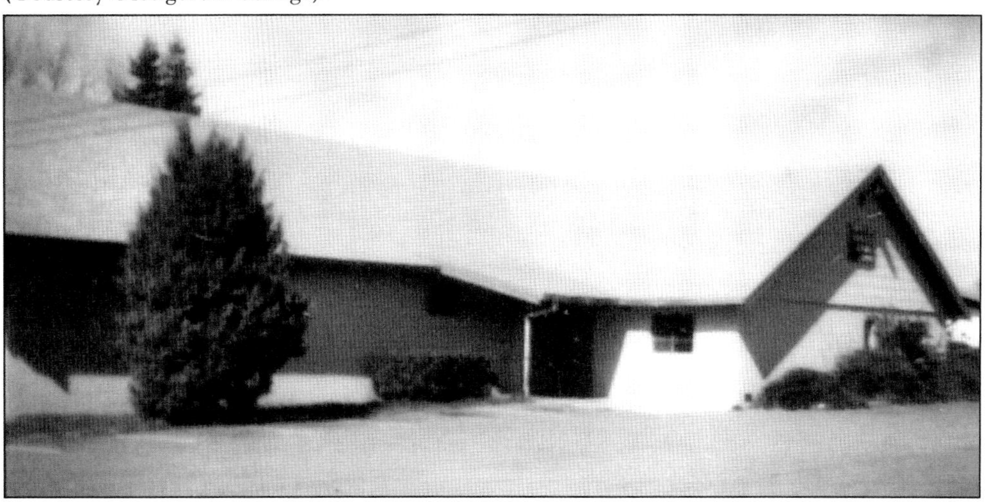

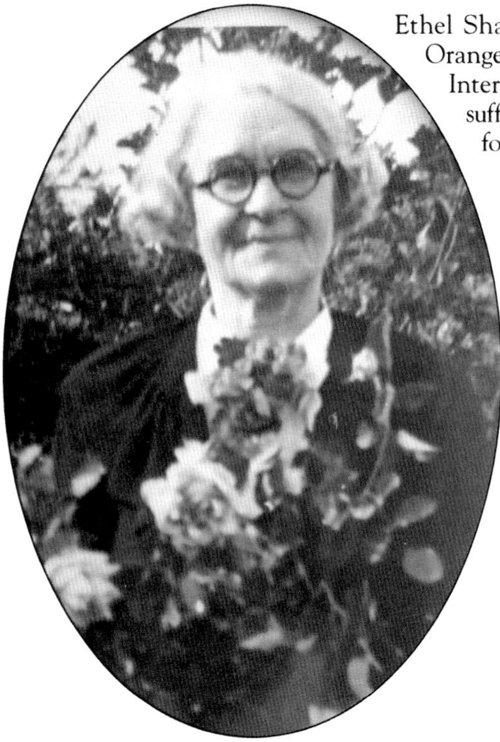

Ethel Shackelton was the first female Master of the Orangevale Grange, serving in 1918, 1919, and 1934. Interestingly, at the time of her first appointment, suffrage continued to remain an unattained civil right for women. (Courtesy Orangevale Grange.)

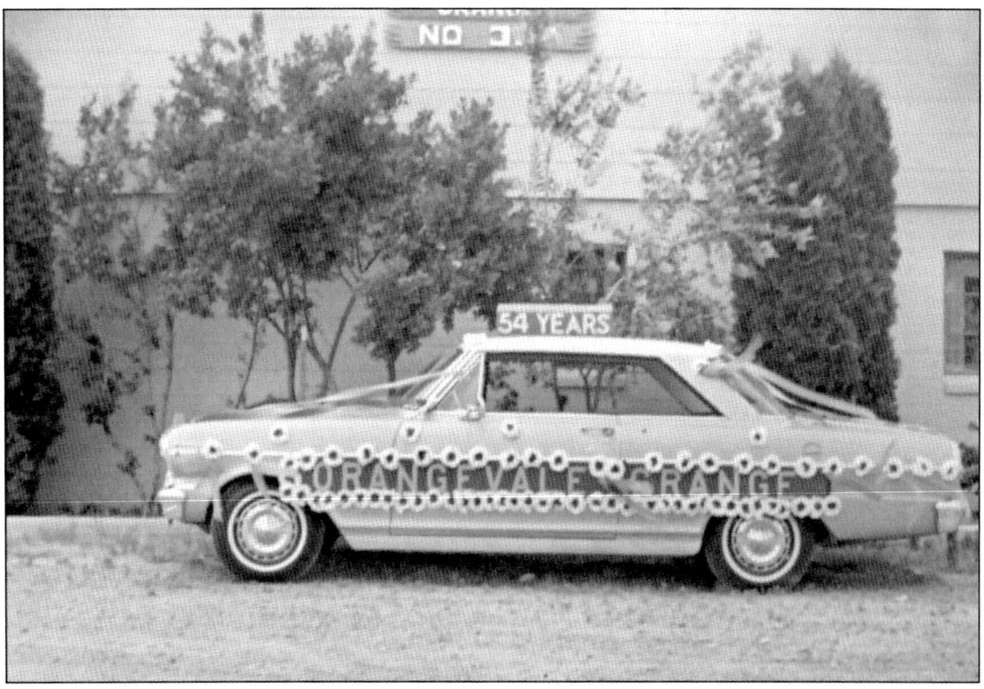

The above car, decorated with green and orange streamers, helped celebrate the Orangevale Grange's 54th anniversary in 1964. The Grange has been an active participant in serving, supporting, and sponsoring the Orangevale community and its residents, old and young, since its formation in 1910. (Courtesy Orangevale Grange.)

Six

Getting from Here to There

In their effect upon human welfare, in the difficult and complex problems lying within the province of almost every department of human endeavor, road improvement may well be said to touch the progress of civilization at every point.

—Logan Page, Director, Office of Public Roads, September 30, 1912

The availability of quality roads, bridges, and other transportation networks play a major role in a community's ability to attract and conduct business. When the Orange Vale Colonization Company promoted Orangevale as a pastoral paradise, they also advertised the construction of roads and bridges. A May 8, 1888, article in the *Sacramento Union* highlights the importance of this infrastructure to Orangevale:

> If the Townsite is attractive, hardly less so is Orangevale avenue, as the approach to this model colony is called, which skirts the bank of the American River as far as the Lincoln cut, and is romantic enough for anything. It is a well-graded road, with the picturesqueness of an avenue or park-walk. In its construction it has been found necessary to erect no less than three bridges, which are open to traffic already.

Greenback Lane, one of the first roads built in Orangevale, is also one of the largest thoroughfares today and has one of the most fascinating stories associated with it. Legend maintains that Chinese laborers built Greenback Lane during the 1860s and 1870s (coinciding with the construction of railroad lines to which the road provided access) and that they received payment in America's first wide-circulating paper money, "demand notes," or "greenbacks." Greenbacks, nicknamed so because of the distinctive green ink on the reverse side, were worth approximately 30¢ to the dollar and were a common form of payment at the time.

Orangevale's other roads, according to the *Sacramento Union*, "are appropriately designated by names signifying the different varieties of fruit for which the colony expects to become famous." Actually, the north-south roads have nut trees for names, and the east-west roads have shade trees for names, with exceptions for Main and Central Avenues, which were named after water lines, and Orangevale Avenue (likely Greenback Lane and not the current road), the town's main line. Greenback Lane, paved in 1916, remained the only major road in Orangevale until Madison and Hazel Avenues became major roads in the 1960s, following the large population growth in the region and the construction of more bridges.

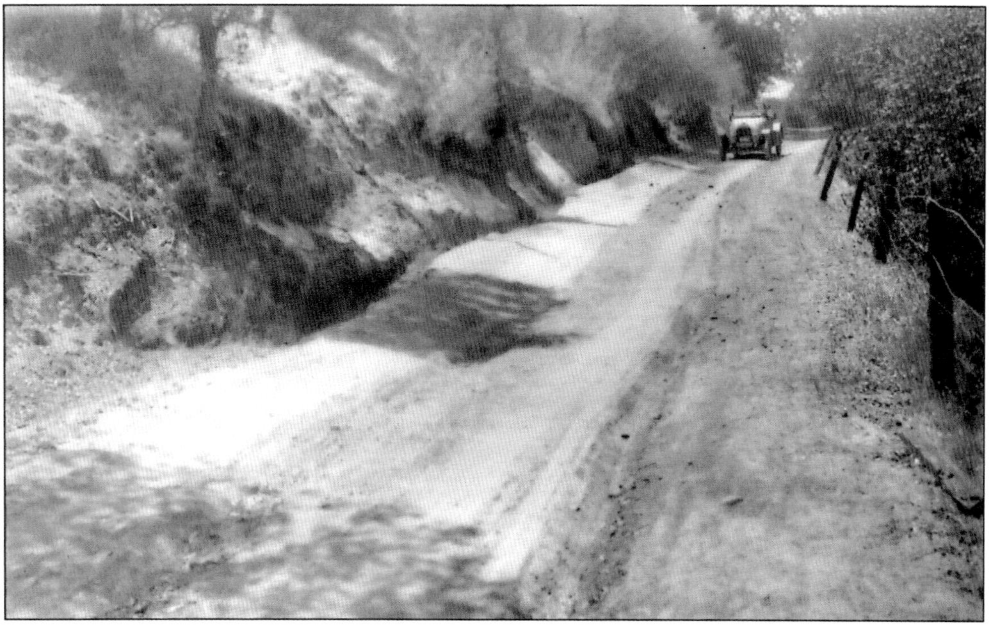

Pictures of the "Lincoln Highway Oldsmobile" passing through Orangevale along the Lincoln Highway show the difficult, but beautiful terrain of Orangevale in 1919. As a young soldier, Dwight D. Eisenhower had trouble traversing the nation in 1919. Following the route of the Lincoln Highway (later U.S. 40), which ran from New York to San Francisco, he and his crew took 62 days to cross the country and often broke down or met with delays caused by the bad road conditions. This experience influenced his understanding of—and desire for—a workable national highway system. In 1956, President Eisenhower authorized the Federal Aid Highway Act to improve the nation's highway system. (Courtesy SAMCC, No. 80/05/5780 and No. 80/05/5785.)

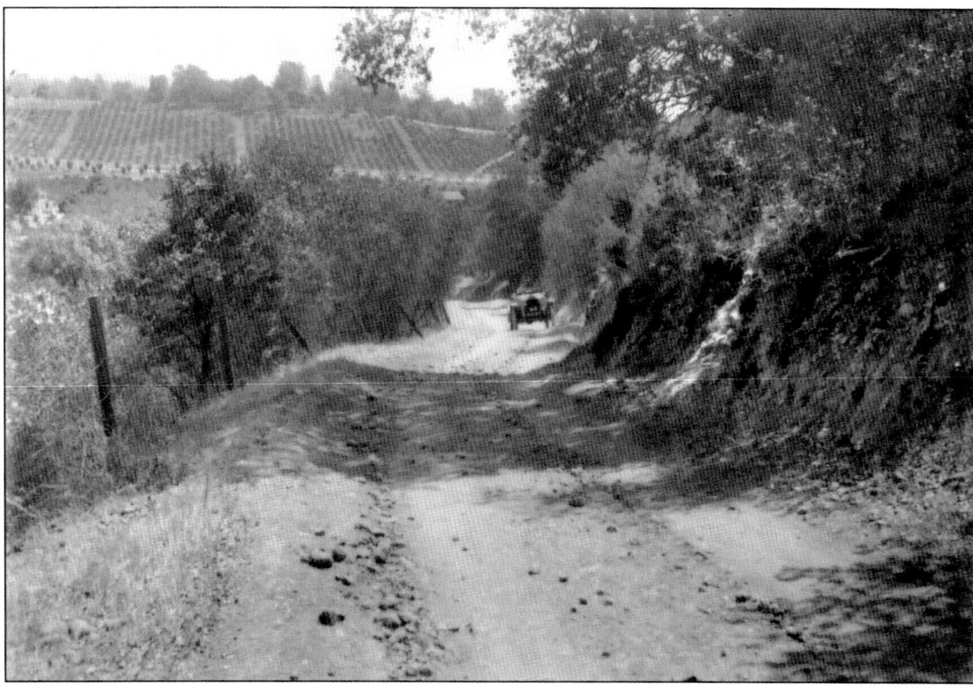

A young Tomich boy is seen here *c.* 1915, walking along one of the many unpaved roads in Orangevale, possibly Pecan Avenue or Chestnut Avenue, where the family's two homes were located. (Courtesy Fred Tomich.)

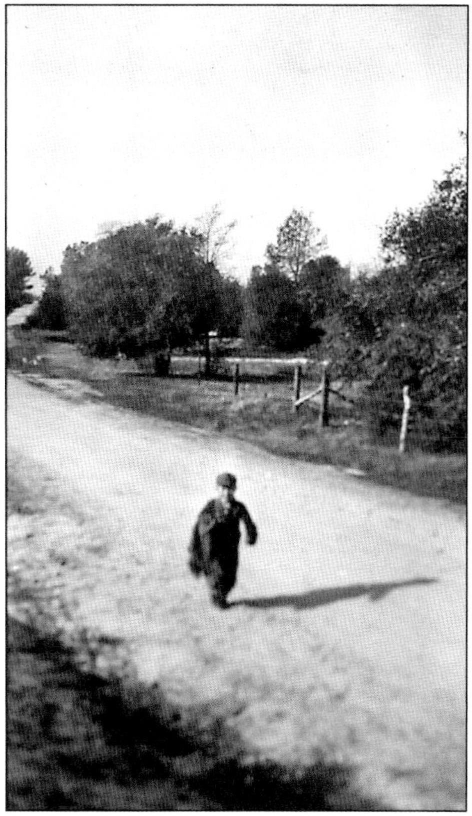

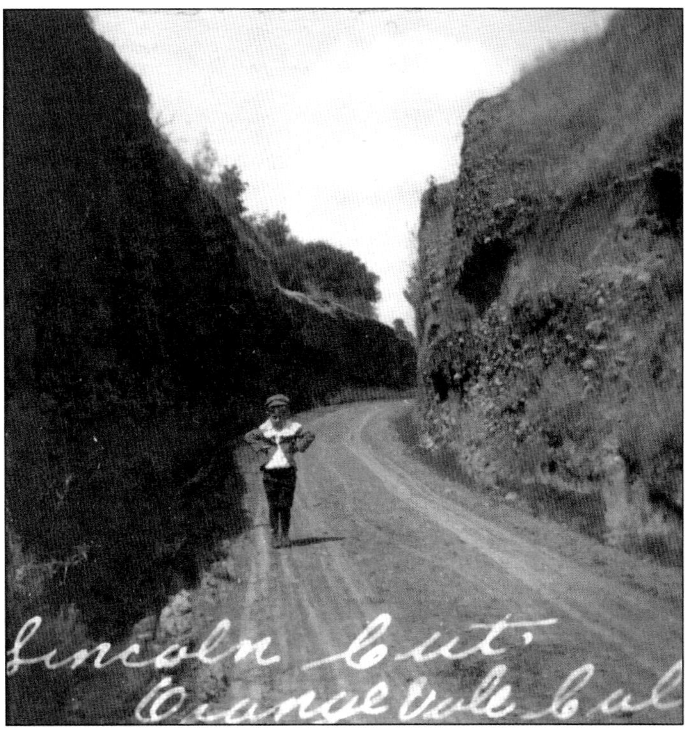

Here a young boy *c.* 1900 strolls along Greenback Lane through the Lincoln Cut before it was paved. Between 1858 and 1861, the California Central Railroad made two cuts along the American River's tough granite bluffs in Folsom to provide access to train depots and a railroad bridge. The Lincoln Cut connected to Orangevale Avenue (likely modern-day Greenback Lane) on the north side of the river. (Courtesy Folsom History Museum, No. 2004.04.12.)

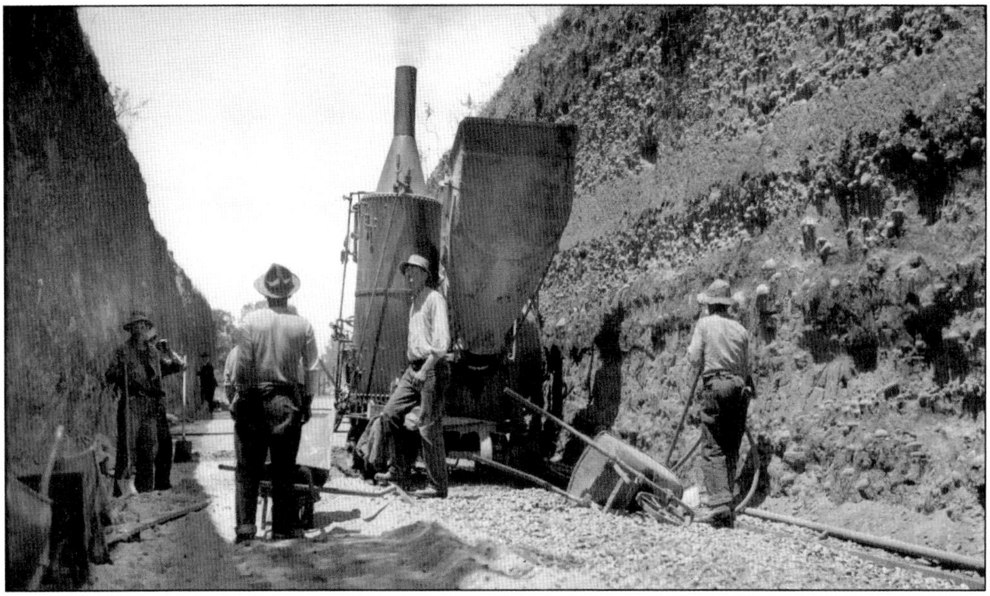

Many of California's highways and public-works employees paved Greenback Lane around 1916, including this section through the Lincoln Cut. The road was referred to as Orangevale Avenue (most likely not the current road) until it was destroyed by the widening and extension of Madison Avenue in the late 1960s. In fact, many of the nation's roads were paved at this time because of the Good Roads Movement, which advocated improved conditions. (Courtesy SAMCC, No. 76/35/283.)

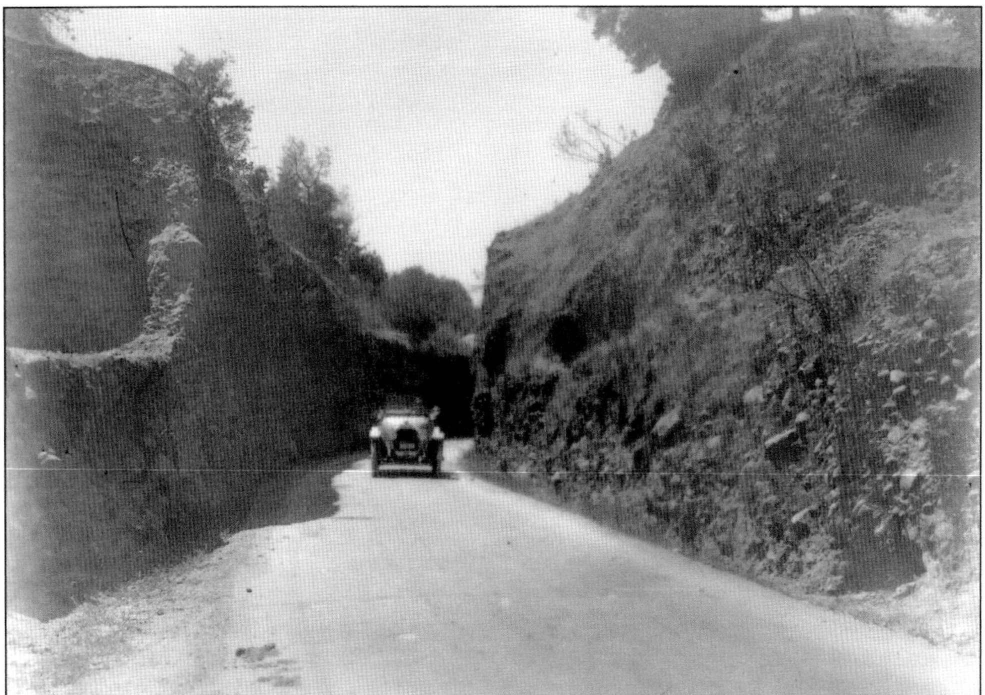

Pictured here in 1919, the "Lincoln Highway Oldsmobile" enjoys a smooth ride through the Lincoln Cut along the paved Greenback Lane. (Courtesy SAMCC, No. 80/05/5786.)

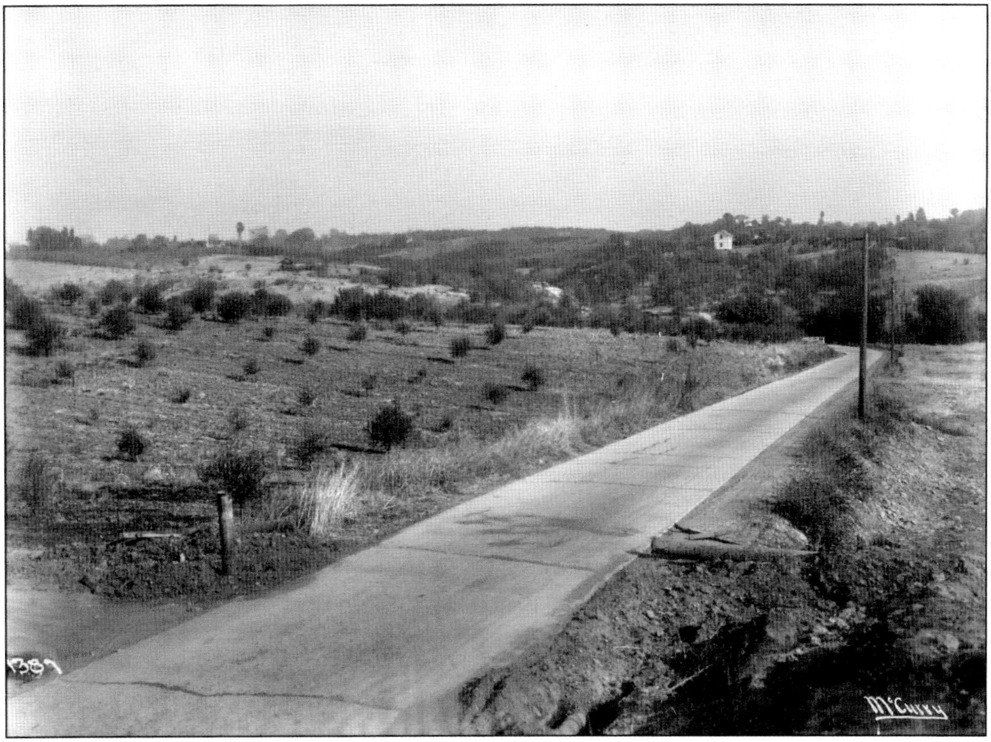

Originally labeled "County Highway, Orangevale," *c.* 1915, this is possibly another stretch of the Lincoln Highway that crossed the beautiful open landscape of Orangevale. It is an example of the quality paved roads in this small community. (Courtesy SAMCC, No. 81/01/352.)

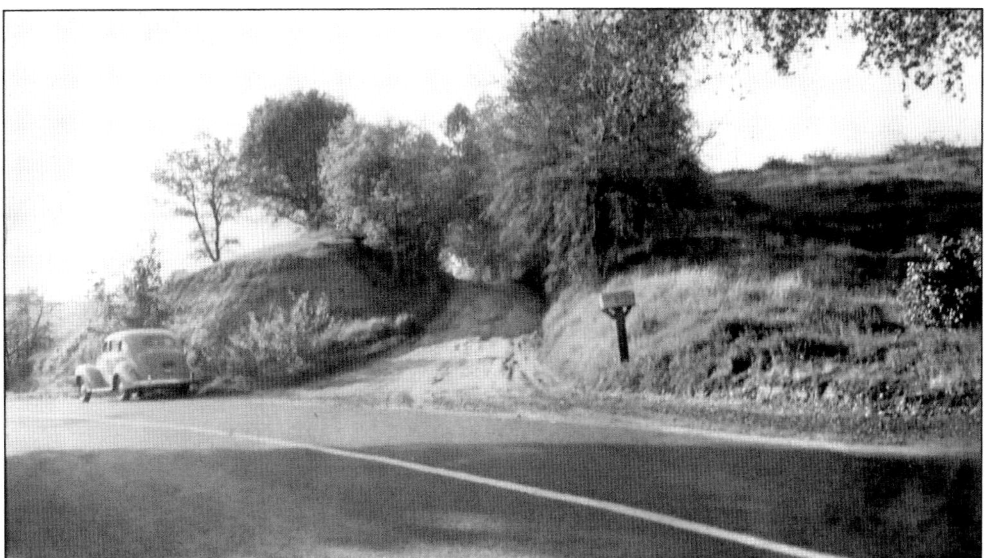

Pictured here in March 1941, this unpaved road, which was abandoned after the railroad bridge collapsed around 1867, is the old roadbed of the California Central Railroad. The two roads, located just to the west of the Lincoln Cut, show the mix of quality paved and unpaved roads in and around Orangevale in the mid-20th century. (Courtesy SAMCC, No. 85/24/5754.)

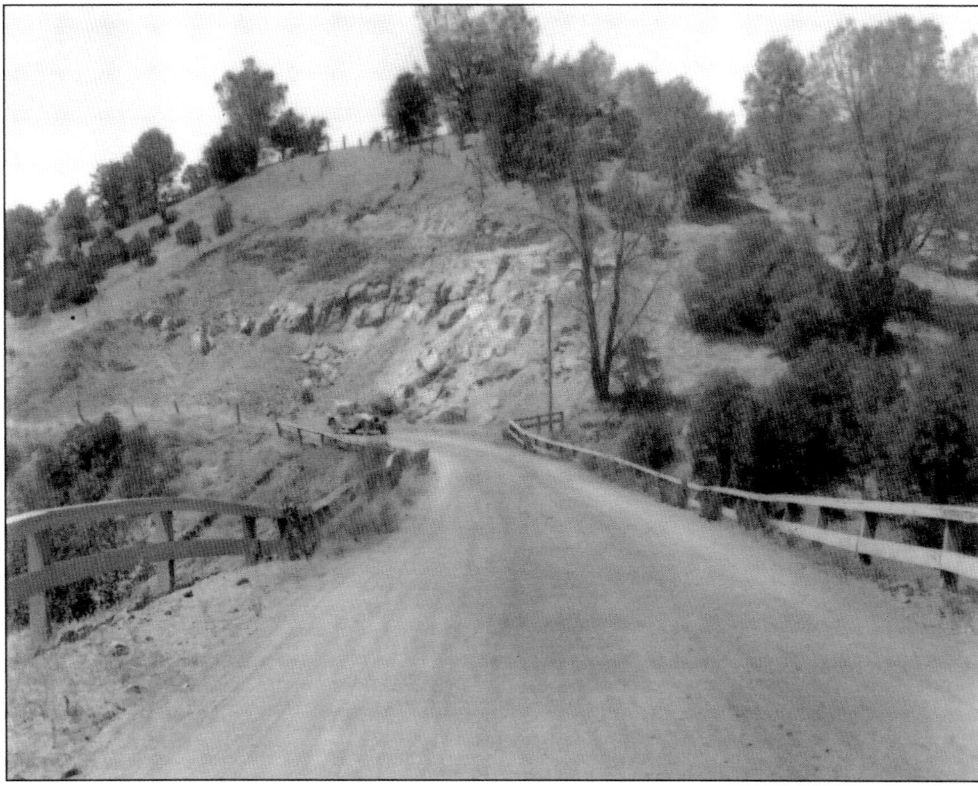

The Lincoln Highway Oldsmobile, seen here in 1919, traverses through the countryside of Orangevale's rolling hills in route to Folsom. (Courtesy SAMCC, No. 80/05/5782.

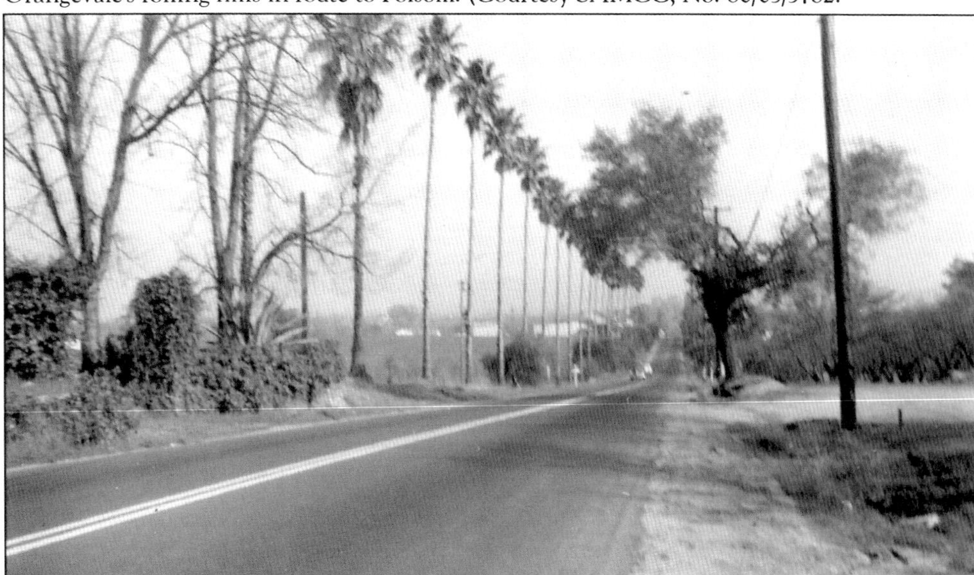

Greenback Lane, even before it became a four-lane thoroughfare, has always served as Orangevale's main road. Pictured here in 1958, two cars drive down the road lined with beautiful palm trees and free from heavy traffic. Widening Greenback Lane to four lanes in the late 1960s required removal of the palm trees. (Courtesy Orange Vale Water Company.)

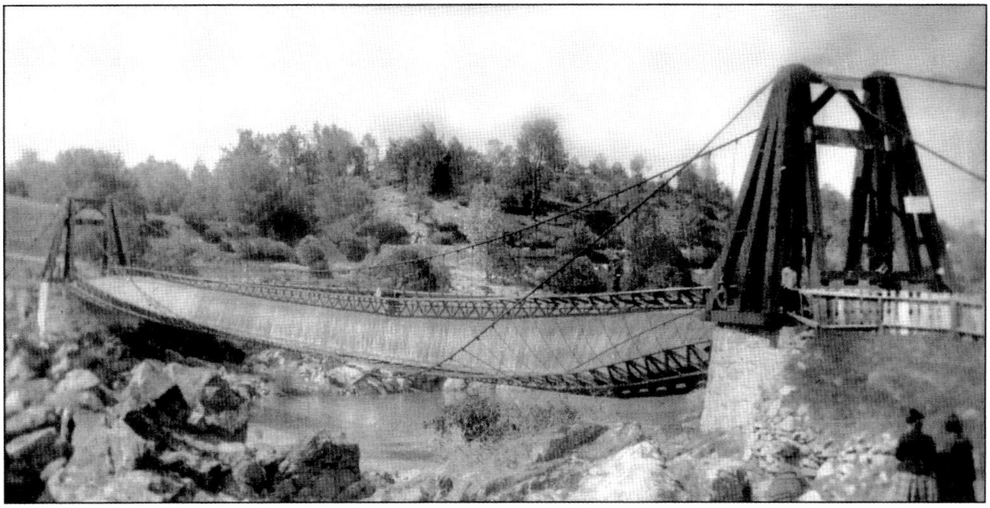

This old suspension bridge (above), built around 1862 just after a major flood, was used in advertisements by the Orange Vale Colonization Company. It crossed the American River to Folsom and serviced the surrounding areas, including Orangevale, for 30 years before it collapsed, as seen below, in 1892. (Courtesy SAMCC, No. 85/24/5662 and No. 85/24/5664a.)

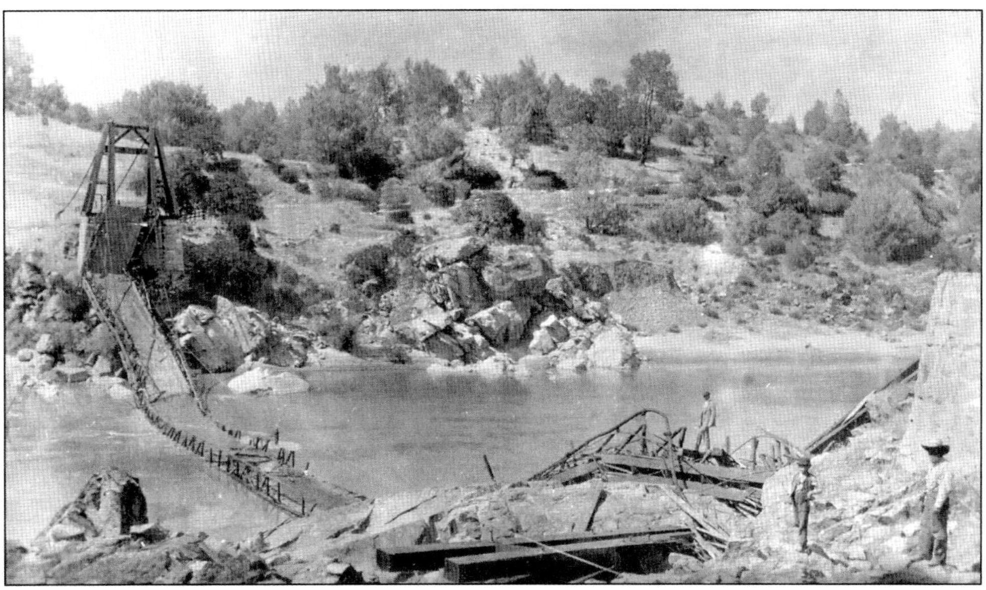

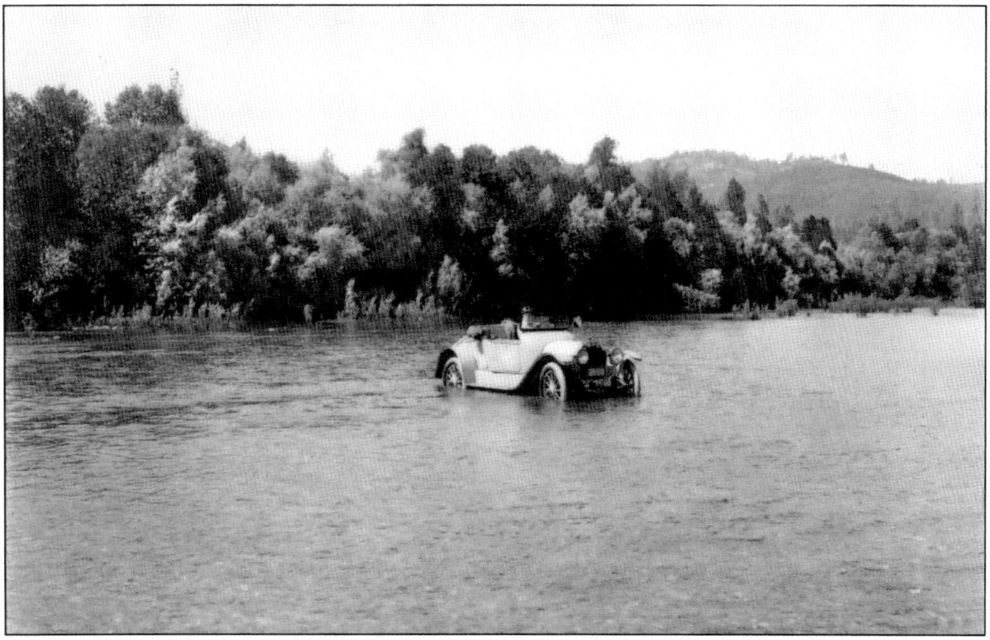

As this 1919 photograph of the "Lincoln Highway Oldsmobile" demonstrates, the river was not always easy to cross and sometimes required drivers to traverse the river's low points. Bridges in Orangevale and across the American River in Folsom and Fair Oaks have been essential for Orangevale to survive, whether used by farmers to ship fruit or by commuters to get to work. (Courtesy SAMCC, No. 80/05/5784.)

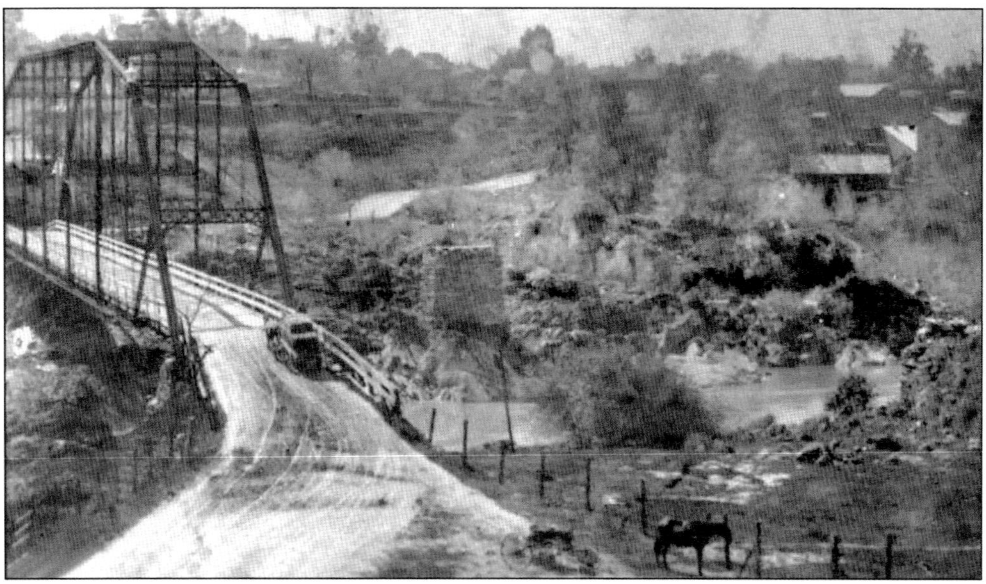

The Orange Vale Colonization Company acted quickly to make sure this old steel truss bridge, a Pennsylvania Petit, pictured in the 1890s, went up in 1893, after the old suspension bridge collapsed. The Orange Vale Colonization Company knew its success at luring potential settlers to the area would depend on access to a bridge over the American River, which farmers needed to reach the railroad in Folsom to transport their fruit. (Courtesy Folsom History Museum, No. 2004.05.04.)

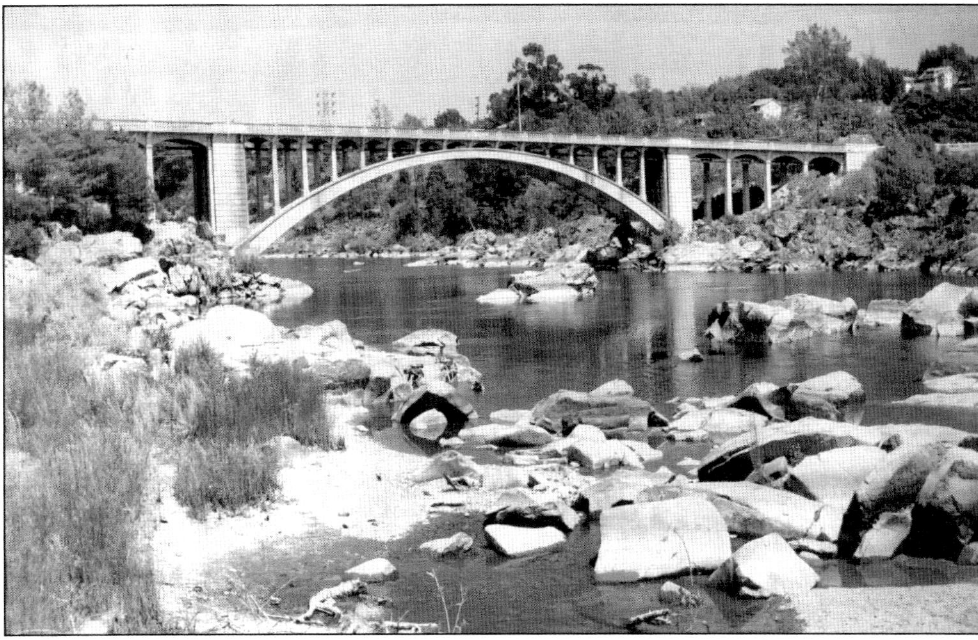

The truss bridge proved inadequate as the automobile became more prevalent, and a new bridge was needed to handle car traffic and weight. The Rainbow Bridge, purportedly unnamed until a resident first called it such in the 1940s, opened in 1917, according to the California Department of Transportation. The bridge, pictured here in the 1970s, is an example of the reinforced-concrete-arch bridge typical of the time. (Courtesy SAMCC, *Sacramento Bee* Photo Morgue, Bridges.)

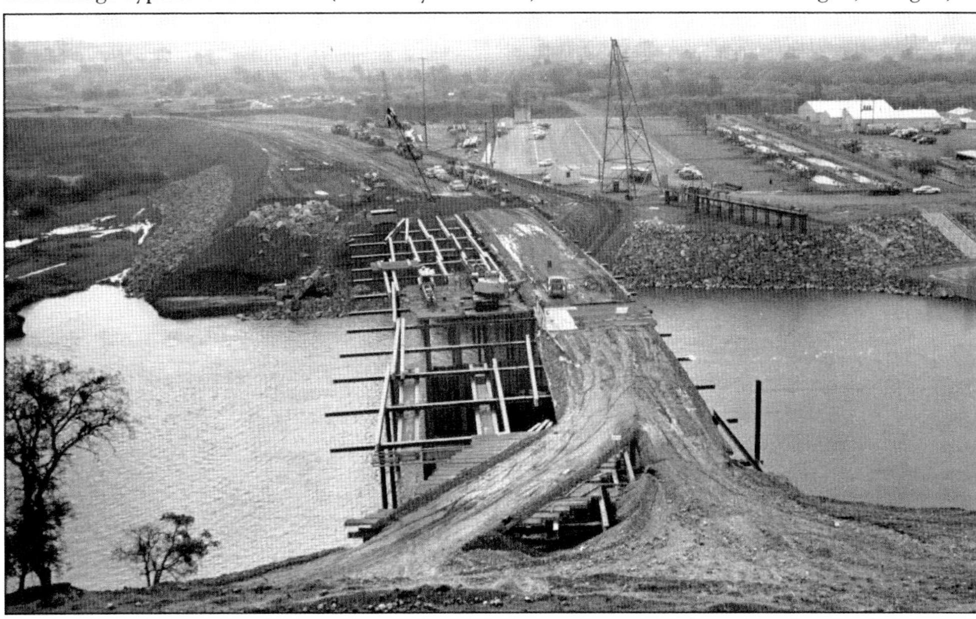

Construction of the Hazel Avenue Bridge over the American River from Rancho Cordova to Fair Oaks began in 1965. Still, as with bridges at Folsom, the Hazel Avenue Bridge provided easier access to and from Orangevale for commuters and has remained a pivotal transportation route for more than 40 years. As seen here on December 2, 1965, a temporary access had been built as construction of the bridge began. (Courtesy SAMCC, *Sac Bee* Photo Morgue, Bridges.)

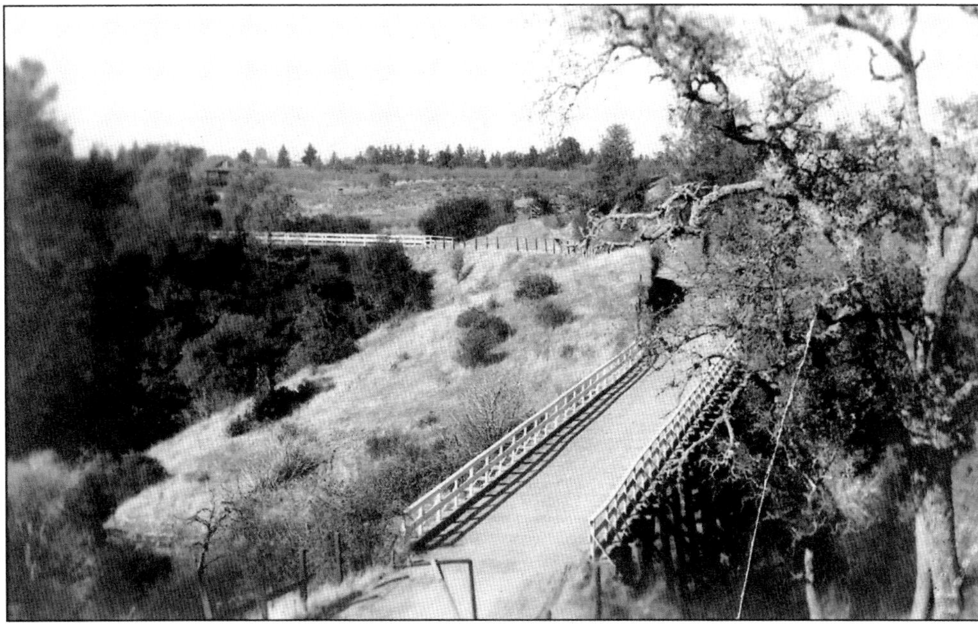

Pictured here sometime in the first two decades of the 20th century, the bridge over Fern Glen near the Lincoln Cut between Orangevale and Folsom provided access for commuters and travelers in and around Orangevale as it connected to bridges over the American River at Folsom. (Courtesy Folsom History Museum, No. 2004.04.14.)

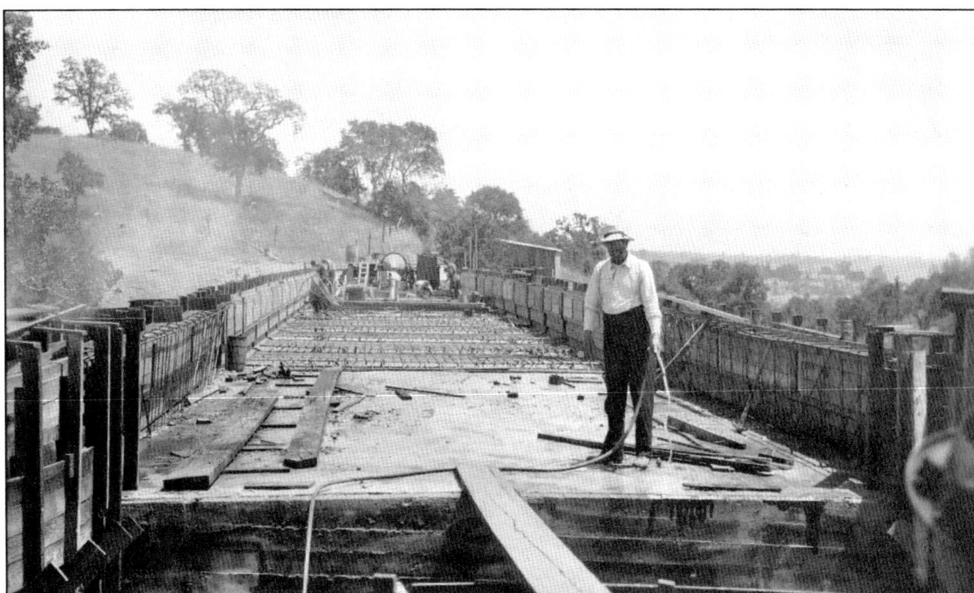

The Orangevale Avenue Bridge, constructed in 1915, is a reinforced-concrete-arch bridge with open spandrel columns and a T-beam superstructure. Here a worker handles the hose as others work in the background in 1915. (Courtesy SAMCC, No. 77/35/505.)

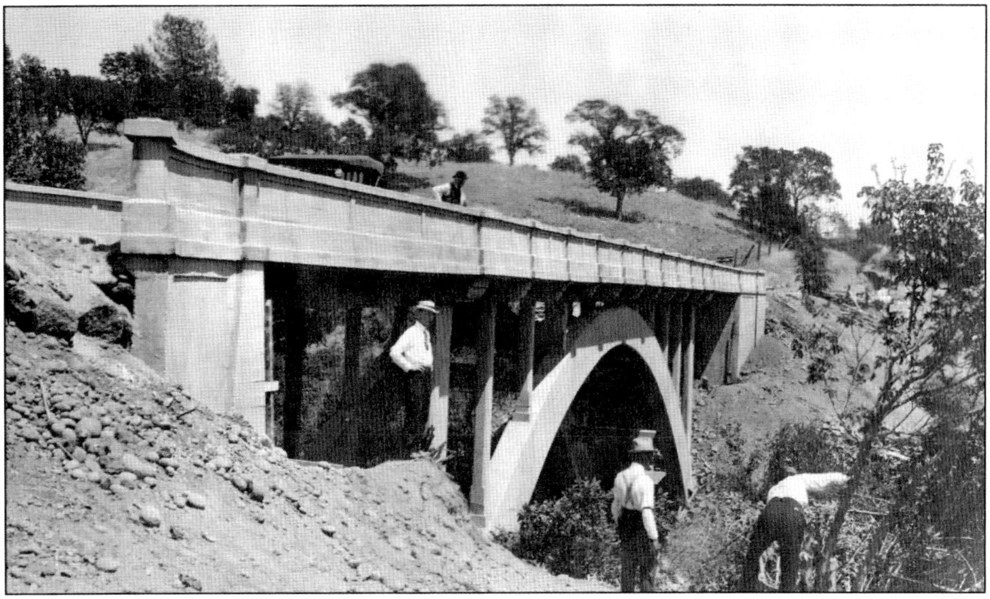

Pictured here in 1915, the Orangevale Avenue Bridge, a reinforced-concrete structure designed to last approximately 50 years, has serviced the community for more than 90 years and allows Orangevale residents and visitors to traverse Orangevale's beautiful rolling hills. (Courtesy SAMCC, No. 77/35/500 and No. 77/35/481.)

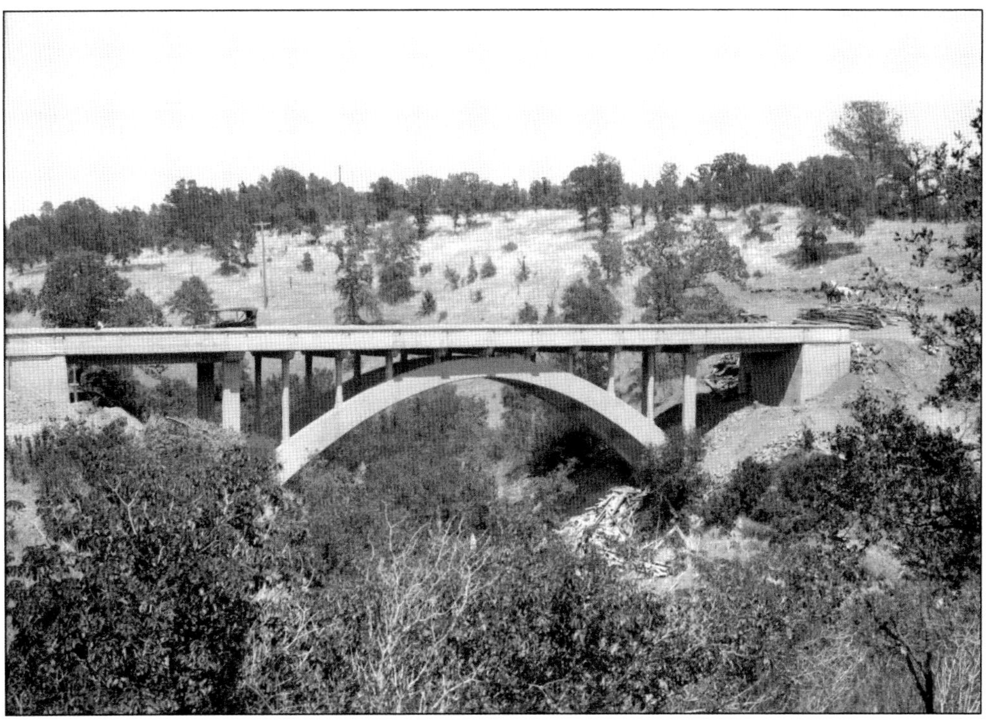

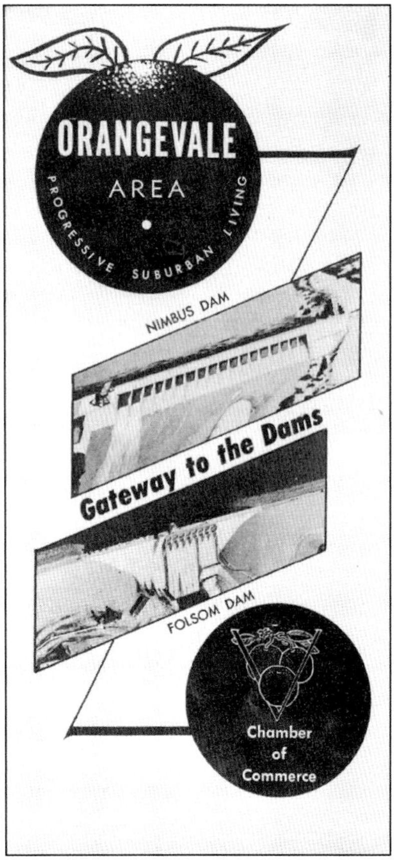

In the 1950s and 1960s, Orangevale's chamber of commerce promoted the community with this pamphlet. They boasted of the modern structures nearby to attract settlers who may have thought of Orangevale as a primitive rural community. (Courtesy SAMCC, unidentified black and white negatives.)

The Hazel Avenue Bridge and Nimbus Dam, finished in 1955, are seen during the bridge's construction in 1965–1966. The Nimbus Dam, seven miles downstream from the Folsom Dam, reregulates the releases for power made through the Folsom power plant and forms Lake Natoma. (Courtesy SAMCC, Sac Bee Photo Morgue No. 1126.)

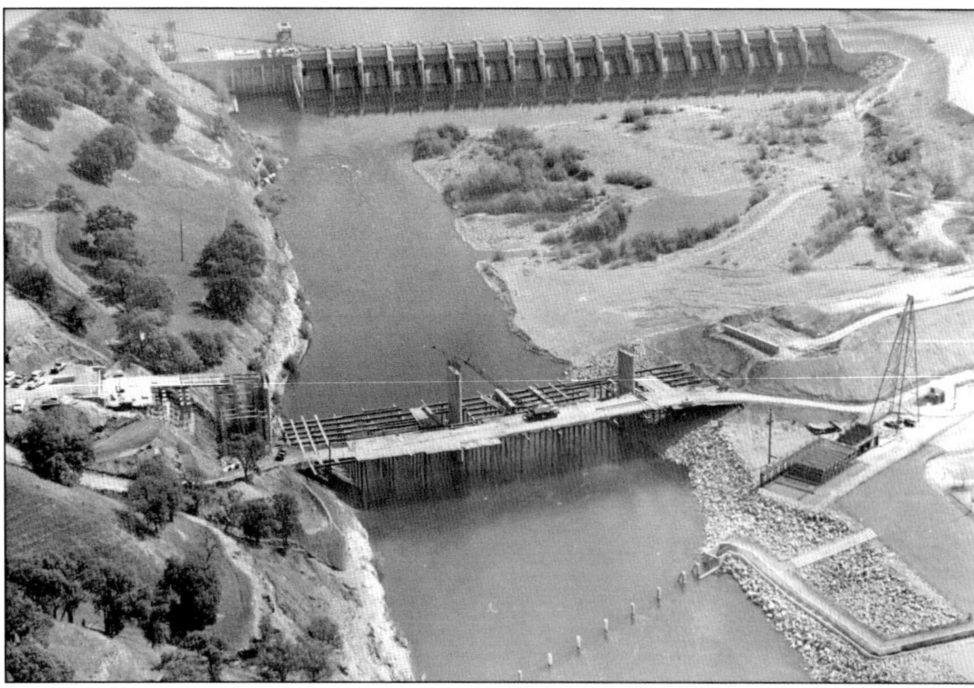

Seven

Growing Up in Orangevale

Children are our most valuable natural resource.

—Herbert Hoover, 1874–1964

Parents in Orangevale worked hard to secure a safe environment where their most prized natural resources, their children, could play, learn values, acquire a good work ethic, and grow.

Early booster publications advertising Orangevale, such as the 1909 publication *Sacramento Valley Sunbeam: Devoted to the Interests of Ideal Country Homes*, highlight small parks, good neighbors, and "lots of work for the boys and girls as well as the grown people." For children, especially within agricultural communities, work is often a necessary component of life. In Orangevale, as recalled by Naida Effinger, with men employed elsewhere, such as at Folsom prison or on dredgers, women and children were a needed labor force. "It was always fun," said Effinger. "Because it was a whole bunch of kids, you were always playing around and still working at the same time. It was all a fun thing."

Parents and community members worked hard to ensure the best experience for their children by supporting the establishment of schools, libraries, and parks. Even with a community center in place as early as the 1940s, Orangevale residents wanted a youth center. Land was purchased, donations made, and every August, carnivals were held at the youth center to raise additional funds. On April 16, 1950, the Orangevale Youth Center was dedicated. Boxer Max Baer acted as the master of ceremonies and Howard Greenhalgh, who served as the first president of the Orangevale Youth Center board from 1948 to 1953, made introductory remarks. Local organizations and community members continued to work toward maintaining and improving the youth center, which is still active today.

Many residents miss the old, spacious Orangevale, where work was fun, exploration encouraged, bare feet common, and creativity essential. Fortunately, those days are not completely lost, as such memories have been captured by the photographic lenses of adoring parents and are presented here.

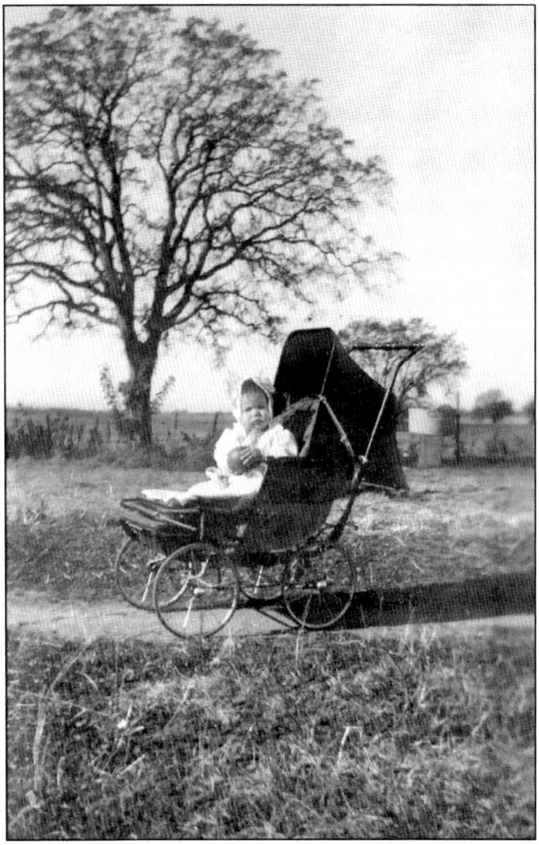

Six-month-old Ivie Odlin sits contented in her baby basket clasping a ball in her hands in front of her parents' home off Pecan Avenue. Odlin was born on March 3, 1910, to proud parents, Ida and Guy Odlin. (Courtesy Jean Kelly.)

Eleanor Tomich holds her firstborn, Nick, born in 1912, on her lap on the porch of their new house on Chestnut Avenue. Nick Tomich grew up to be an apprentice for the notable Sacramento firm of Dean and Dean Architects in 1931 and retired in 1988. Tomich helped design nearly 1,000 buildings. (Courtesy Tom Tomich.)

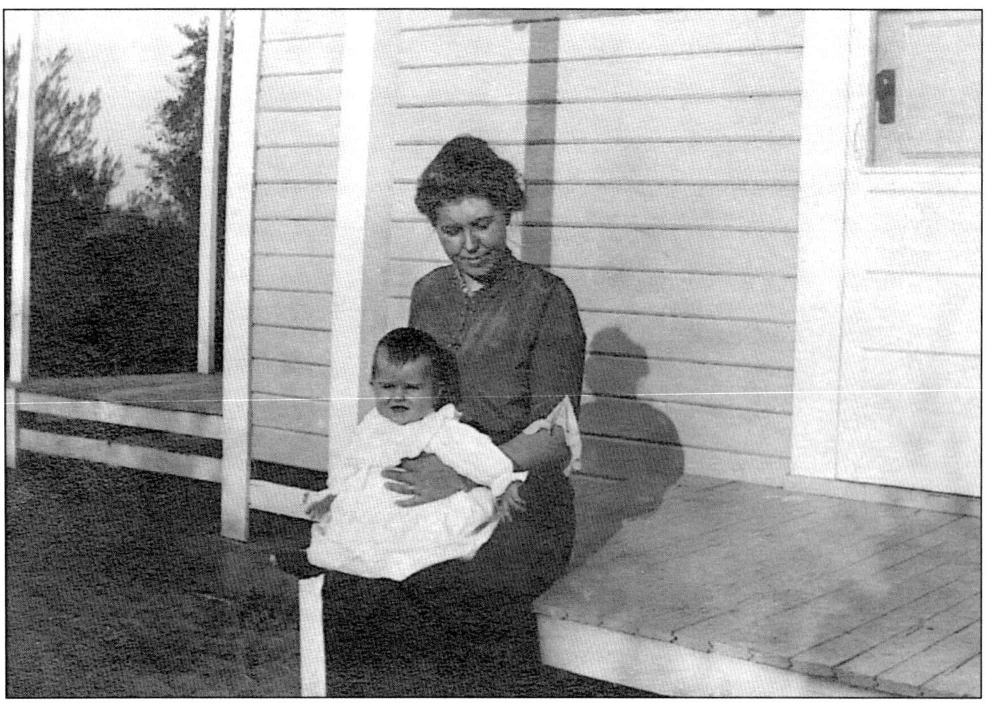

Ida Odlin holds her daughters, three-year-old Ivie (left) and two-year-old Ione "Marjorie" (right), in 1913. (Courtesy Jean Kelly.)

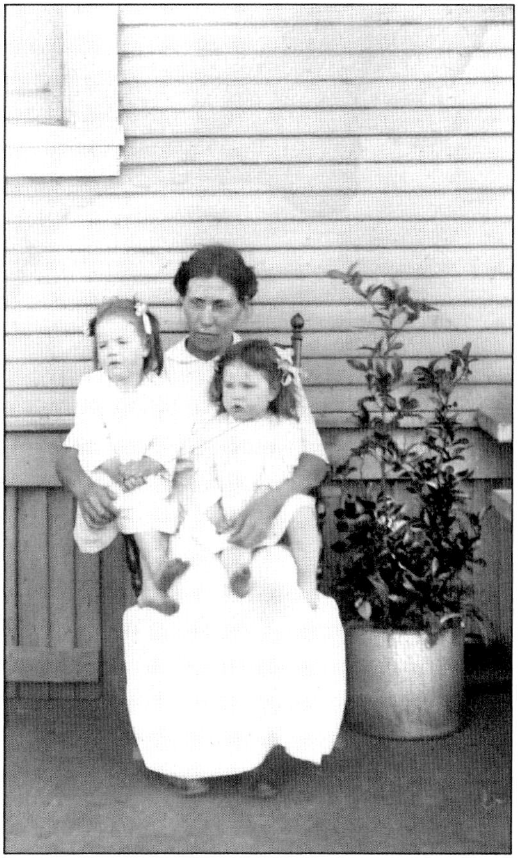

Pictured here are Nick Tomich and younger sister Frances, playing with a goat in front of their house on Chestnut Avenue c. 1916. (Courtesy Tom Tomich)

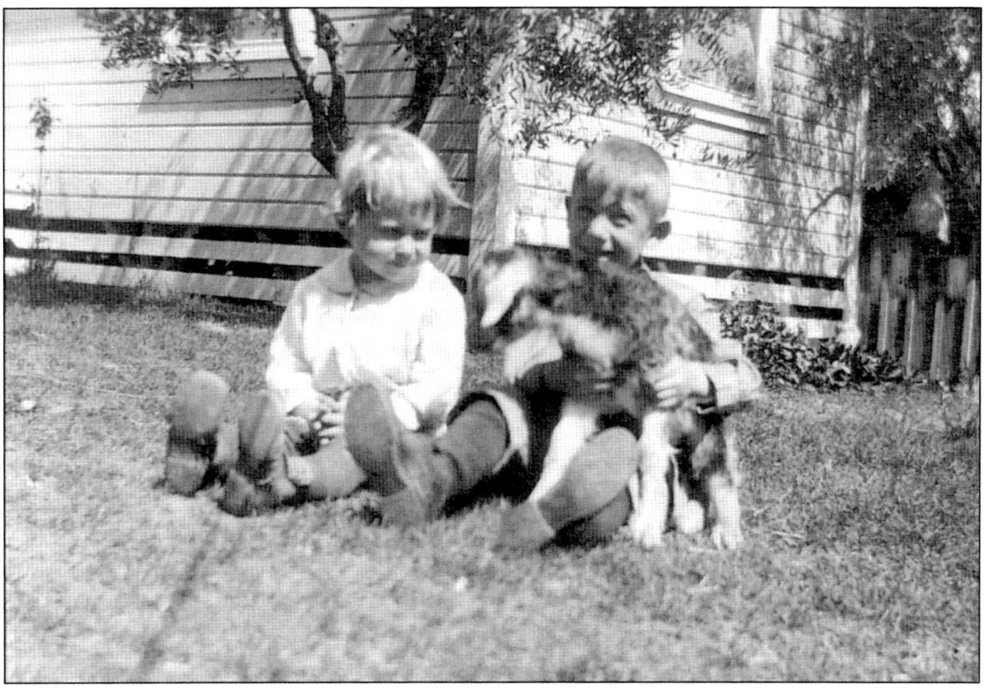

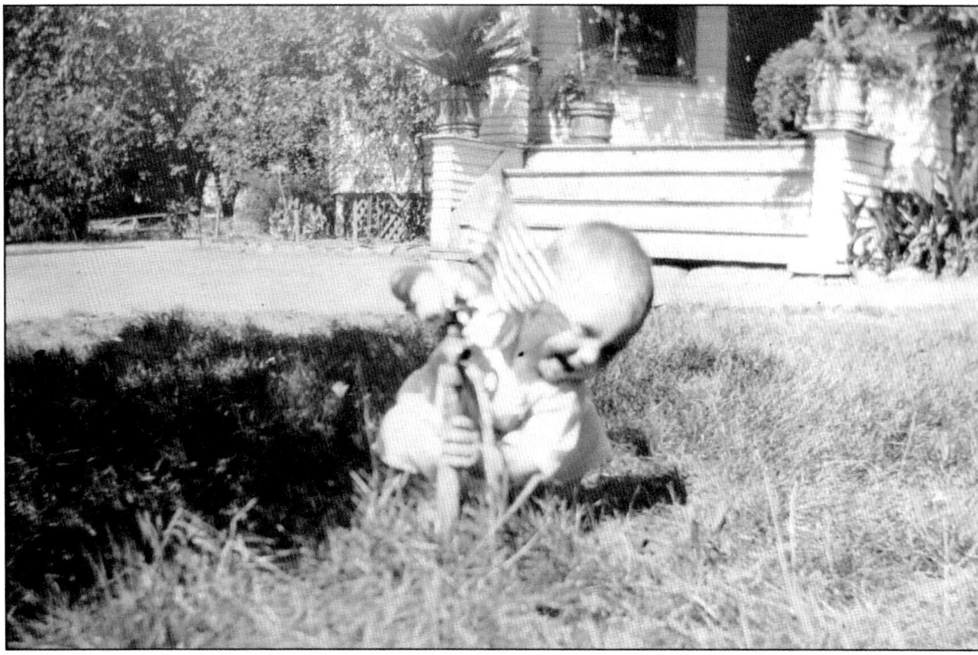

Baby John "Jack" Tomich happily grasps an American flag in the front yard of his Grandma Wickstrom's residence on Pecan Avenue in 1918. (Courtesy Fred Tomich.)

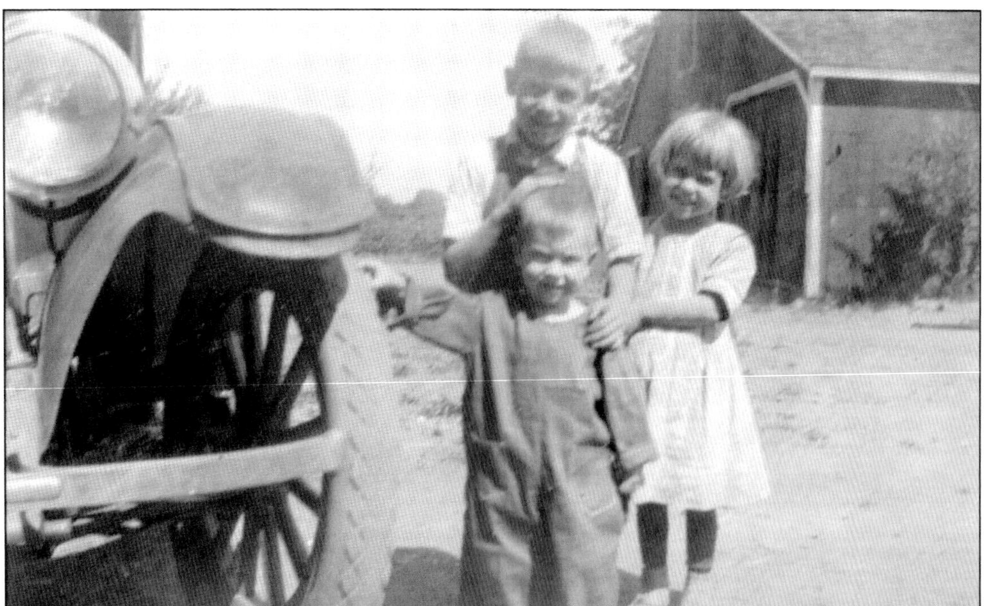

Proud big brother Nick Tomich stands with his younger siblings Frances and Jack around 1925. (Courtesy Fred Tomich.)

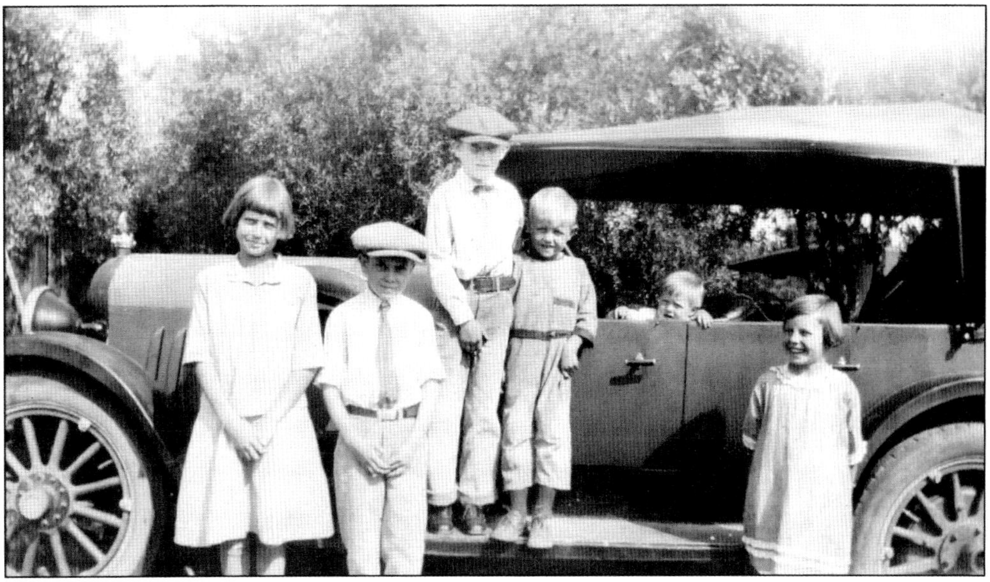

Standing contented in front of Aunt Ruth Kirsten's Hapmobile in 1927 from left to right are Frances Tomich, John Tomich, Ray Johnson, Quentin Tomich, Tom Tomich, and Eleanor Tomich. Aunt Ruth loved to drive. An account kept at the Orange Vale Water Company describes her love of driving: "As a young lady, she and a few other girl friends in flowing white dresses drove the unpaved and muddy roads to Tahoe on more than one occasion." (Courtesy Fred and Tom Tomich.)

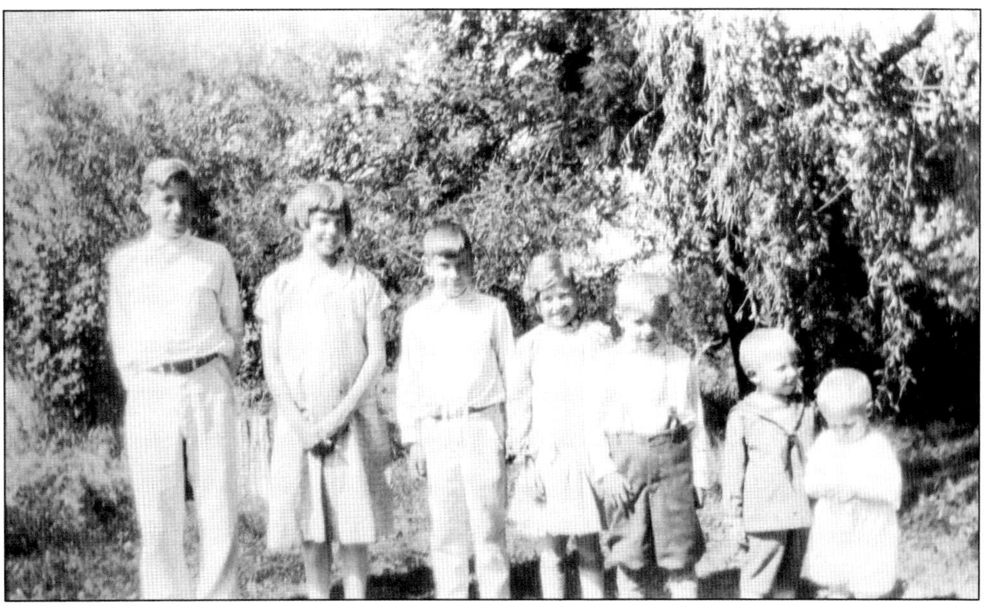

Pictured here c. 1925, Prosper and Eleanor Tomich's children are lined up in the order of their birth. From left to right they are Nick, Frances, John, Eleanor, Quentin, Fred, and Tom. (Courtesy Fred Tomich.)

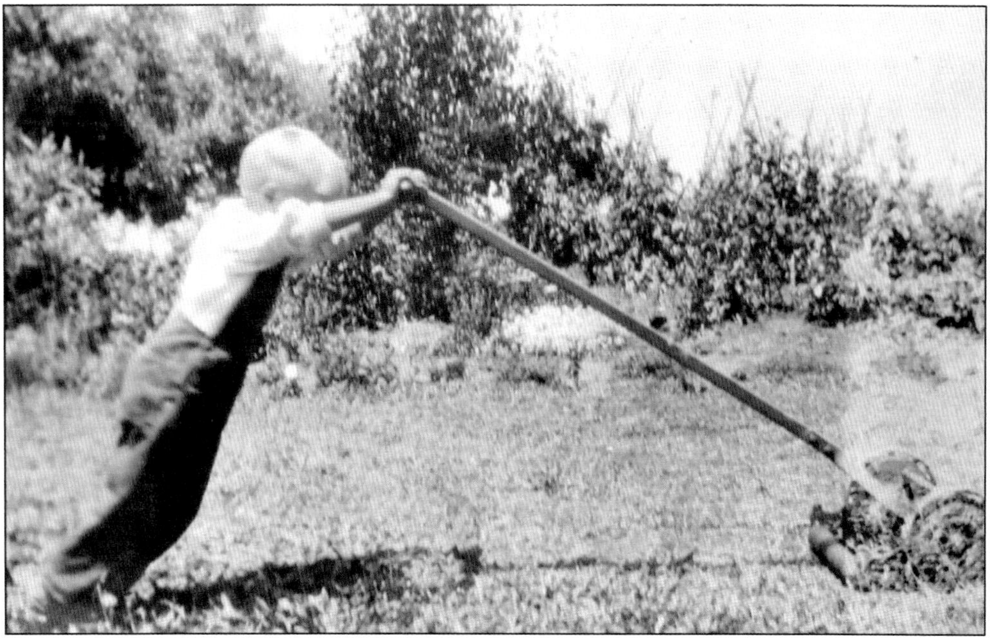

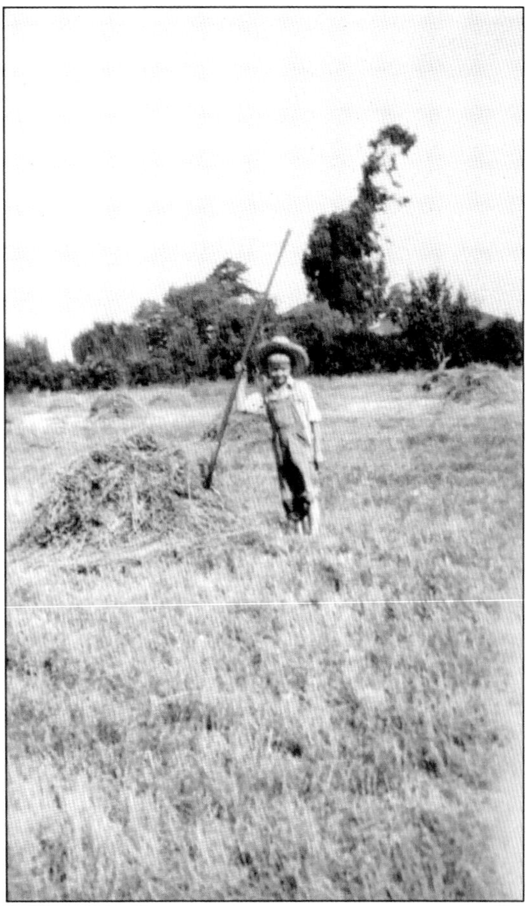

Typical of the work ethic found in young Orangevalians, a young Tomich boy mows the lawn. The picture is believed to be of Fred Tomich in the mid-1920s. (Courtesy Fred Tomich.)

Always industrious, a Tomich youngster works away at a pile of hay with his pitchfork. (Courtesy Fred Tomich.)

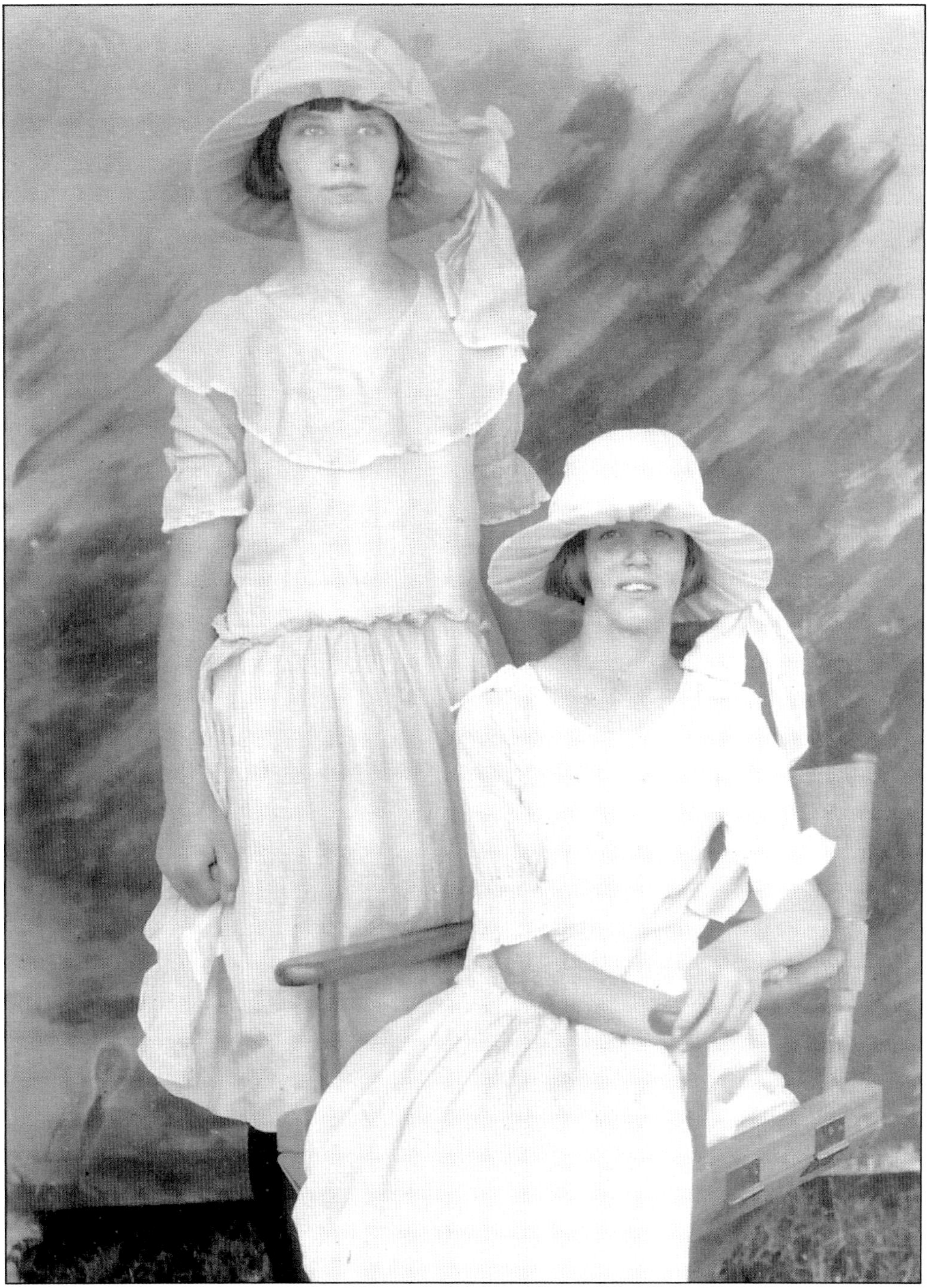

Sisters Ivie, 13 (sitting), and Marjorie, 12, are pictured here in 1923. Both born in Orangevale, Ivie stayed for most of her life, until moving to Folsom, and Marjorie stayed her entire life. (Courtesy Jean Kelly.)

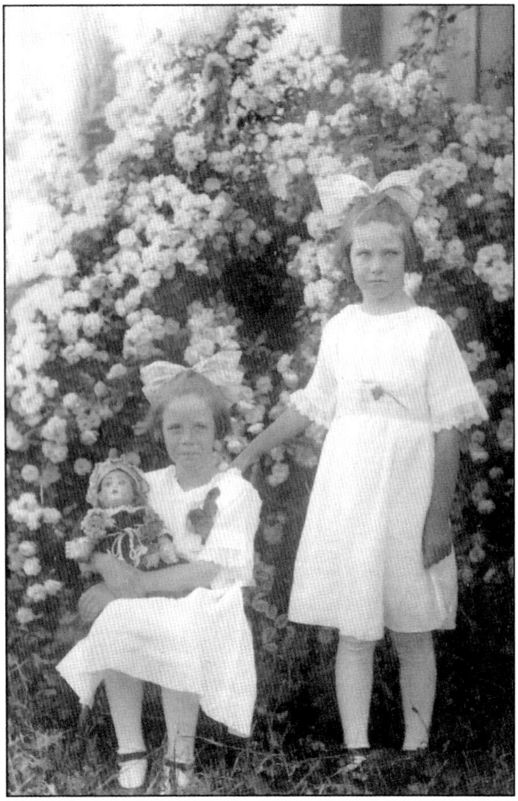

Guy and Ida Odlin often made postcards from the photographs of their beautiful daughters, pictured here in the late 1910s or early 1920s. They decided to hold back Ivie (clasping the doll) from beginning school for one year so that she could be in the same grade as her younger sister Marjorie. (Courtesy Jean Kelly.)

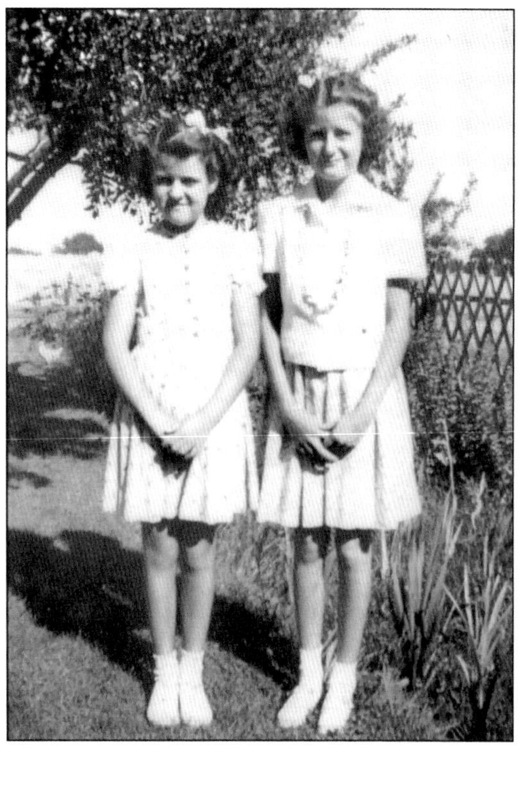

Sisters JoAnn Field Allred and Donna Field Matthews stand in front of their house on Illinois Avenue in the 1940s. (Courtesy JoAnn Allred.)

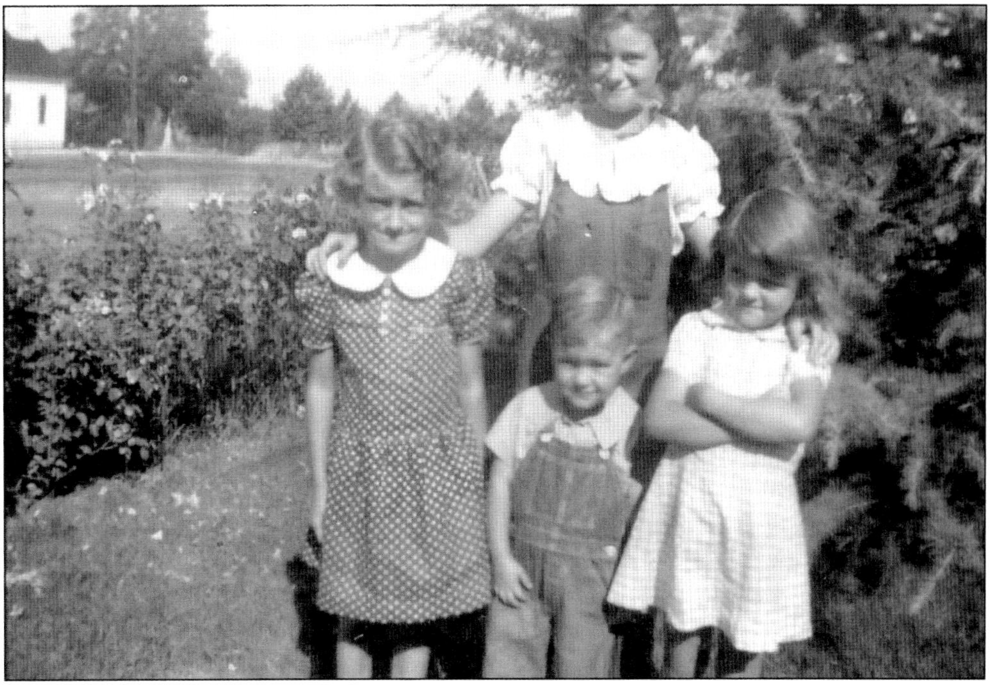

Norma Field stands proudly behind her three younger siblings—who are, from left to right, Donna, LaMoine, and JoAnn—in the front yard of their home on Illinois Avenue in 1940. Later they would welcome another brother Lawrence. (Courtesy JoAnn Allred.)

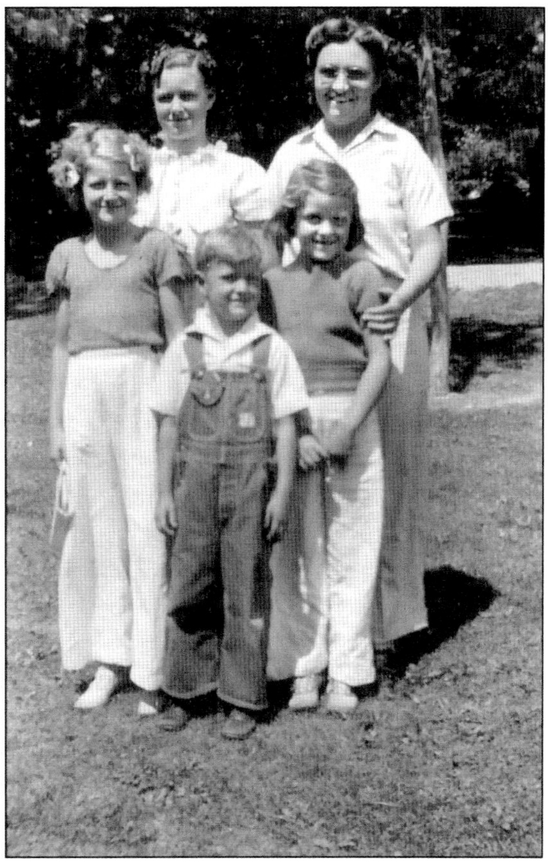

Ora Field stands proudly with her children sometime in the 1940s. They are, clockwise from Ora, JoAnn, LaMoine, Donna, and Norma. Missing from the picture, and perhaps taking the photograph, is father Floyd Field. Ora Field celebrated her 100th birthday in Orangevale in October 2006. (Courtesy JoAnn Allred.)

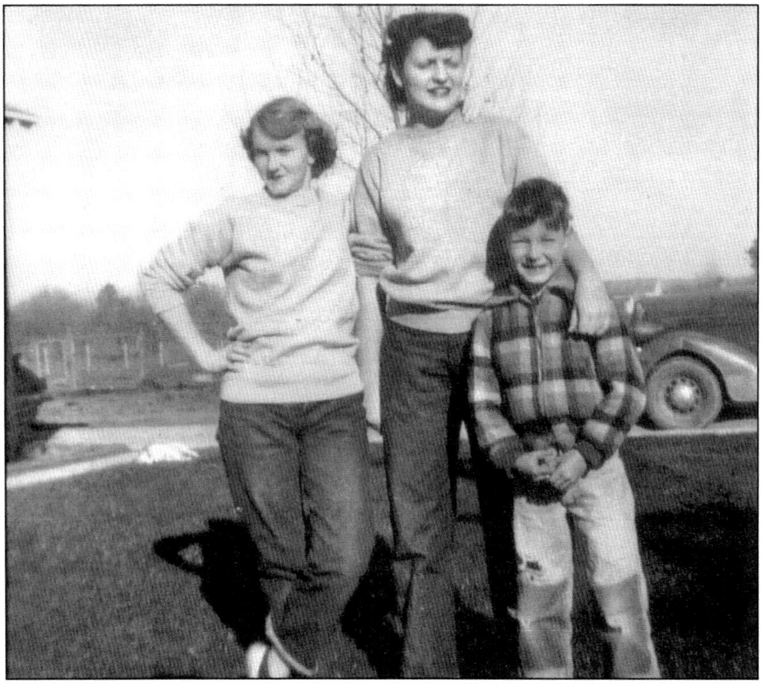

If there's such a thing as inseparable pals, then Thore Ann Peterson and JoAnn Field were such. The two friends, pictured here with JoAnn's little brother LaMoine, stand in front of the Field house on Hazel Avenue (now Naranja Way) c. 1945. (Courtesy JoAnn Allred.)

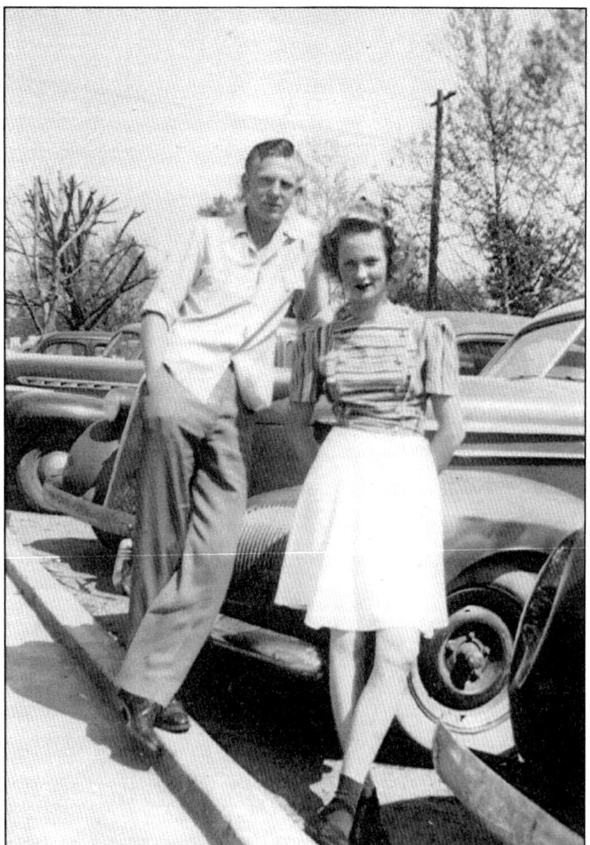

Pictured here are Garth Peterson and Shirley Smith in the early 1940s. (Courtesy JoAnn Allred.)

Proud Grandpa Floyd Field holds his first grandchild, Vicki Lynn Apostolas, in 1952. This photograph, taken in front of the Field home off Hazel Avenue (now Naranga Way), shows proud Uncle LaMoine and his future wife, Diane, in the background. (Courtesy JoAnn Allred.)

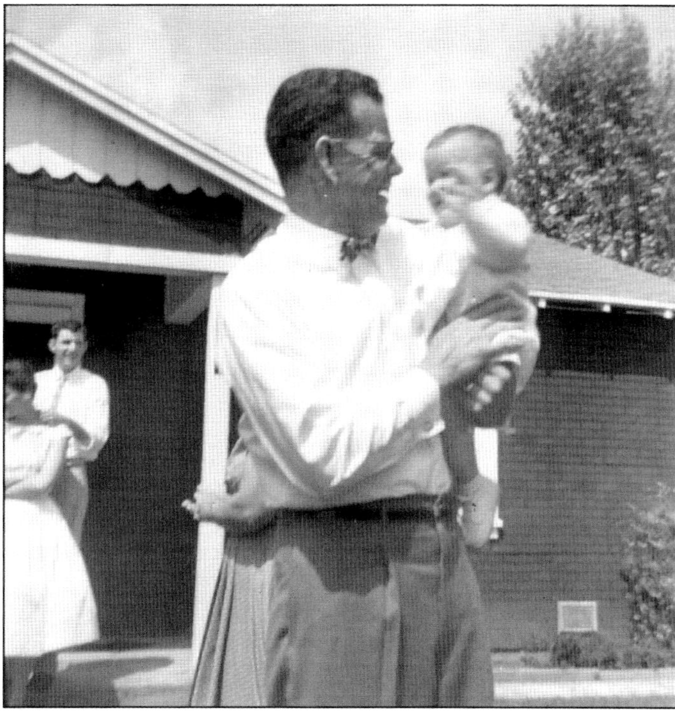

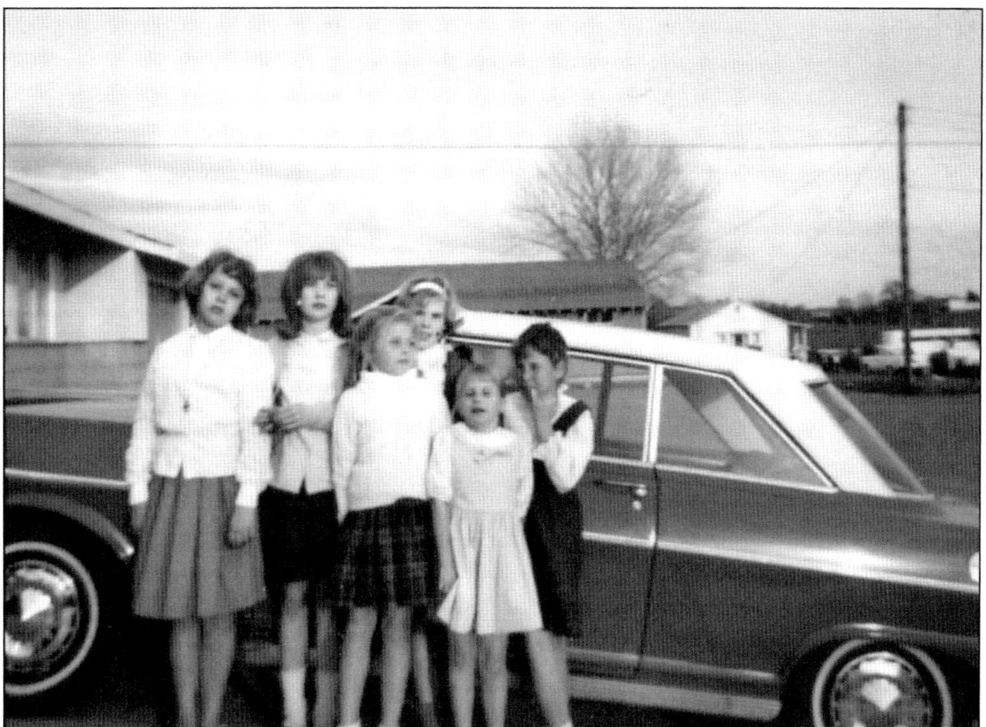

Standing around 1965 in front of Bob and Glenda Lewis's Chevy at their home on Polly Avenue are, from left to right, Denise Terry, Ramona Wright, Pamela Lewis White, Jacqueline Lewis Martin, Ann Collinsworth, and Pamela Miller. (Courtesy Glenda Lewis.)

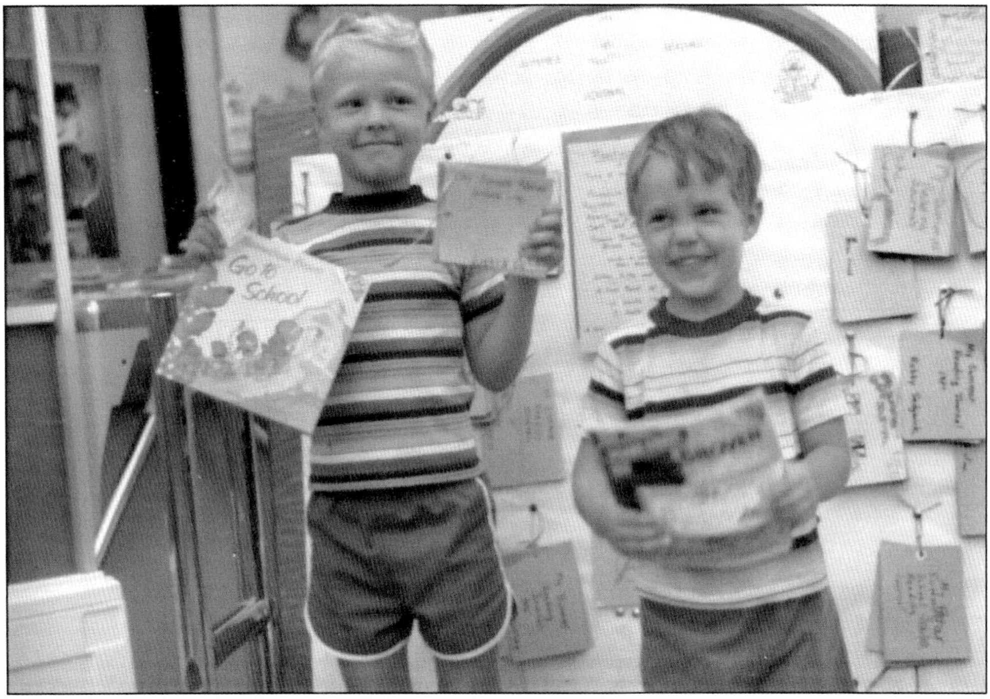

The excitement and enthusiasm that books bring to children is captured in the faces of book winners Jeremy and Justin at the Orangevale/Casa Roble Community Library in 1980 (above). In fact, books have been readily available for the children of Orangevale ever since the establishment of a library in Adelaide Morse's dining room in 1912. True, the number of books has grown from the modest start of 50, and the location of the library has changed over the years, but a library for Orangevale children and adults alike has persisted due to the perseverance of concerned parents and community members. Also pictured in 1980, Judy Randall and her daughter (below) bond through the sharing of a story at the Orangevale/Casa Roble Community Library, which served as Orangevale's library from 1978 to 1983. (Courtesy Orangevale Library.)

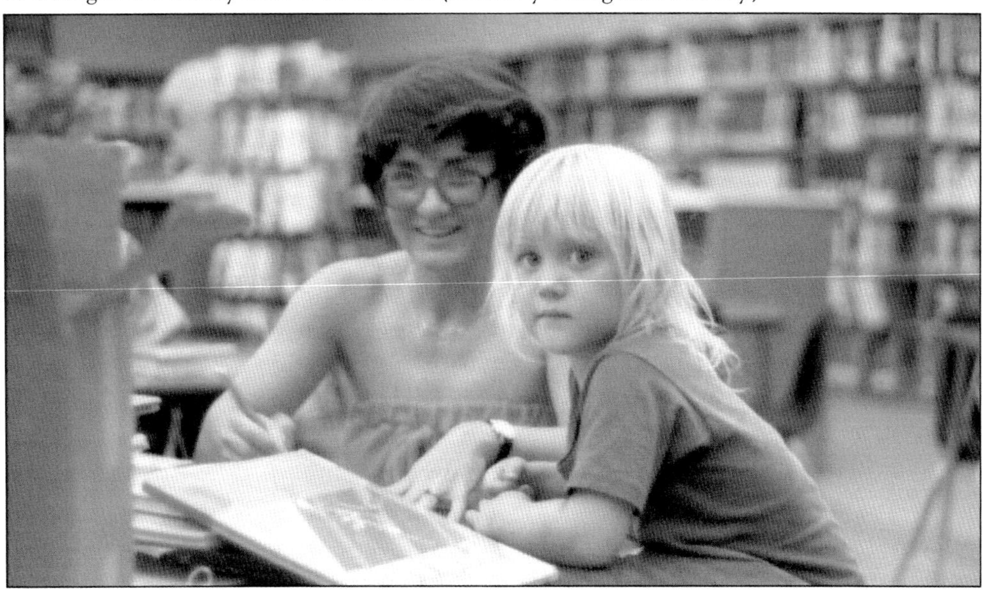

Eight

Pencils, Books, and Teachers' Dirty Looks

I believe that education is the fundamental method of social progress and reform. . . . I believe that the community's duty to education is, therefore, its paramount moral duty.

—John Dewey, "My Pedagogic Creed," 1897

Education has been a cornerstone of American values since the nation's founding. From the Land Ordinance in 1785 that established a mechanism for funding public education to the *Brown v. Board of Education* decision in 1954 that guaranteed all children, regardless of race, equal rights to education, Americans have defended the right to learn. Indeed, education provides people with the tools and knowledge they need to understand their world and to be responsible and informed citizens. Education is the catalyst for human development, the "great equalizer" that gives one the potential to overcome harsh conditions, such as poverty, disability, and ignorance. Likewise, education is vital to economic development, for it allows people to be more productive and to earn a better living.

Determining when Orangevale opened its first school is a bit tricky. Most local histories report that the Orangevale School, affiliated with the present-day Orangevale Open Elementary School, built in 1890, served as the community's first such institution. Nevertheless, cultural resource specialist Catherine Heck credits Roberts School for having been the first, stating that it opened sometime between 1883 and 1890. Regardless, a May 8, 1888, article in the *Sacramento Union* says, "there is a good school on the colony," which clearly indicates a school in operation before Orangevale School opened its doors. Still, the article later declares, "a school house *will be* erected." This indicates that no actual school building existed and that the Orangevale School perhaps truly was the first school building while this other "good school," possibly Roberts or some other, simply functioned though a private residence or public building.

Shortly after World War II and because of the baby boom, "old" Roberts and Orangevale Schools merged and eventually three new schools, Roberts (the old Roberts burned down), Central (Coleman), and Twin Lakes, opened their doors. In the 1960s, eight more schools were constructed, including Orangevale's first high school, Casa Roble (before this, students attended San Juan High School in Citrus Heights and Bella Vista in Fair Oaks). In the 1980s, Orangevale opened two more elementary schools, Trajan and Ottoman Way, and Coleman closed its doors in 2006.

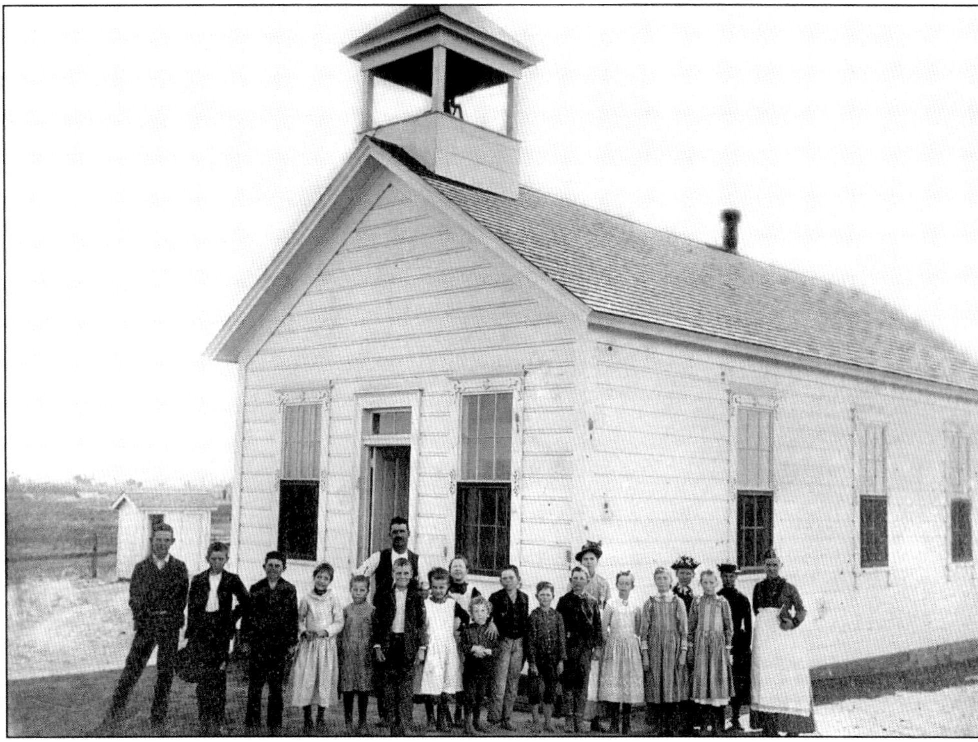

The Orangevale School, built in 1890, is certainly one of the community's oldest schools and has been in operation for more than 100 years. The old schoolhouse (above), which was replaced by a larger facility in 1904 (below), as Orangevale's population slowly grew, still stands across the street from the current school built in 1938 and is a private residence today. (Above courtesy Orangevale Open Elementary School; below courtesy Orange Vale Water Company.)

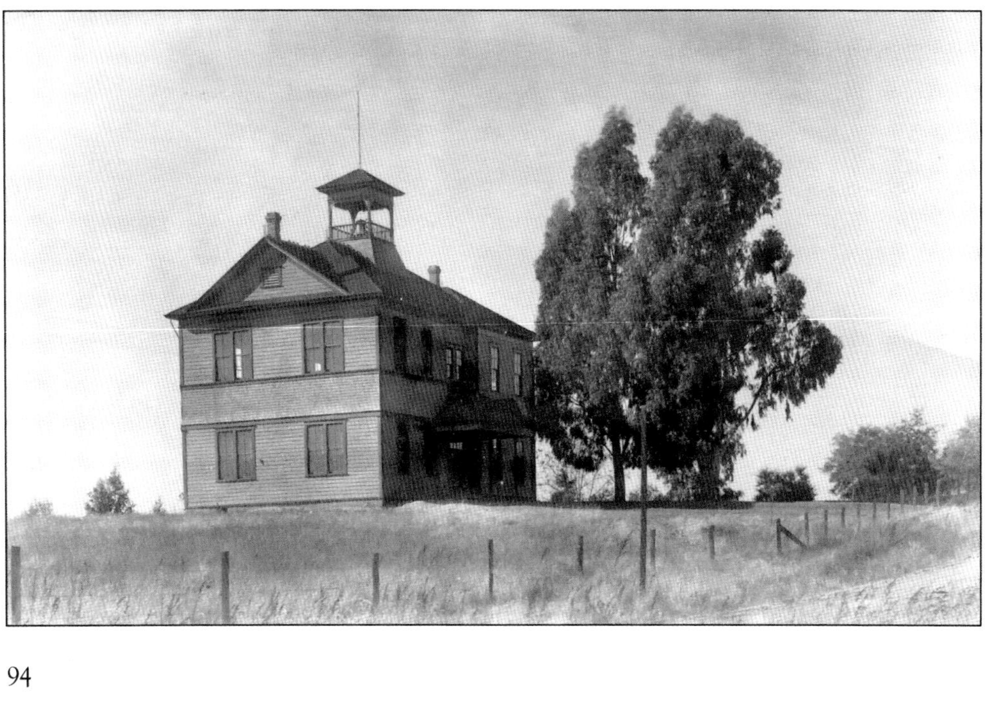

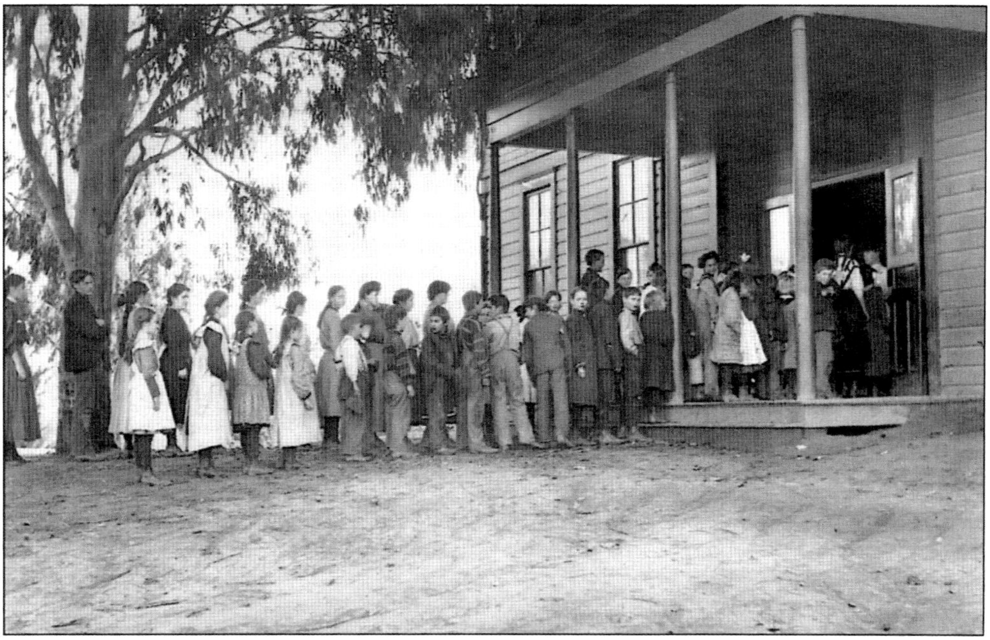

Orangevale School students, pictured here *c.* 1915, like so many others around the United States, eagerly line up in front of the school to go to class. The two-story structure was built in 1904 with materials hauled by wagon from Roseville. Two classrooms served children on the ground floor, while a large hall upstairs held dances and entertainment. (Courtesy Tom Tomich.)

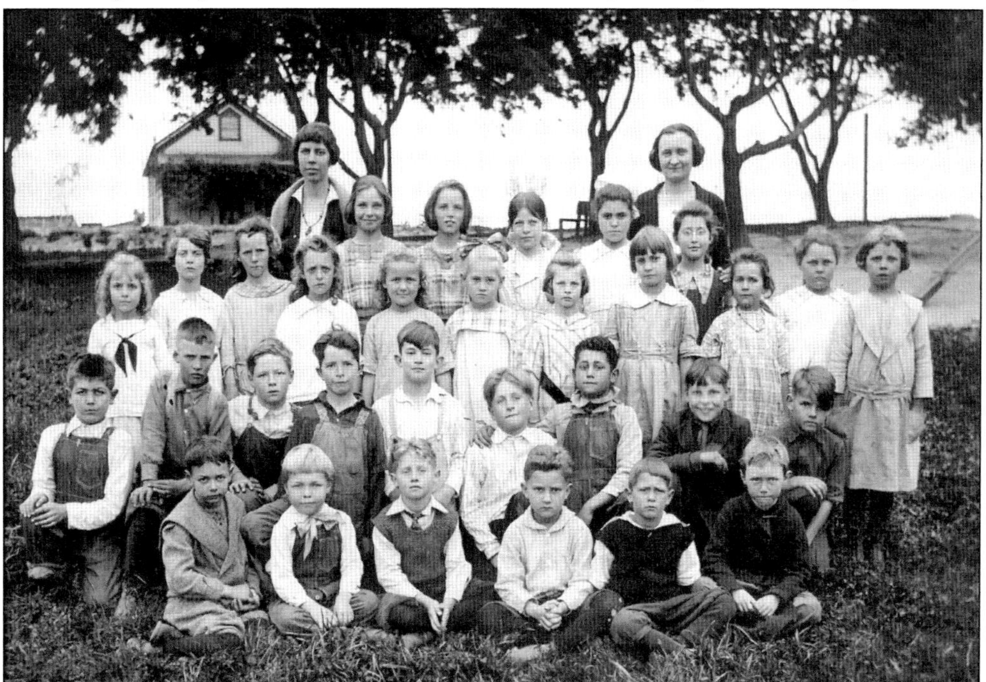

Orangevale School students pose for their class portrait sometime around 1920. Of the few identified (in the top row wearing matching dresses) are Ione "Marjorie" Odlin, born in 1911, and her sister Ivie, born in 1910. (Courtesy Jean Kelly.)

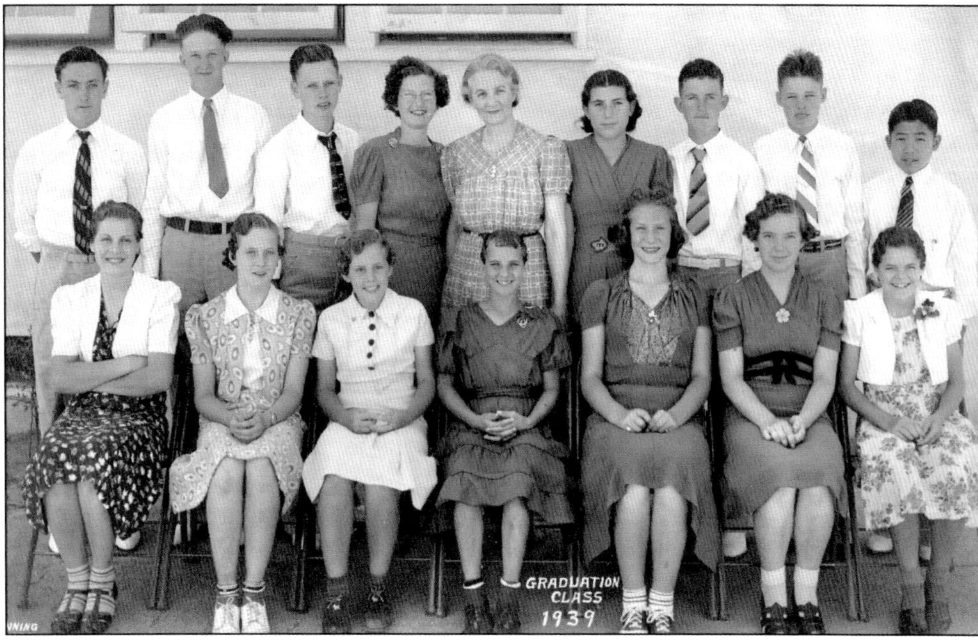

Pictured here is the 1939 Orangevale School class. They are, from left to right, as follows: (first row) Elizabeth Coppinger, Dorotha Wyatt, Naida Stevenson-Effinger, Rosa Brock, Gloria Odlin, Lorna Cooley, and Catharine Mums; (second row) Stewart Mcgee, Robert McKenzie, Donald Morton, Edna Mae Wilky, Sadie Cable, Margaret Zanetta, Jimmy Bain, Alan Hogaboon, and Jimmy Takeyata (sp?). Only a year before, in 1938, the school erected its current building, which started with three classrooms, a library, kitchen, and storage room. (Courtesy Naida and Andrew Effinger.)

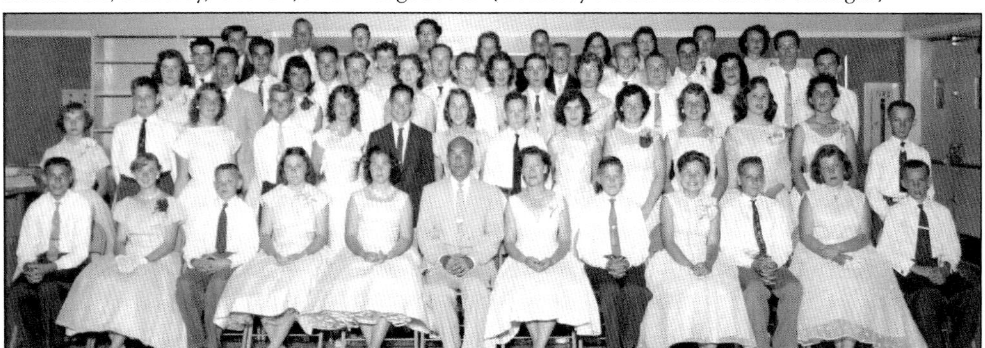

The 1957 Orangevale School graduates are pictured, from left to right, as follows: (first row) Joel Danenberg, Patricia Hicks, Ben Quick, Gretchen Erickson, Connie Mullenaux, Fred Lynn, Thelma Douglass, Bobby Wicks, Bernice Hendrix, Larry Rice, Louise Rosevear, and Rodney Hutchison; (second row) Vivian Wolpert, Michael Rankin, Jean Bruins, Raymond Norton, Donna White, Gregory Steck, Judy Price, Junius Brooks, Patricia Ellis, Willa Carman, Janet Jorgensen, Virginia Whale, Frances Canales, and James Fox; (third row) Judy Laurin, Sam Hull, Carol Coughran, Jerry Leverett, Sally Pickrel, Robert Shepherd, Robert Council, Lynette Wolpert, John Woolsey, Linda Zeno, and Fred Arritt; (fourth row) Ronald Nolting, John Kroger, Albert Legg, Pamela Stone, Jon Simpson, Suzanne Merton, Victor Overholt, Joe Buster, Benjamin Prall, and Stanley Sanstad; (fifth row) Bryan Roediger, Darryl Bailey, Wayne Young, Elaine Vandercook, Sharon Ewton, Steven Schutte, Gloria Neal, Helen Cook, Emmett Harless, and Donna Langley. (Courtesy Orangevale Open Elementary School.)

This close-up of Sadie Cable comes from the 1956 Orangevale School graduates portrait. Cable, who came with her parents, Theodore and Eva Greenhalgh, and eight siblings from Crookstown, Minnesota, in 1903, taught in Orangevale for about 30 years. (Courtesy Orangevale Open Elementary School.)

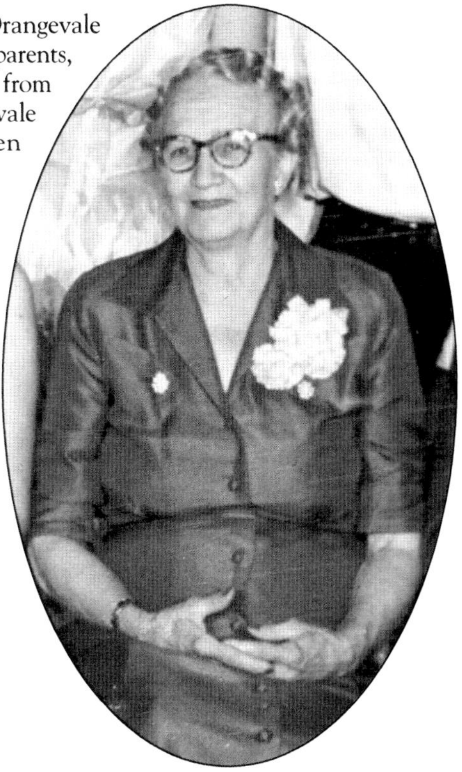

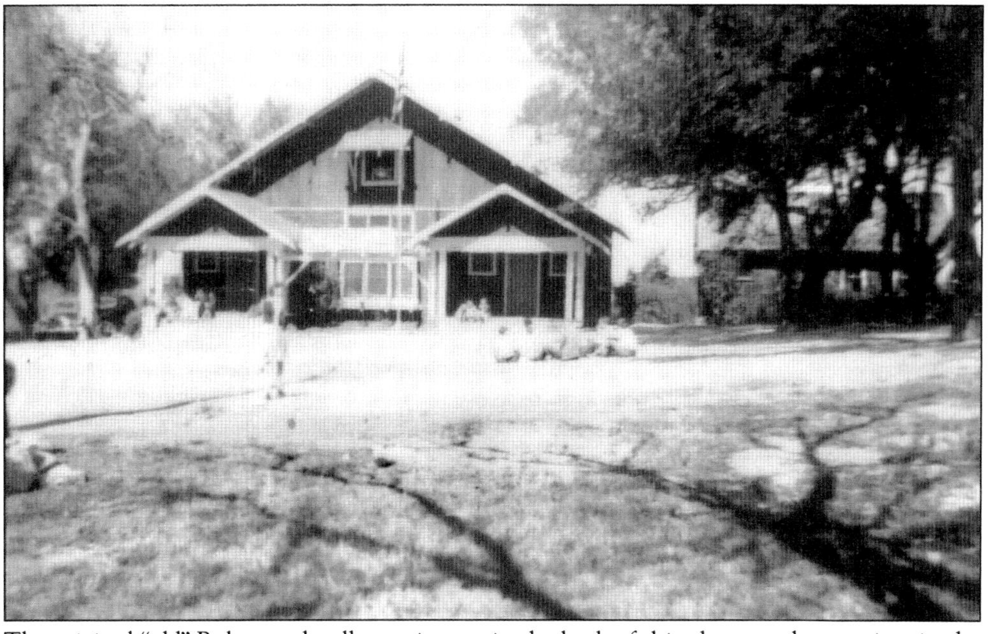

The original "old" Roberts schoolhouse is seen in the back of this photograph sometime in the 1940s. The schoolhouse, possibly built before the old Orangevale School, served the community before it burned down through an unfortunate act of arson in the fall of 1953. Nevertheless, with the building of a new schoolhouse in the mid-1950s, Roberts School has been able to serve the community for approximately 100 years. (Courtesy JoAnn Allred.)

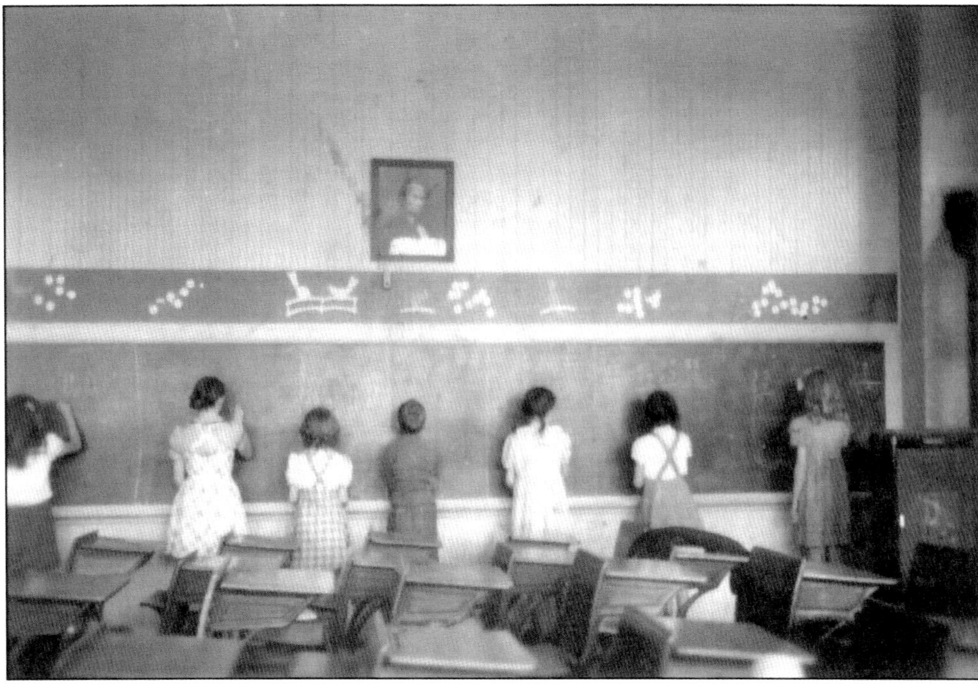

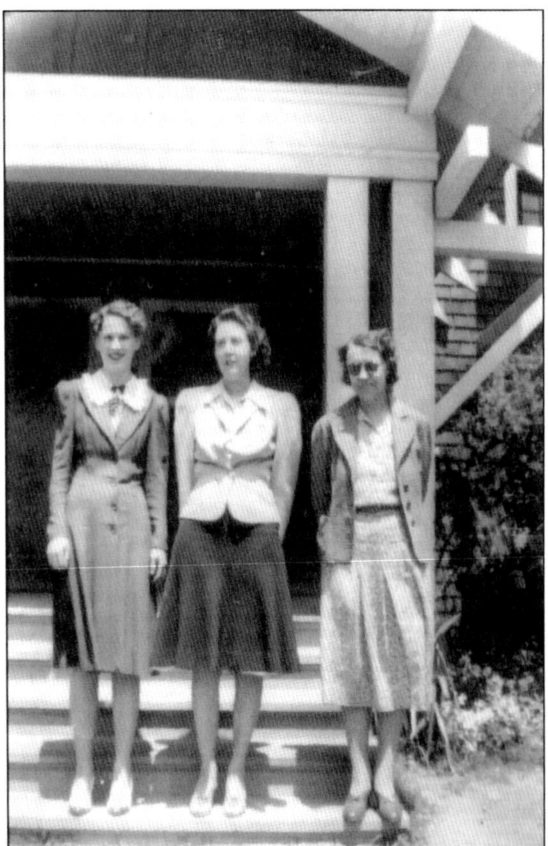

This extremely rare glimpse into the interior of the old Roberts School, above, shows children in Ruth Kirsten's class during the 1940s working on the blackboard. Pictured at left, Roberts School teachers Inez Cahoone, Mrs. Vance, and Ruth Kirsten, stop to pose on the steps of the schoolhouse in the 1940s. (Courtesy JoAnn Allred.)

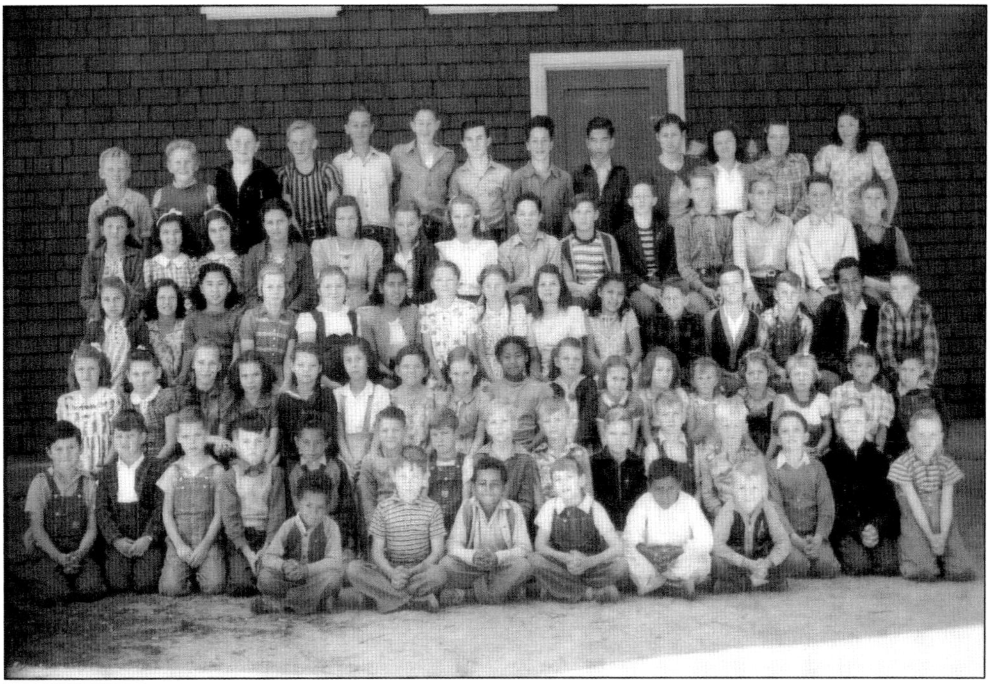

Pictured here is the 1942 Roberts School class, first through eighth grades. Those identified include Thore Ann Peterson, fifth from the right in the second row; Joann Field-Allred, eighth from the right in the second row; Donna Field Matthews, first on the left in second row; LuBeth (sp?) Thomas, second from the left on third row; and Lynn Thomas, sixth from the left in the fourth row. (Courtesy JoAnn Allred.)

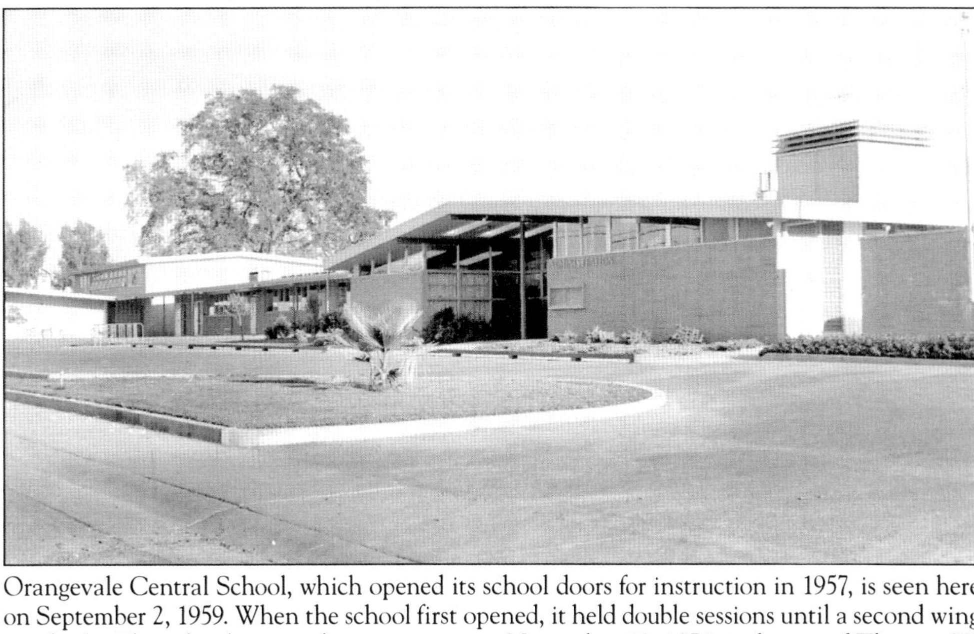

Orangevale Central School, which opened its school doors for instruction in 1957, is seen here on September 2, 1959. When the school first opened, it held double sessions until a second wing was built. The school received a new name on November 18, 1974, in honor of Thomas W. Coleman, a longtime Orangevale teacher and principal. (Courtesy SAMCC, Drawer 88, Row 5, Piggott, Sept. 59.)

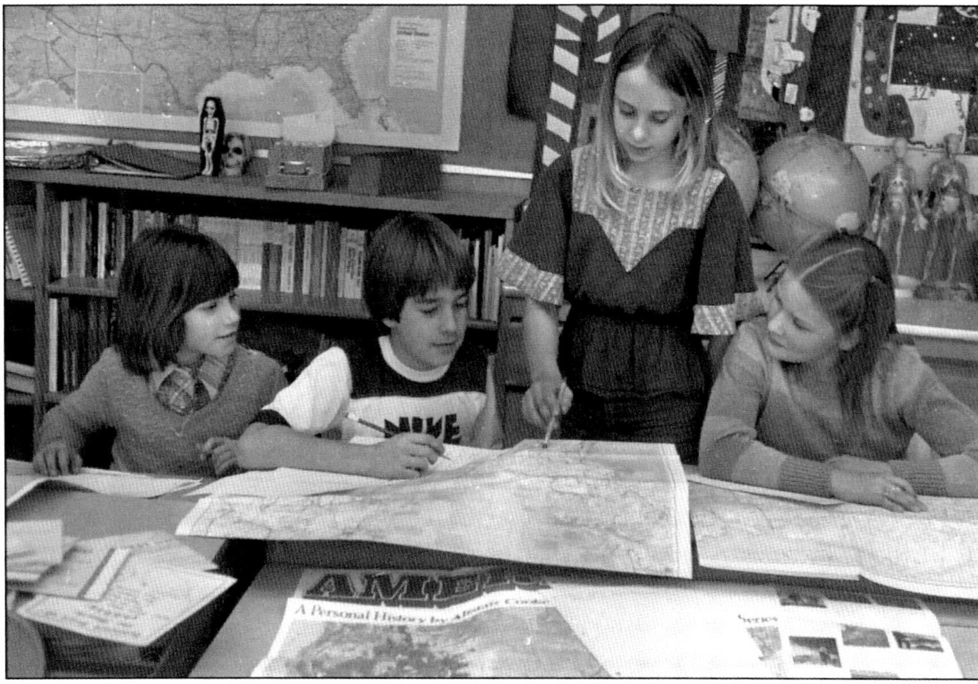

Pershing Elementary School, one of eight schools built during the 1960s, opened to meet the needs of the growing population in Orangevale because of the baby boom and rapid suburbanization that took place after World War II. Here students work over a map in 1981. (Courtesy Orange Vale Water Company.)

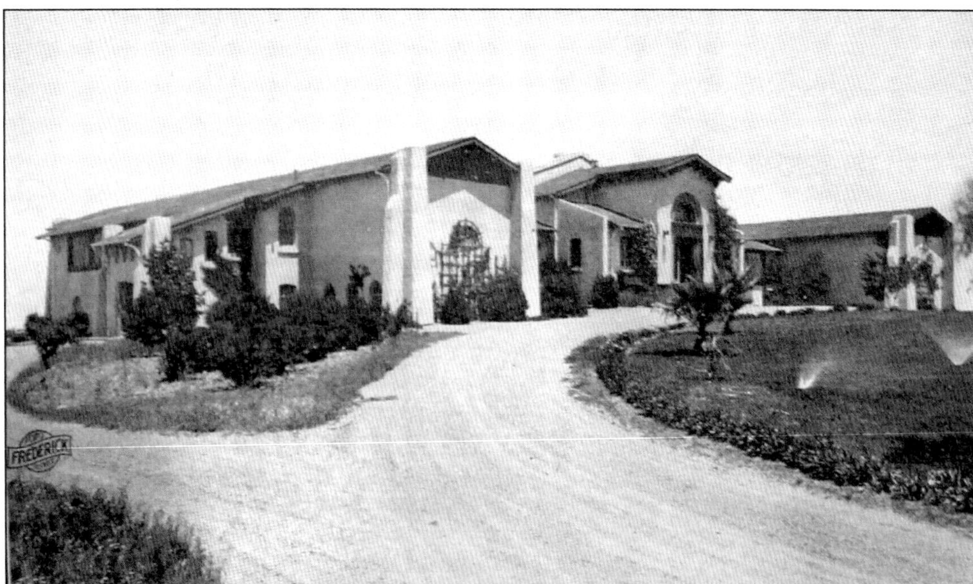

The San Juan High School, which first began on the upper floors of the Fair Oaks schoolhouse (now the community clubhouse in the Fair Oaks Village) in 1913, moved to its present location off Greenback Lane in the early 1920s. The school, pictured here in 1922, served students from Fair Oaks, Orangevale, and Citrus Heights. (Courtesy Sacramento Room, Sacramento Public Library.)

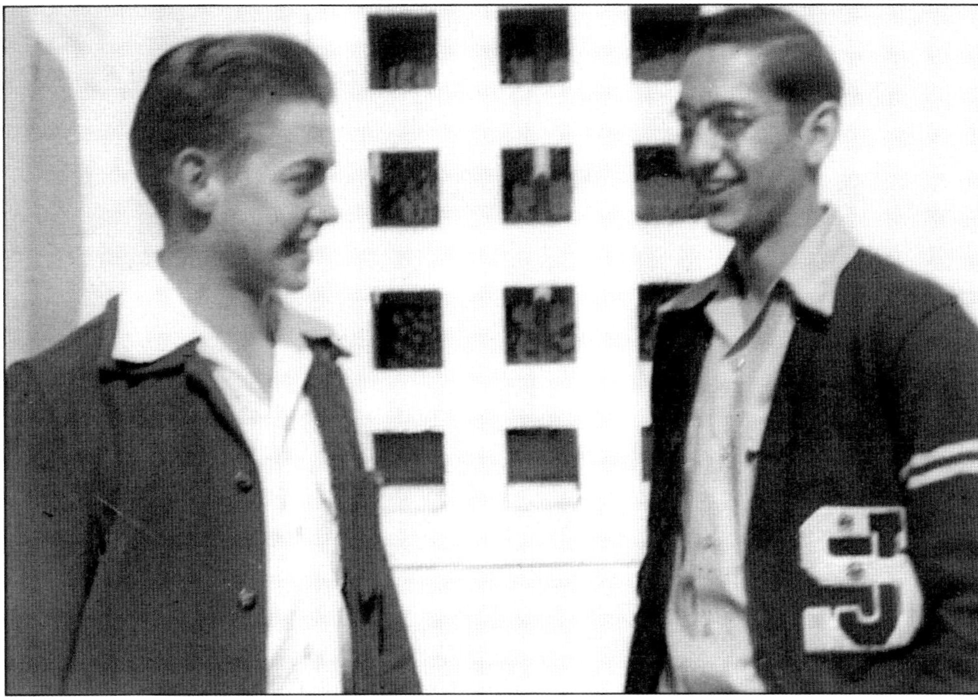

Tom Tomich and Tom Zanze are seen here at San Juan High School in 1942. Tom Tomich served as the president of the San Juan High School senior class before he left following graduation to join the fight in World War II as an 18-year-old soldier in Gen. George Patton's Third Army. (Courtesy Tom Tomich.)

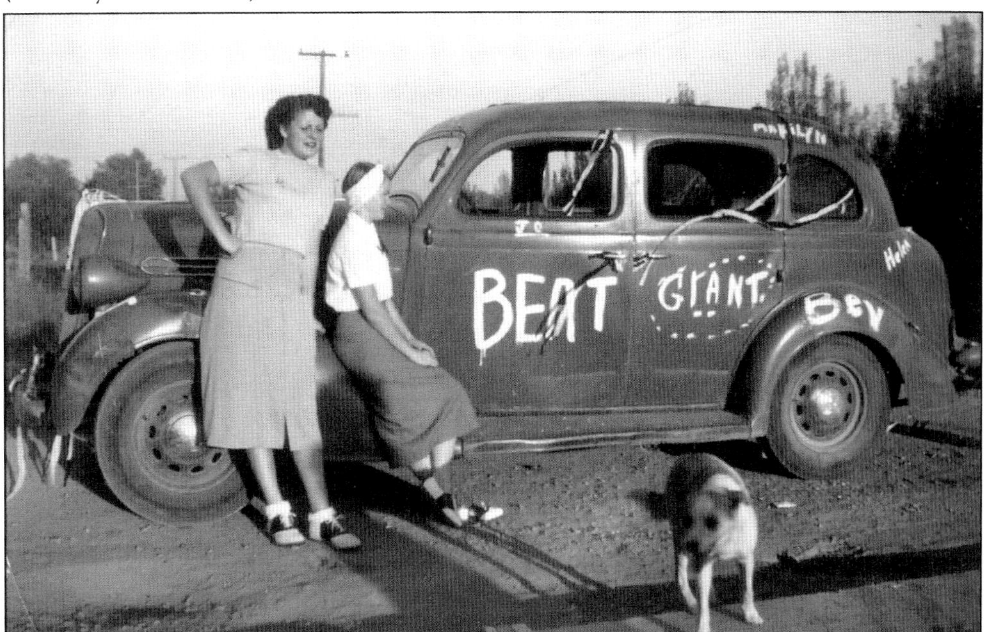

Joann Field-Allred, standing, and Thore Ann Peterson celebrate in front of their aptly decorated car after the San Juan High School football team beat Grant Union High School in 1952. (Courtesy JoAnn Allred.)

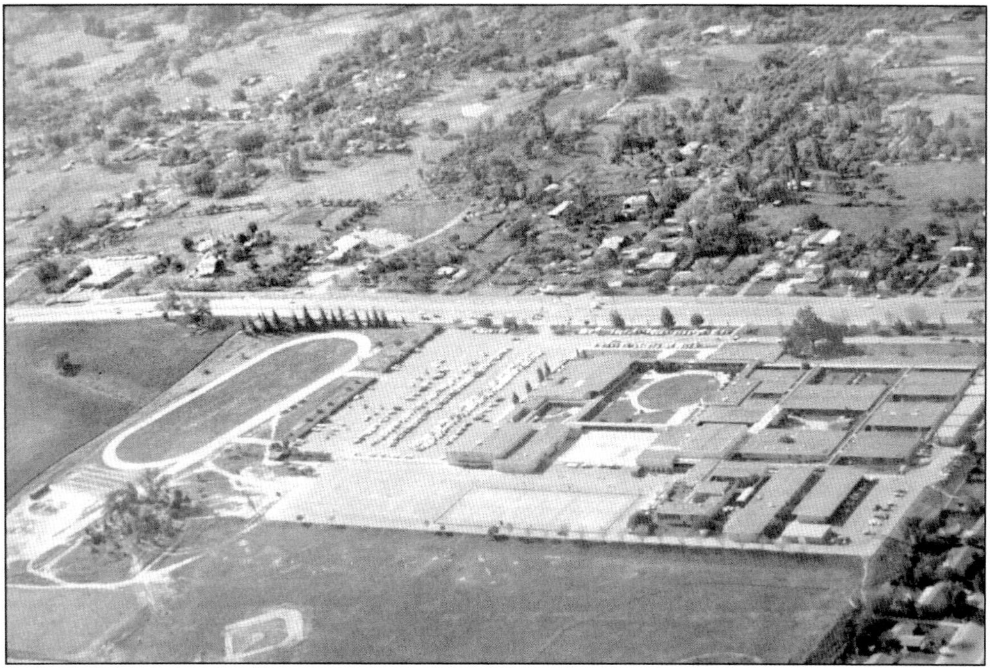

Bella Vista High School, which opened in 1962, in Fair Oaks, continues to serve many students from Orangevale and Fair Oaks. This aerial view, looking south, taken sometime in the 1970s, shows the open landscape surrounding the school and the school's major thoroughfare, Madison Avenue, on the south side. (Courtesy Bella Vista High School.)

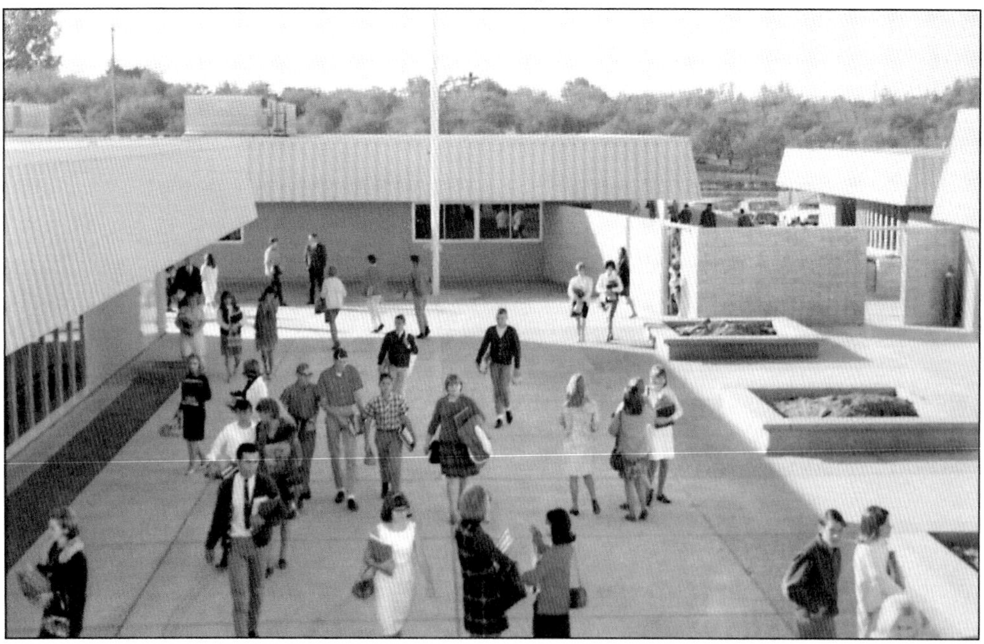

Casa Roble High School, which opened in 1966 and saw its first class graduate in 1969, is the first and only high school actually in Orangevale. This aerial view (likely taken from the roof of one of the school's buildings) shows students interacting as they rush from class to class, soon after the school opened in 1966–1967. (Courtesy Casa Roble High School.)

Nine

The Many Faces of Orangevale

I am a part of all that I have met.

—Alfred Lord Tennyson, *Ulysses*, 1842

Whether studying the lives of the early captains of industry who formed the Orange Vale Colonization Company, those who took a chance on Orangevale and moved their families thousands of miles west to settle, or those who have kept their family orchards running for generations, each personal story contributes to Orangevale's history. Indeed, during the 1930s, historian Perry Miller challenged previous ideas that conditions, not people, made history. Miller argued that because individuals are agents in history, then it is the individual who needs to be studied. Since the 1960s and 1970s, social history has become a field that captures the various experiences of individuals regardless of socioeconomic class, race, or gender.

People were already beginning to set down roots in Orangevale by 1893, such as the Wahrhaftig, Boyarsky, Edward, Sager, Landis, and Moncur families. Around this time, Orangevale's first doctor, Dr. Edith Beauchamp from Ohio, arrived and operated out of the Villa. More families continued to cast their lots in Orangevale and relocated their families—often thousand of miles from home—throughout the late 19th and early 20th centuries. Theodore Greenhalgh brought his wife and nine children from Minnesota in 1903, and Albert Wickstrom brought his family from Minnesota in 1904. Wahrhaftig, Wickstrom, Landis, and Greenhalgh all served in some capacity with the Orange Vale Water Company. With the support and help of their families, they established orchards and packinghouses, and their descendants continue to live in the Orangevale area today.

The Great Depression and the freeze of 1932, however, did not deter others from migrating to Orangevale. For example, after emigrating from Yugoslavia in 1938, the Salle brothers established a farm on Filbert Avenue. The history of Orangevale is a history of individual action and interaction among its residences. While only a few can be profiled here, these pictures provide a rare glimpse into the lives of the people who have become a part of Orangevale's culture and history.

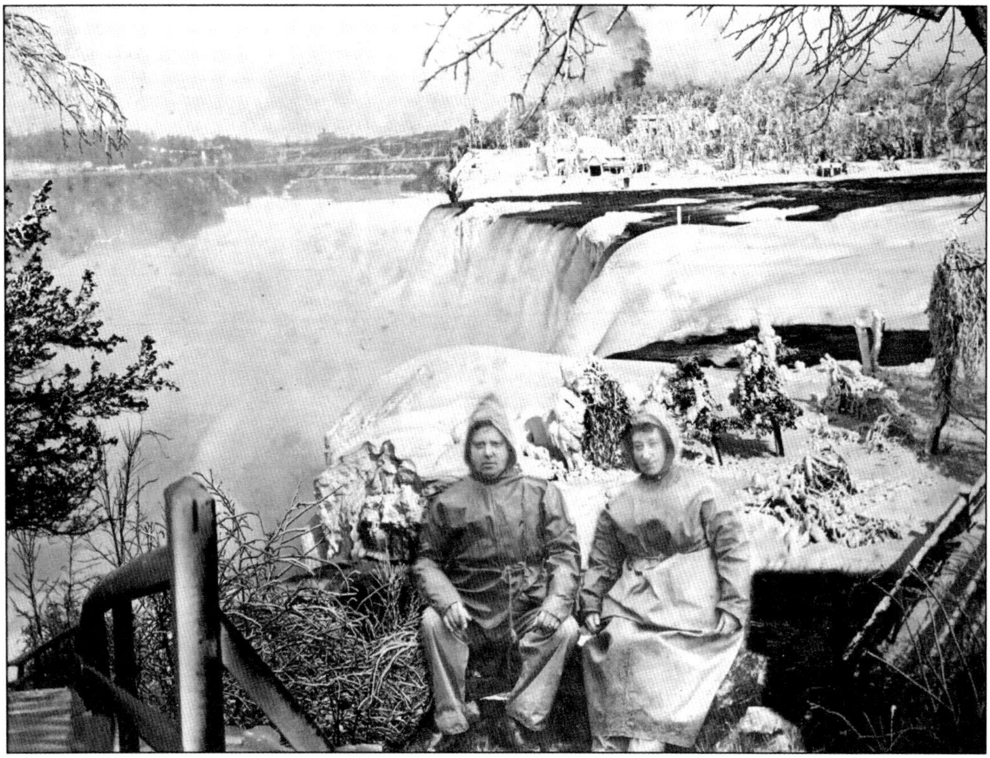

Pictured here are William and Mary Alice Calder at what an inscription on the back of the original photograph claims as Niagara Falls (or possibly a studio backdrop) in the 1890s. William, a Shakespearean actor and producer, immigrated to the United States from Scotland just prior to the Civil War. William, also a veteran of the Civil War and manager of a theatrical company, settled in Orangevale on a fruit ranch. He served as secretary, and later director, of the Orange Vale Water Company. (Courtesy SAMCC, No. 2003/001/070.)

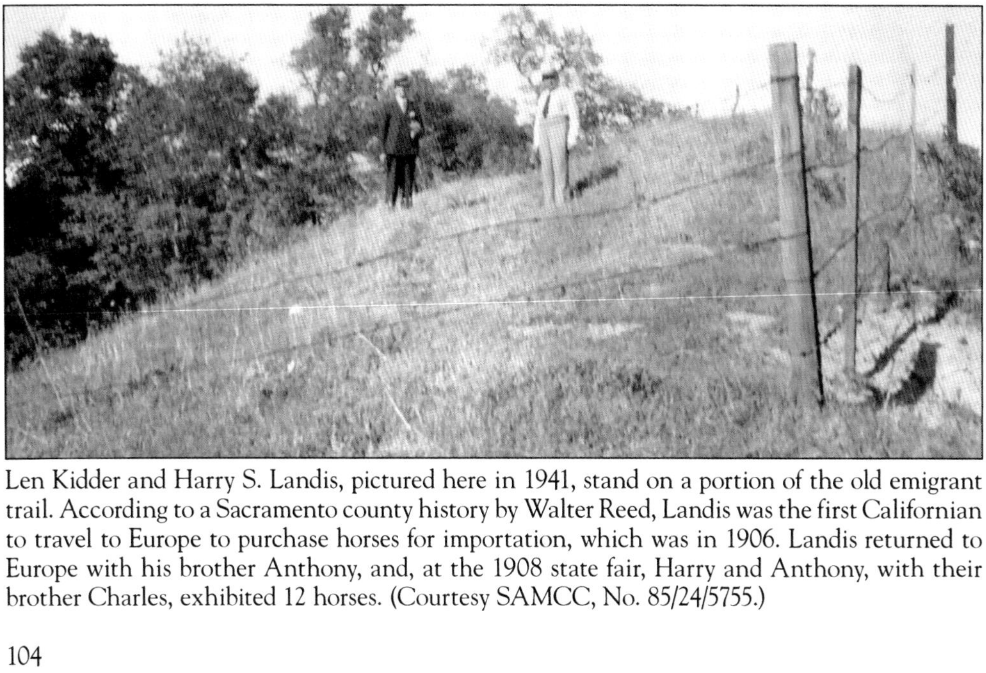

Len Kidder and Harry S. Landis, pictured here in 1941, stand on a portion of the old emigrant trail. According to a Sacramento county history by Walter Reed, Landis was the first Californian to travel to Europe to purchase horses for importation, which was in 1906. Landis returned to Europe with his brother Anthony, and, at the 1908 state fair, Harry and Anthony, with their brother Charles, exhibited 12 horses. (Courtesy SAMCC, No. 85/24/5755.)

Albert Wickstrom purchased two 10-acre tracts from Lizzie B. Sager in 1904 and brought his family from Minnesota to Orangevale. Wickstrom, pictured at right around 1905, wasted little time in becoming involved in the community, assuming a position on the Orange Vale Water Company board of directors in 1905. (Courtesy Orange Vale Water Company.)

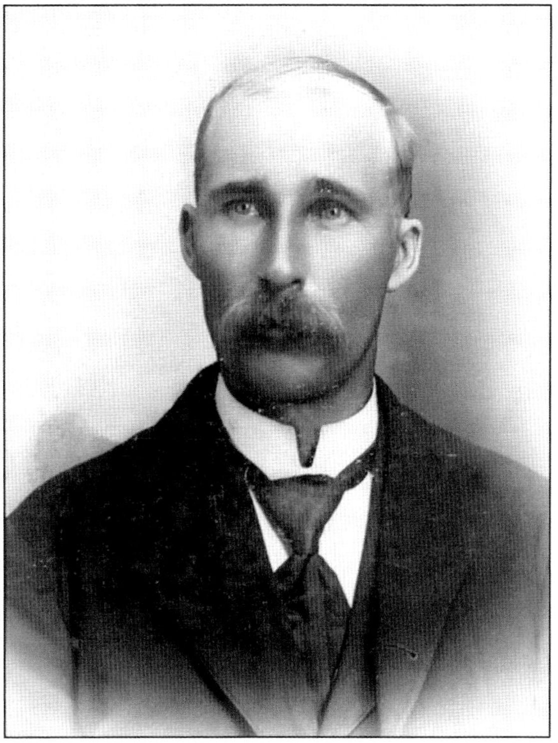

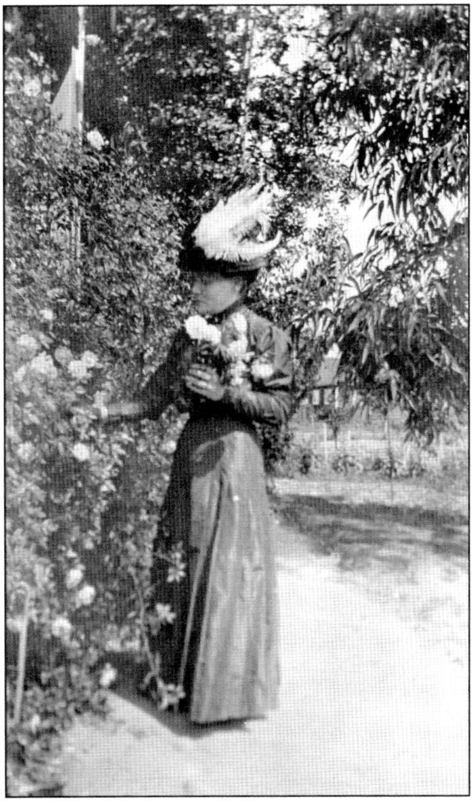

Albert Wickstrom brought his wife, Hannah, pictured at left around 1915, and children from Minnesota to the "friendlier climate" of Orangevale in 1904. Hannah, widowed in 1910 after Albert suffered fatal injuries from a horse, continued to manage the family orchards with help from family. (Courtesy Fred and Tom Tomich.)

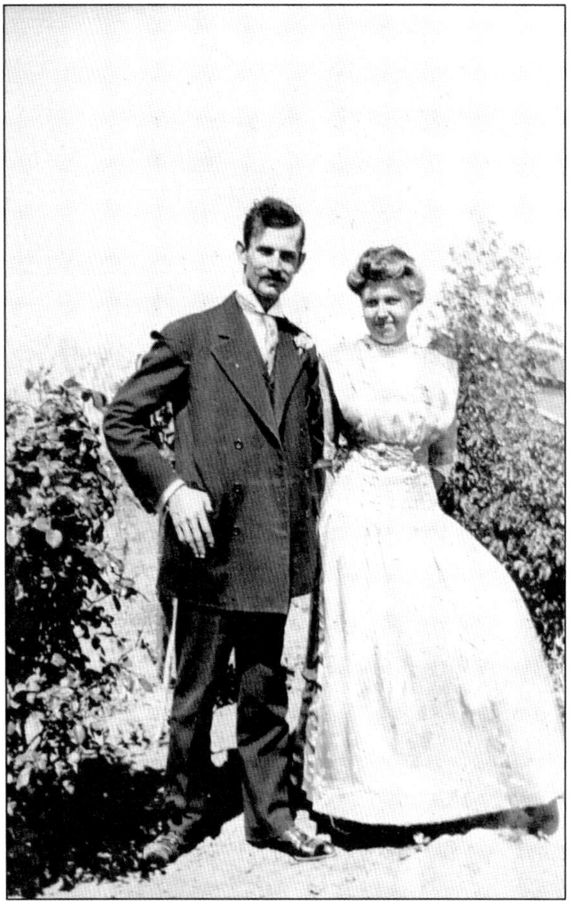

Pictured here in the 1910s or 1920s are Prosper and Eleanor Tomich. Prosper, a native of Yugoslavia, moved to Orangevale in 1911. In addition to farming in Orangevale, Prosper served as a trustee of the Orangevale Elementary School District and the San Juan Union High School District. Prosper and Eleanor, the daughter of Albert and Hannah Wickstrom, had seven children: Nicholas, Frances, John, Eleanor, Quentin, Frederick, and Thomas. (Courtesy Fred Tomich.)

Albert and Eleanor Tomich's daughter Frances Tomich Sarich is pictured here sometime in the 1930s or 1940s, sitting gracefully at the piano. Musically talented, Frances also played the violin. (Courtesy Frances Sarich.)

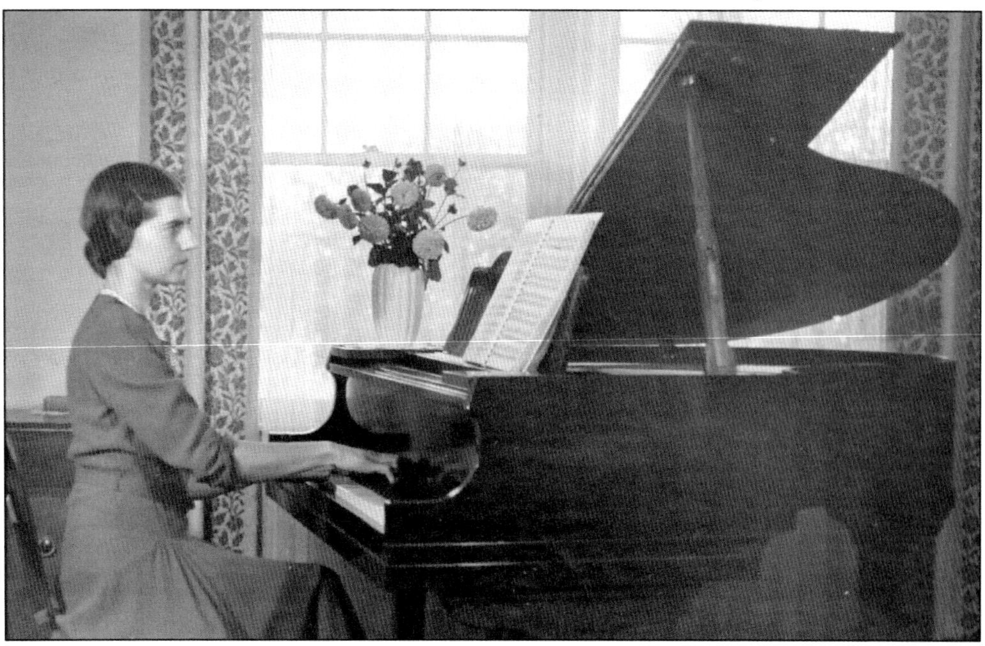

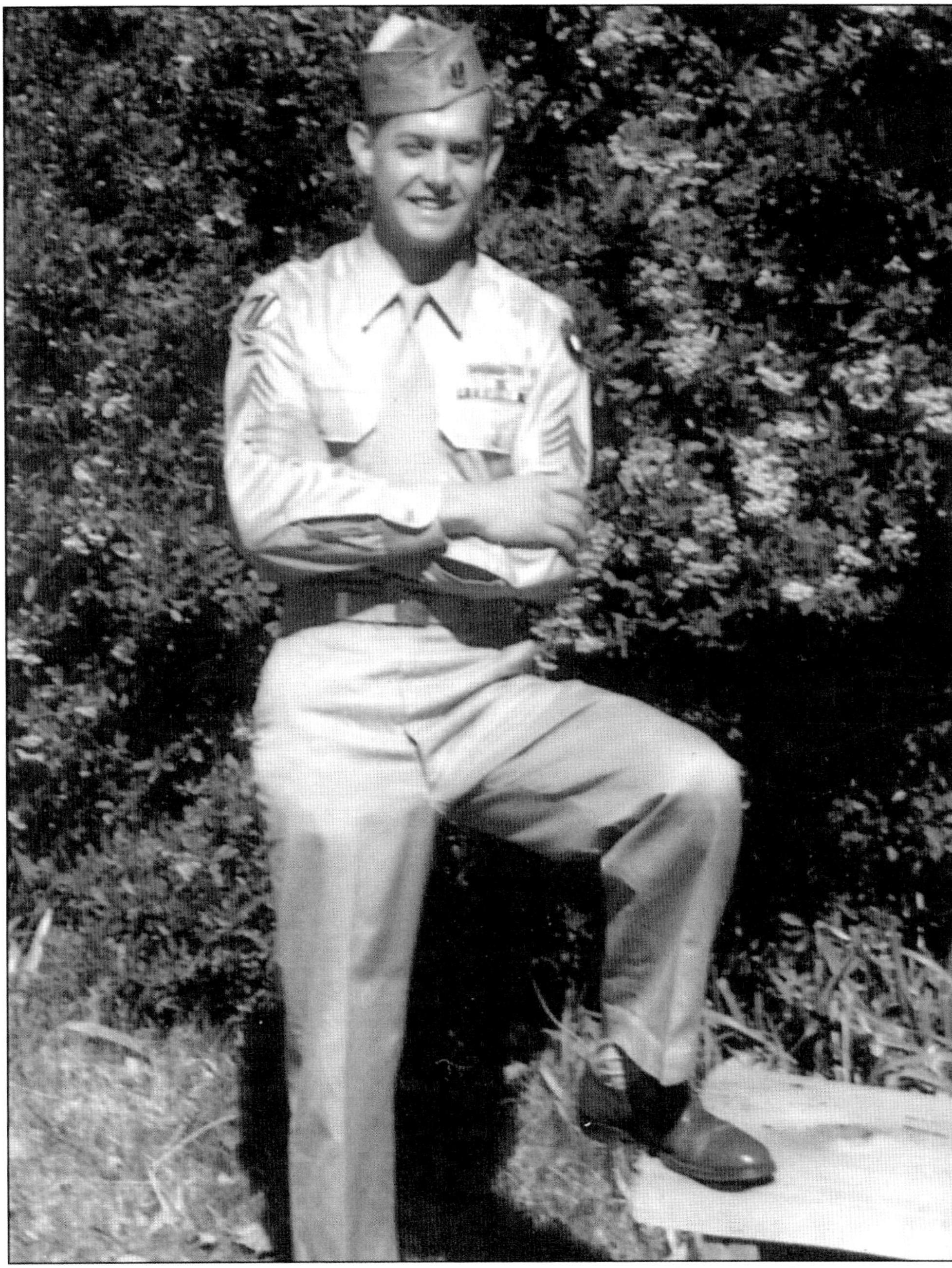

Above stands local fruit grower and horticulturist Tom Tomich, son of Prosper and Eleanor Tomich. Often referring to himself as, "The Skinniest Kid in George Patton's Third Army," Tom served from 1944 to 1946 in the 66th Infantry, part of the 71st Division. (Courtesy Tom Tomich.)

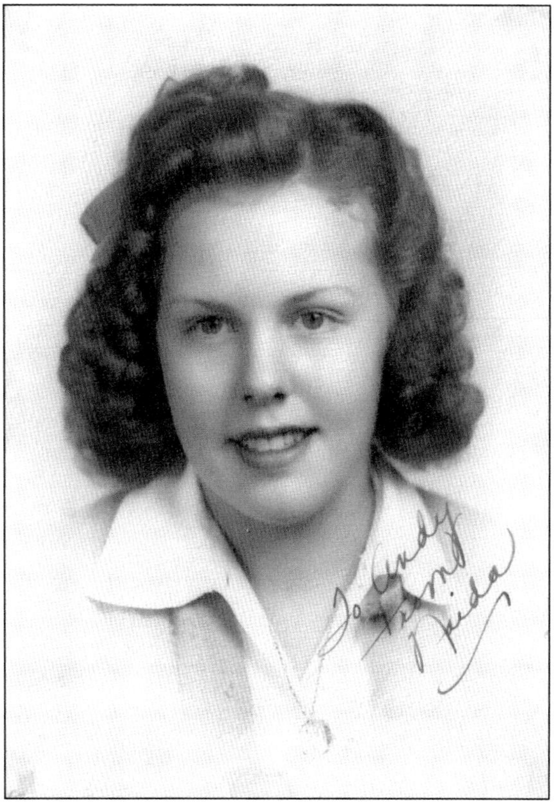

Naida Stevenson (left), 15, worked, along with other kids, at Sol Warhaftig's packing shed in 1941. Following Warhaftig's suggestion, Stevenson wrote her name and address on a piece of cardboard that separated the plums in the box to see if she could get a pen pal. Her plums ended up in Philadelphia, Pennsylvania. There they were unpacked by young Andrew Effinger, who worked as a "huckster," driving a truck filled with fresh fruit and vegetables for sale. After finding Stevenson's note, Effinger sent a letter to Stevenson asking who she was and for her to send a picture. Stevenson complied, and a seven-year courtship resulted. Enlisting in the navy in 1942, Effinger transferred to California in 1945 and met Stevenson for the first time. During another visit (below), they met at the Tropic Club in Sacramento. (Courtesy Andrew and Naida Effinger.)

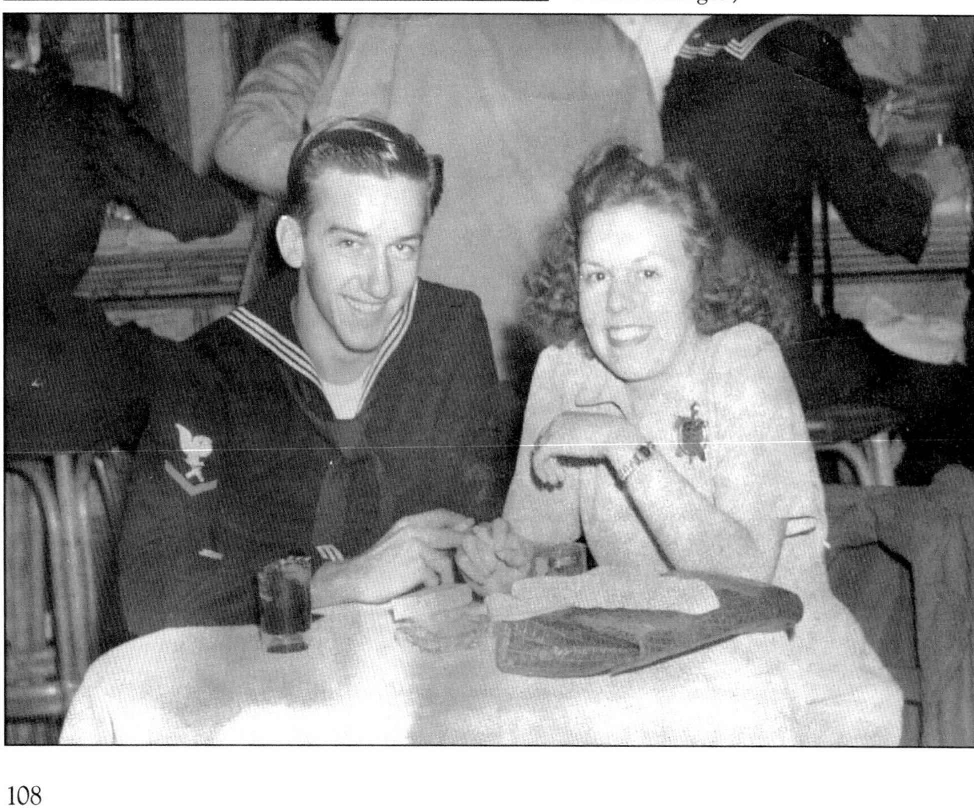

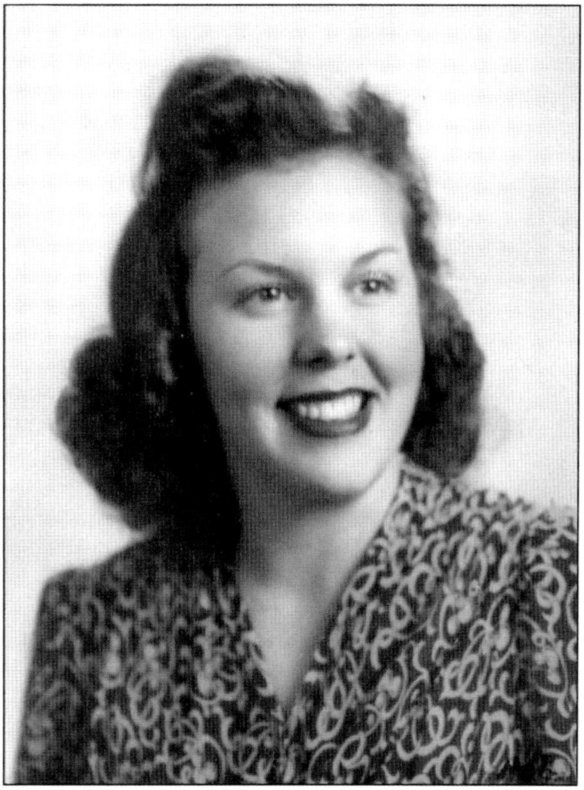

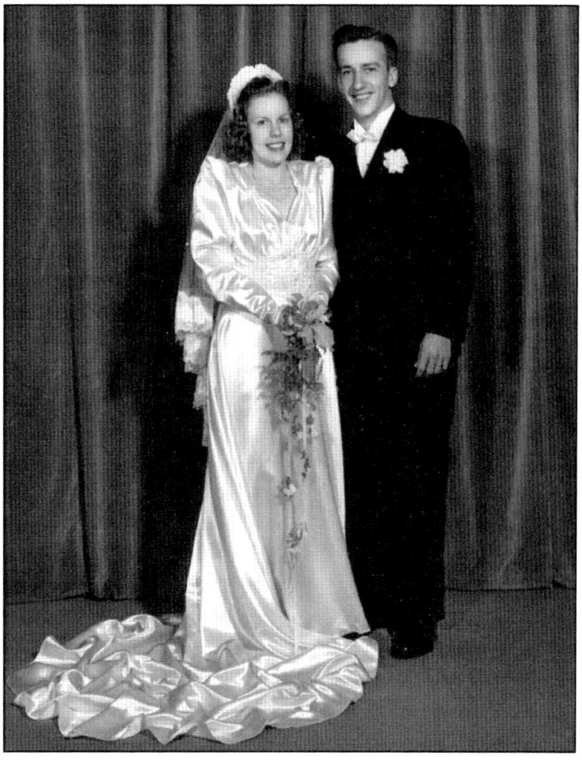

During the war, Andrew Effinger carried a photograph of Stevenson (above) with him in his wallet. It is still in that wallet today. After the war, Andrew saved money and moved to Orangevale. He began work with the Division of Highways and was assigned to work in Eureka. Alternately, once a month, Effinger and Stevenson endured long 12-hour bus trips to visit each other. They married on April 3, 1948, at St. John's Catholic Church in Folsom (below). After living for a short while in Eureka, the Effingers returned to Orangevale in April 1949, and Andrew began work for Sacramento County. The Effingers still live in Orangevale and have three sons. Happy and content, Andrew, as he recently stated, "doesn't open boxes of plums anymore." (Courtesy Andrew and Naida Effinger.)

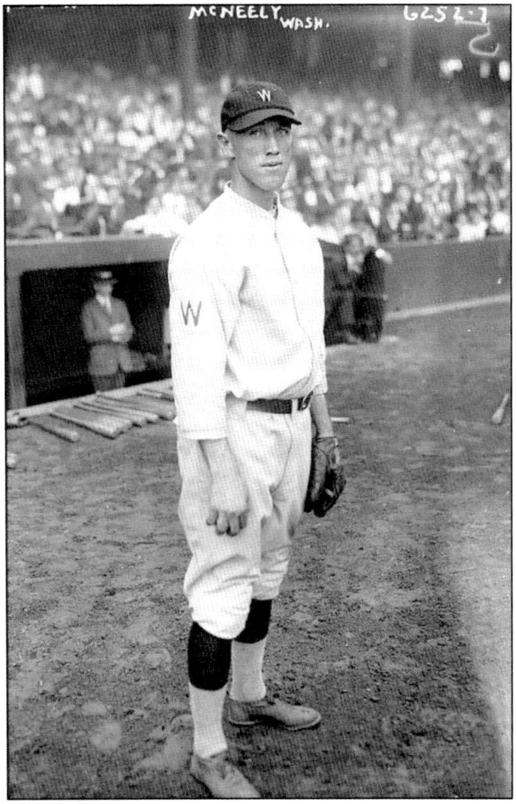

Professional baseball player Earl McNeely and his wife, Ethel Greenhalgh (daughter of Mr. and Mrs. Theodore Greenhalgh), bought 50 acres in Orangevale in 1928 when they purchased William Calder's "The Palms." In 1931, Earl McNeely, with Lloyd and Howard Greenhalgh, started a dehydration plant, which McNeely claimed to be the first in this part of the country until another opened in 1956. (Courtesy Library of Congress, Prints and Photographs Division, LC-DIG-ggbain-37508.)

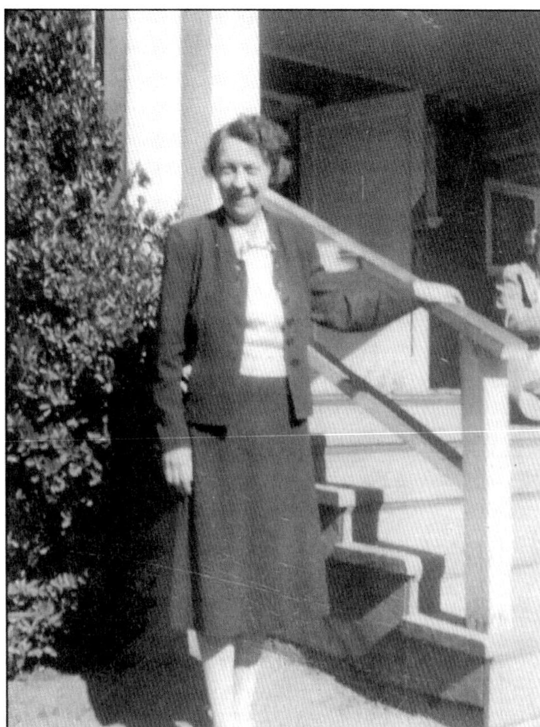

Teacher Ruth Kirsten touched the hearts of children in Orangevale for decades. Born Ruth Wickstrom, her family moved from Minnesota to Orangevale in the spring of 1904. Kirsten began teaching at the Orangevale Elementary School before moving to the old Roberts Elementary School, where she spent the majority of her career. Retiring in 1958, she taught for more than 40 years. (Courtesy JoAnn Allred.)

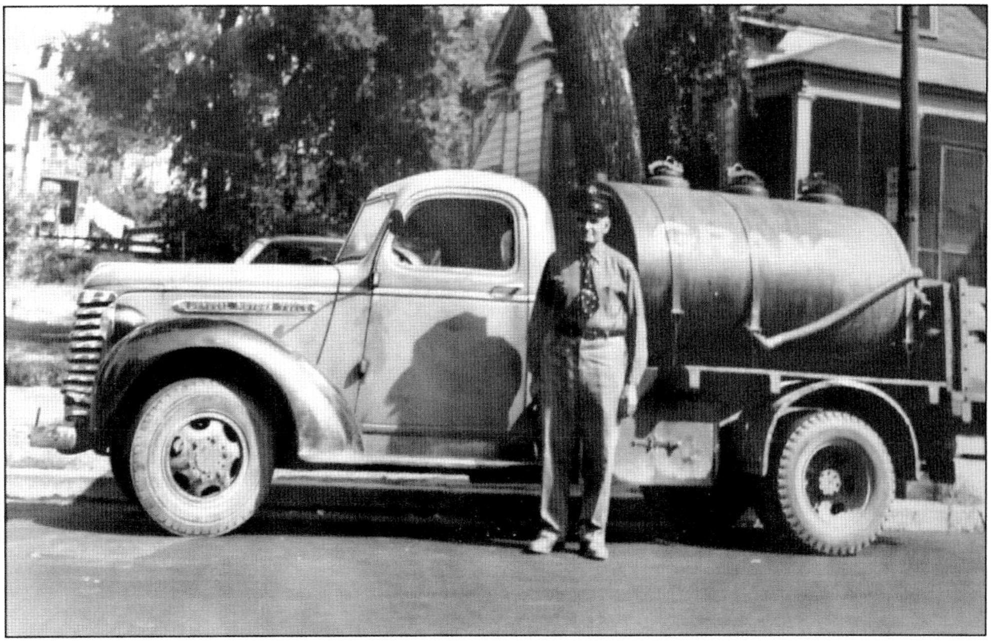

The Orangevale Grange's membership grew between 1935 and 1960, in large part because of the oil-distribution program provided by Elmer Binning (above). Elmer Binning was the grange master from 1941 to 1945 and then again in 1954. Fuel oil within this program was sold only to grange members. (Courtesy Orangevale Grange.)

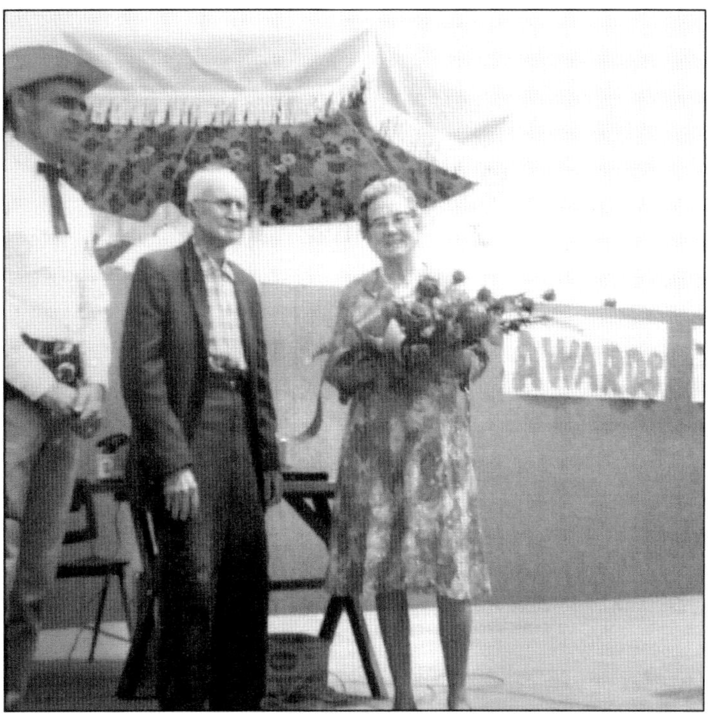

Pictured here in 1968, Grange Master Gene Moberg stands next to Martin and Rose Schaefer, 94 and 83 respectively. Here the Schaefers received the award of "oldest couple in Orangevale." The Schaefers married in 1915 and moved to Orangevale in 1940. In 1950, they started Schaefer's Nursery. Both actively participated in the Orangevale Grange, with Martin as treasurer and gatekeeper and Rose as pianist and secretary. (Courtesy Orangevale Grange.)

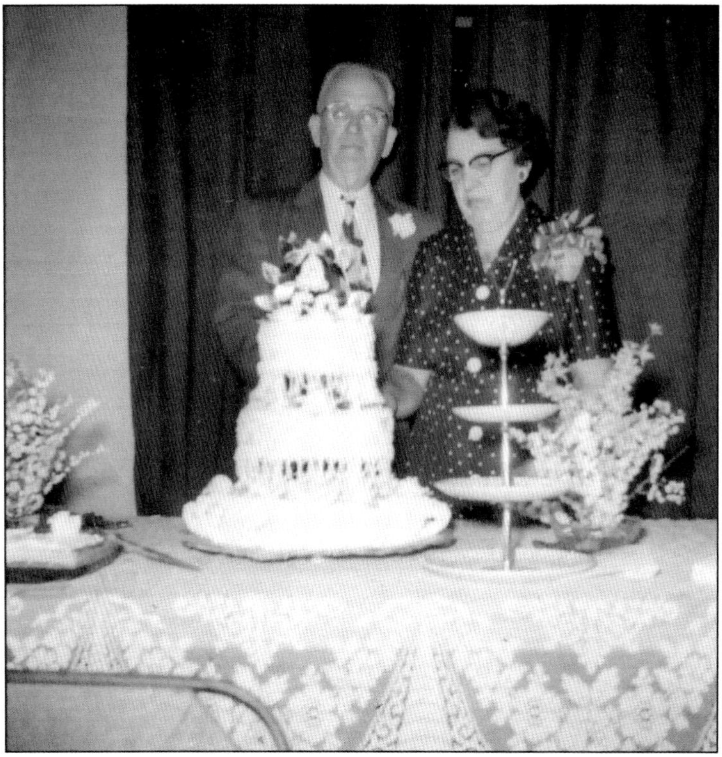

Mr. and Mrs. Fred Wagner celebrate their 50th wedding anniversary in 1956 at an open house given by friends, the Gust Westbergs, in their honor. Guests, totaling 75 in all, signed the guest book, including friends and relatives traveling from Sacramento, Roseville, Millbrae, Garberville, and Burlingame. The evening included this three-tiered wedding cake, a program of reminiscences and songs, and comments by Rev. D. G. Decherd. (Courtesy Orangevale Grange.)

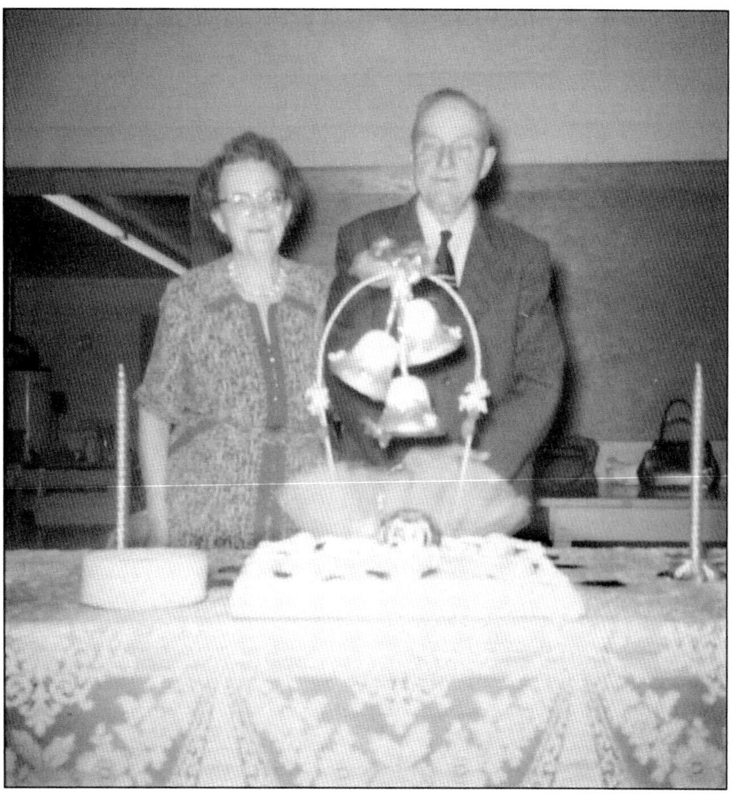

Viola and Earl Binning celebrate their golden wedding anniversary party at the Orangevale Grange hall in the late 1950s or early 1960s. The Binning family has been active in the Grange and the Orangevale community for decades. Exemplary of their importance and contributions to the community and named in honor of the family, Binning Court is located off Main Avenue. (Courtesy Orangevale Grange.)

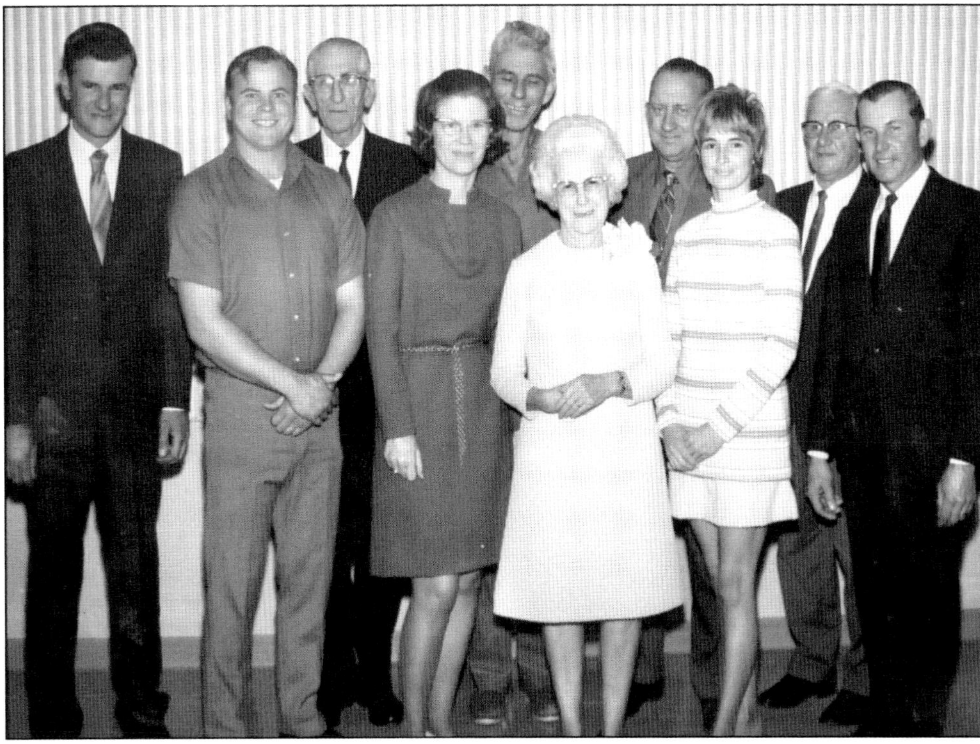

This 1971 photograph (above) captures the friendly faces of the Orange Vale Water Company. Pictured from left to right are Victor Salle (board member), John Wingerter (assistant field superintendent), Ward Cooper (board member), Ruth Conners (manager), Iven Mayfield (superintendent), Ferne Schrader (secretary of the board), Richard Bacon (board member and owner of Orangevale Glass), Sharon Wilcox (billing clerk), Clyde Lampson (board member), and Frederick Tomich (board member). (Courtesy Orange Vale Water Company.)

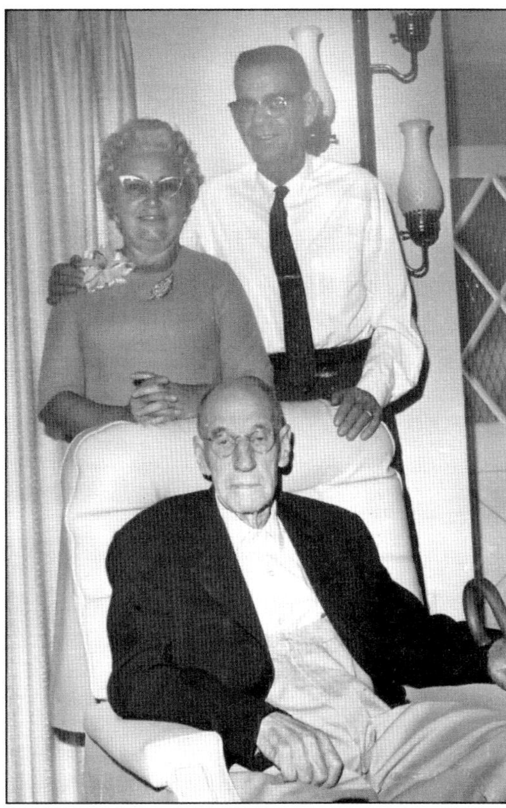

Ora and Floyd Field stand proudly behind Grandpa William Field on their 40th wedding anniversary in 1966. (Courtesy JoAnn Allred.)

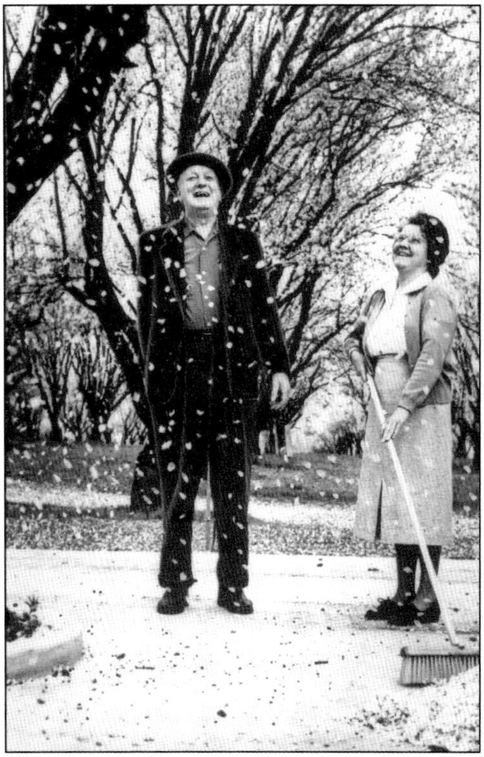

John and Alberta Lammerding enjoy the rarity of snow outside their house, located off Pardillo Avenue, in 1961. Carefully kept from view behind his back is the mallet that he used to knock snow off of the tree for the shot. (Courtesy Gerald Lammerding)

Pictured at center in May 1984, Carol Leever is installed as the Orangevale Woman's Club district president. Roger and Carol Leever moved to Orangevale in 1948 and built a home out of adobe brick in 1951 on their 20 acres. The Leevers were extremely involved in Orangevale, with Carol serving as president of Serve our Seniors and Roger as a board member of the chamber of commerce. (Courtesy Marcia Clark.)

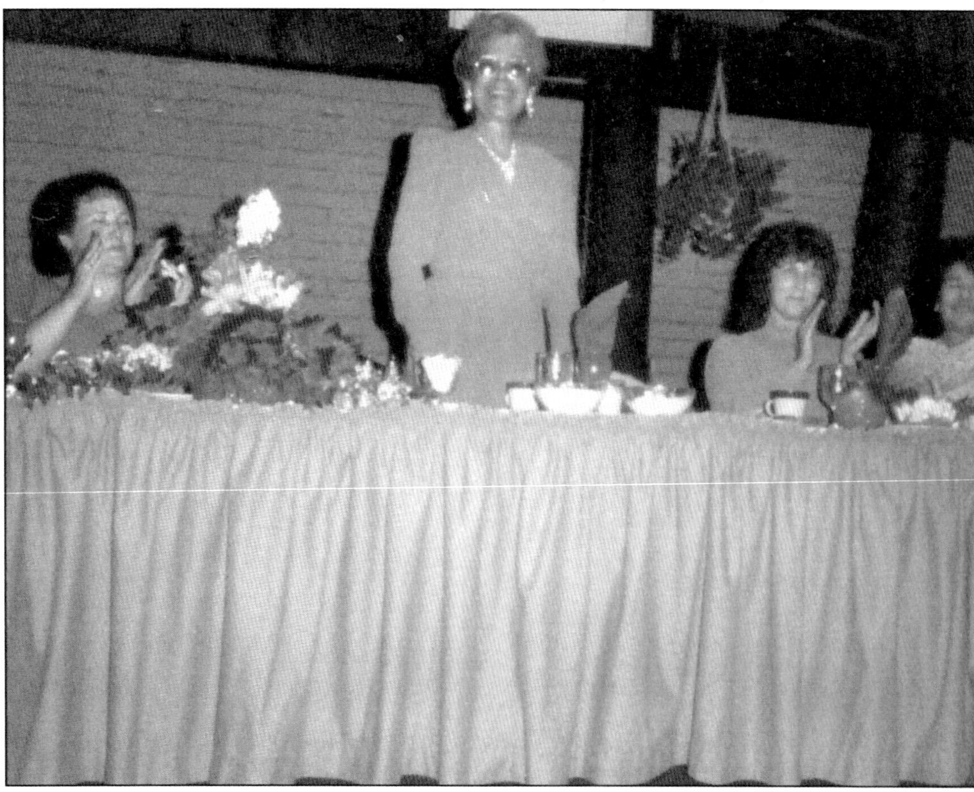

Ten

Orangevale at Play

You can discover more about a person in an hour of play than in a year of conversation.

—Plato, Greek philosopher, 427–347 BCE

The history of sports and recreation is a growing and varied scholarly playing field for historians. As the English author Joseph Strutt argued in 1801, "In order to form a just estimation of the character of any particular people, it is absolutely necessary to investigate Sport and Pastimes most generally prevalent among them." Generations of historians after Strutt, however, ignored this subject, perhaps because of intellectual snobbery, career concerns, or a conviction that a detailed analysis of sports and recreation does not increase historical knowledge. Nevertheless, since the 1980s, a flood of quality academic research has shown sports and recreation to be a legitimate course of study for understanding the human experience. These topics open a window for historians and scholars to examine social attitudes and relationships and cultural definitions and meanings.

Sporting and recreational events allow, even if just for a fleeting moment, those of differing socioeconomic classes and races to join in a common event, whether as spectators or as participants. In addition, sports and recreation provide the exercise so esteemed by modern American culture and purportedly instills such values as teamwork, commitment, and dedication. Walt Whitman declared, "Baseball will take our people out-of-doors, fill them with oxygen, give them a larger physical stoicism. Tend to relieve us from being a nervous, dyspeptic set. Repair these losses, and be a blessing to us. . . . I see great things in baseball."

Residents in Orangevale, like others around the nation, have discovered a variety of ways to enjoy the sporting life over the years. Orangevale residents have found fun and relaxation in playing baseball, football, and tennis, biking, swimming in the American River, cutting loose on the dance floor, or picnicking along the beautiful Orangevale Bluffs. For more than 40 years, residents have also enjoyed an annual parade and fair each spring, called Pow Wow Days. Likewise, the Orangevale Park and Recreation District maintains nine parks and has playground facilities at 12 schools, where residents can play baseball or soccer or participate in one of the many youth programs, including camps, carnivals, and dance classes.

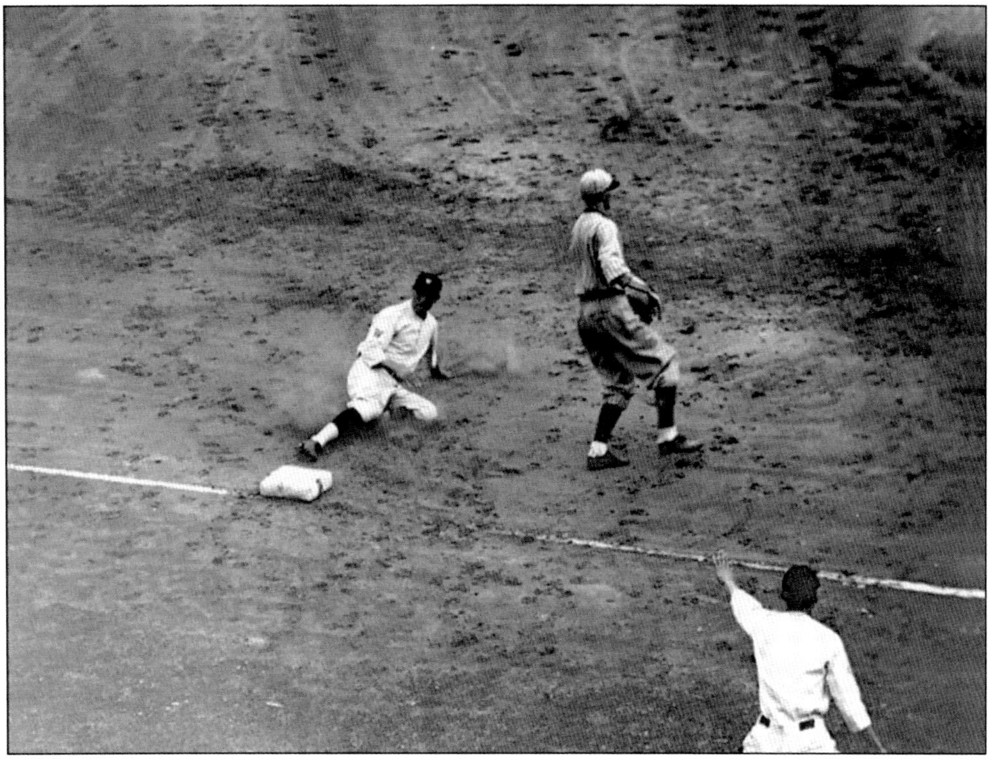

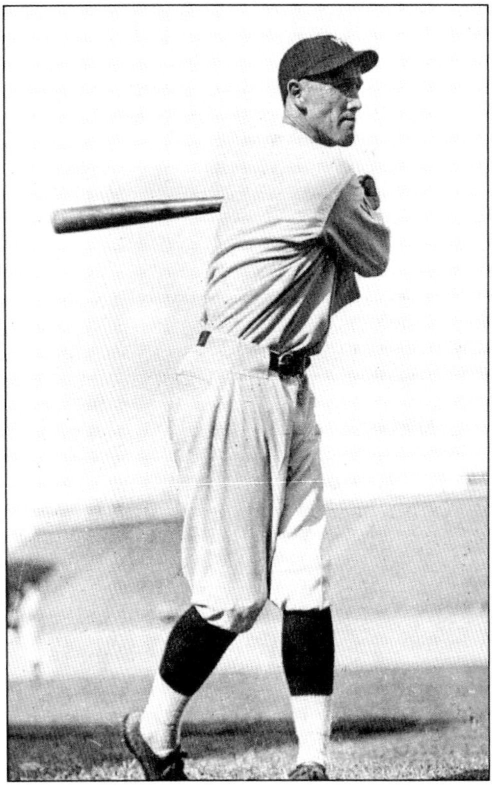

Orangevale's Earl McNeely broke into the majors in 1924, when he played for the Washington Nationals (later the Minnesota Twins). He helped the Nationals win the World Series against the New York Giants with a clutch hit in the 12th inning; with bases loaded and nobody out, McNeely hit a grounder, which took a bad hop, scoring the series-ending run. McNeely, a center fielder, played for eight years. He was with the Nationals from 1924 to 1927 and with the St. Louis Browns (later the Baltimore Orioles) from 1928 to 1931, playing alongside Hall-of-Famers Walter Johnson and Bucky Harris. He had a career .272 batting average and 214 RBIs. During game one of the 1924 World Series, before a crowd of 35,760 at Washington's Griffith Stadium, he made it to third, fielded by Fred Lindstrom (seen above). (Courtesy Library of Congress, Prints and Photographs Division, LC-USZ62-123038 and LC-USZ62-101603.)

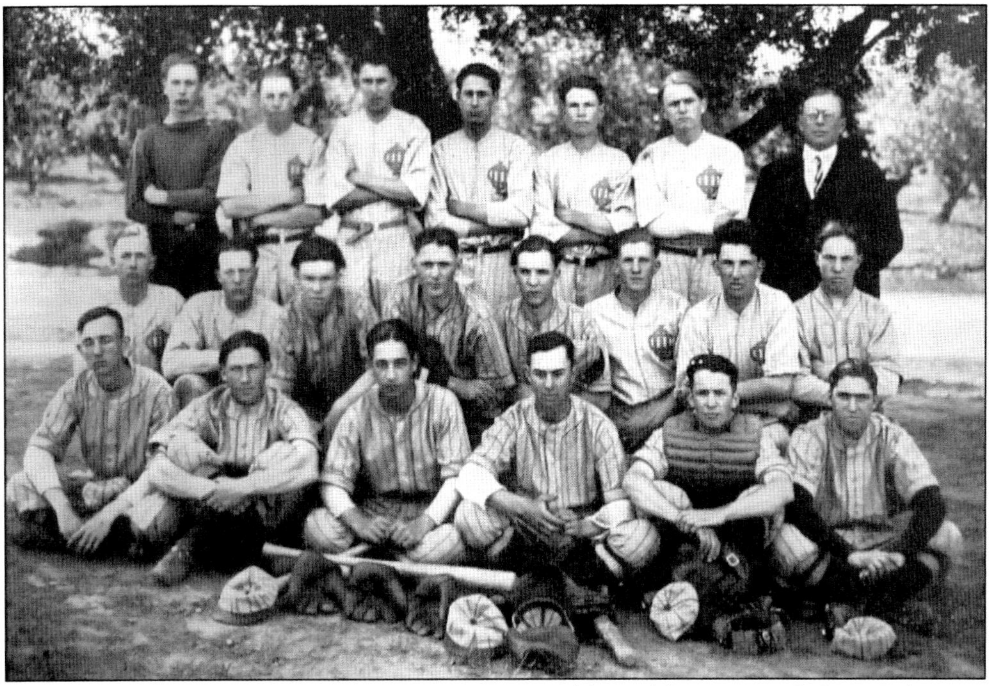

The 1924 San Juan High School baseball team was part of the California Interscholastic Federation League, along with teams from San Juan, Lincoln, Roseville, and Placerville. Though not all identified, the yearbook accounts for the following players on the team: Cochrane, P; Stephens, LF; Lemon (captain), 3B; Bunker, SS; Barber, 2B; Baker; C; Weaver, RF; Cooper, CF; Clark, P; Beauchamp, P; Whitsell, 1B; Braden, C; and Rice, 3B. (Courtesy Sacramento Room, Sacramento Public Library.)

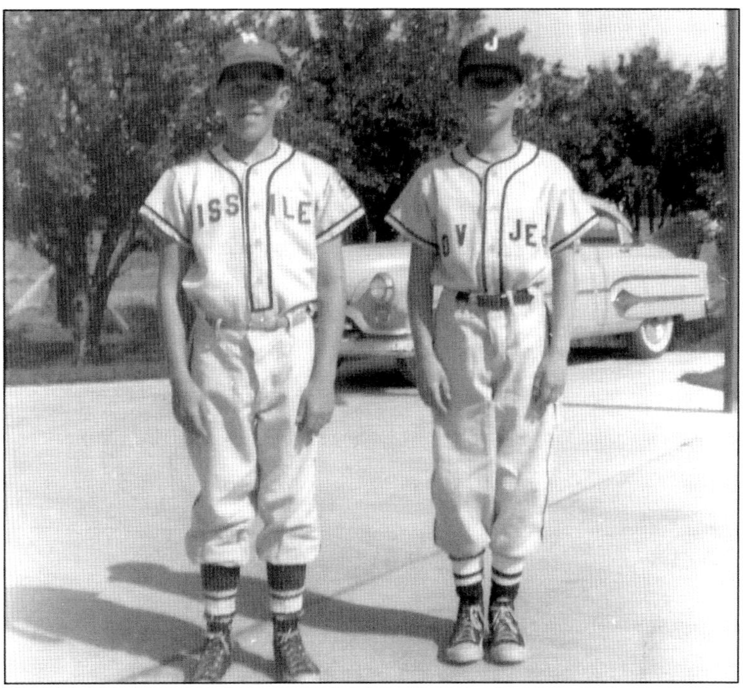

Many of Orangevale's children, like many around the world, have dreamed of growing up playing baseball, like Earl McNeely. Here Curt and Kent Baldwin, age 12 and 10 respectively, pose in their uniforms before the big game in front of their home off Hazel Avenue and Greenback Lane in May 1957. (Courtesy Richard Harke.)

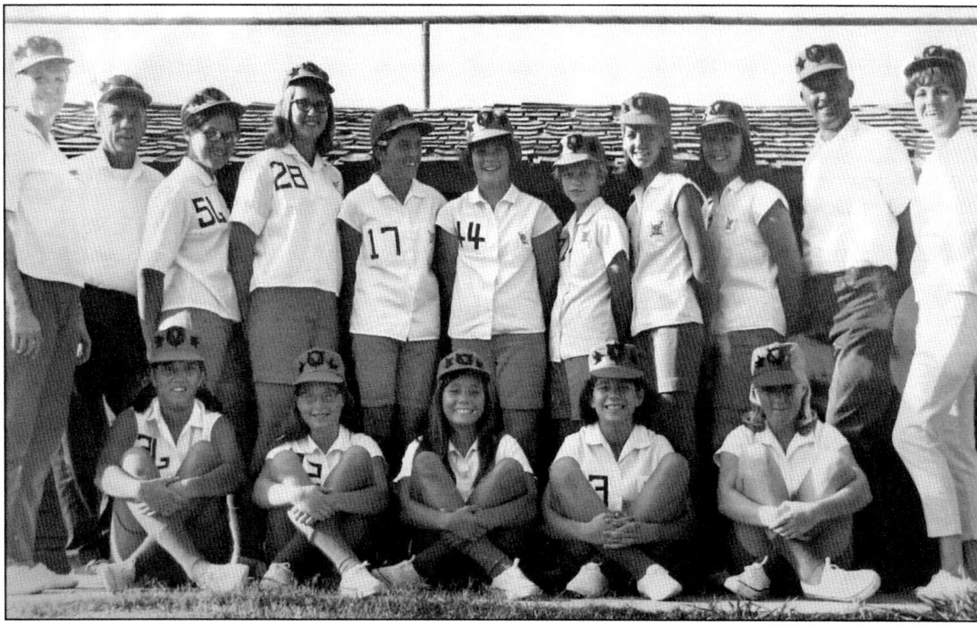

Not to be outdone by the boys, longtime Orangevale resident Glenda Lewis (far right) is seen here with her team in the 1970s. Lewis helped to organize the first girls' league in Orangevale and helped to make the fun of playing baseball available to everyone in the area, regardless of gender. (Courtesy Glenda Lewis.)

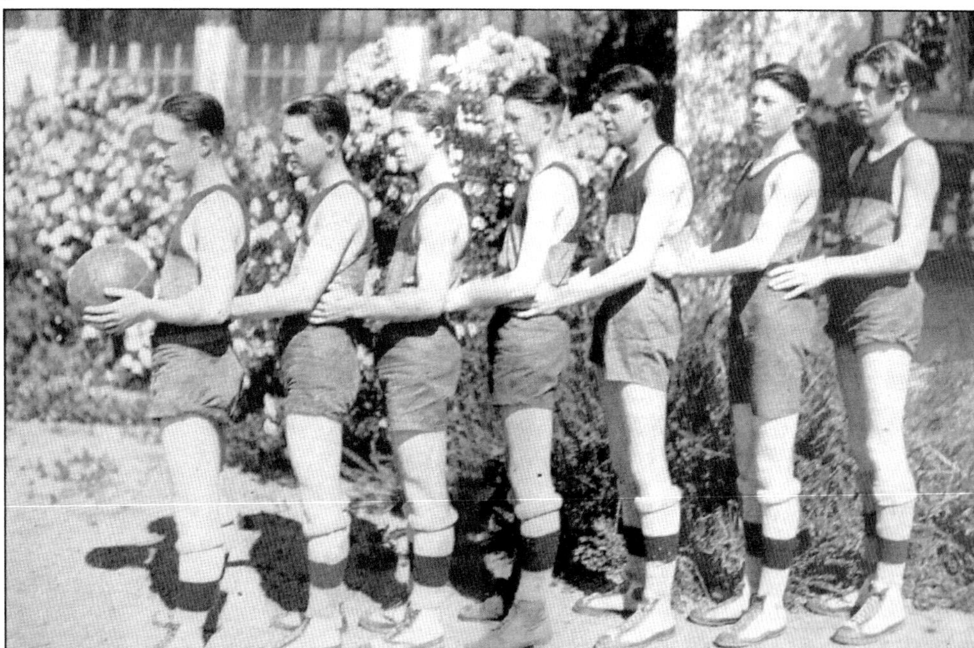

The 1925 San Juan High School boys' basketball team "B" joined the California Interscholastic Federation League and competed against schools from El Dorado, Folsom, and Sacramento. The team finished with a 4-2 record, with the highest scoring game coming in a loss against El Dorado at 23-16. (Courtesy Sacramento Room, Sacramento Public Library.)

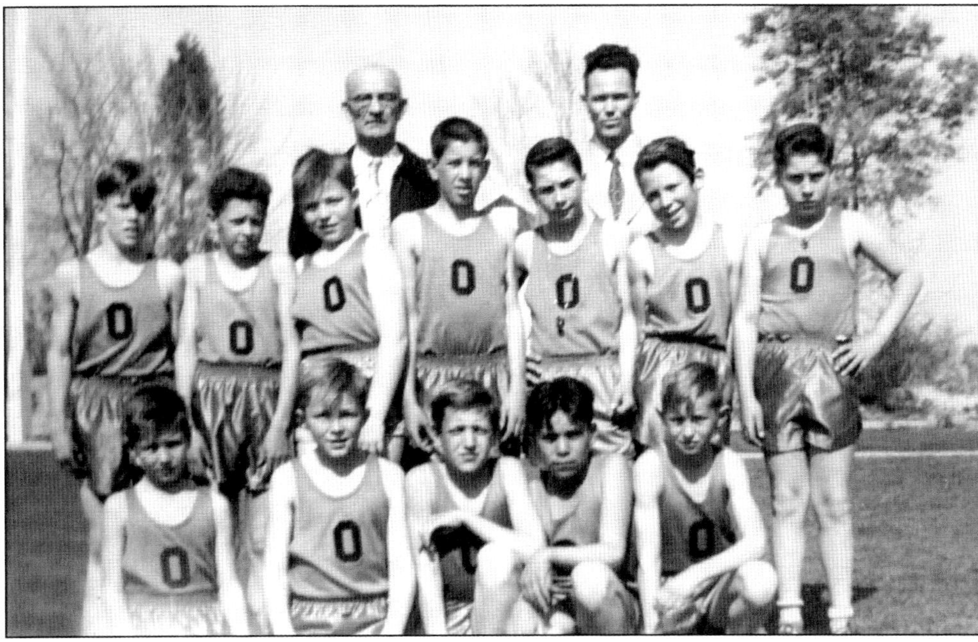

Pictured is the 1952–1953 Orangevale School boys basketball team "C." As seen here, the sporting life has been a part of every grade level, not just for high school students. (Courtesy Orangevale Open Elementary School.)

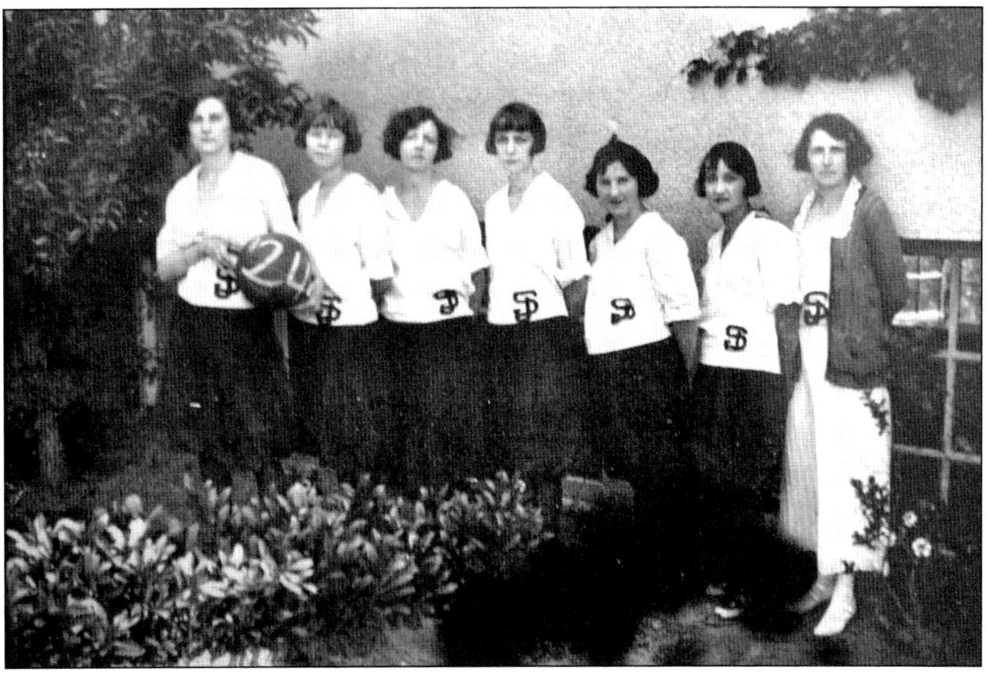

The 1924 San Juan High School girls' basketball team was the first basketball team at San Juan to play in the newly built gymnasium at the school. The team finished with a winning record, suffering only one loss to Galt. According to the yearbook, the team consisted of Katherine Cochrane, Carolyn Bunker, Beatrice Scott, Erla Blair, Grace Whitney, and Dorothy Dixon. (Courtesy Sacramento Room, Sacramento Public Library.)

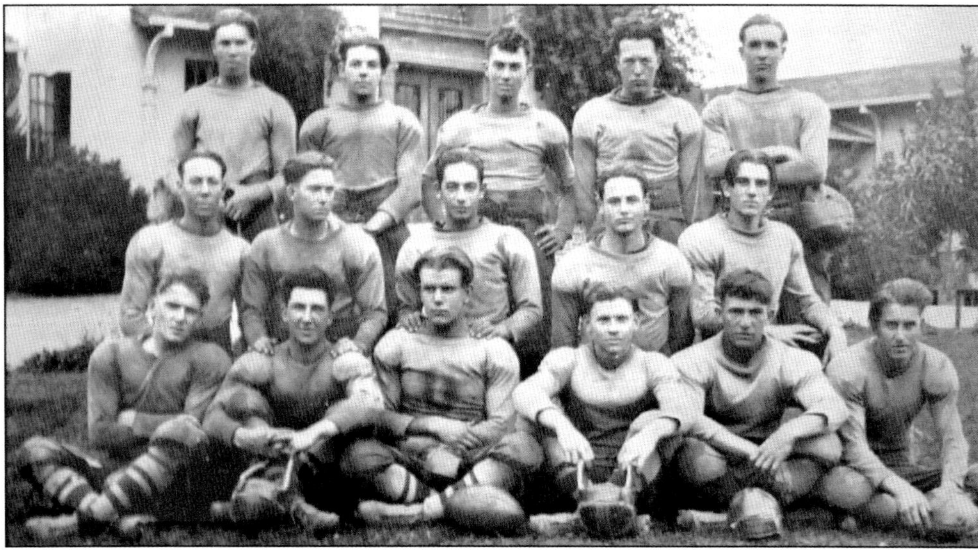

The 1923–1924 San Juan High School football team went undefeated and beat Nevada City High 36-6 to win the California Interscholastic Federation Championship. According to the yearbook, the team, "averaging 150 pounds," consisted of Earl Weaver, Cecil Braden, Jack Loughbridge, Ernest Barber, Victor Imel, Raul Sullivan, Charles Cochrane, Lloyd Altland, Osborn Clark, Ben Evans, Henry Lemon, George Houx, Harvey Moore, and George Francis. (Courtesy Sacramento Room, Sacramento Public Library.)

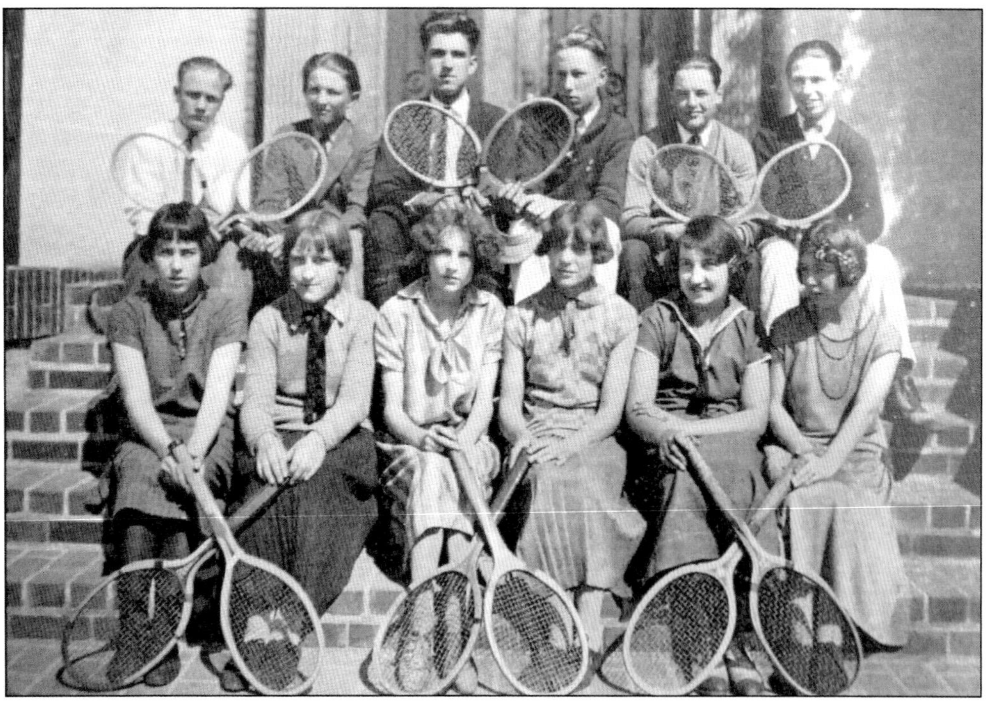

Tennis has long been a favorite sport of Orangevale residents and of surrounding communities. In fact, according to Orangevale cofounder Valentine S. McClatchy's notebooks, he enjoyed tennis along with boxing. Here the San Juan High School tennis team poses for their 1925 yearbook photograph. (Courtesy Sacramento Room, Sacramento Public Library.)

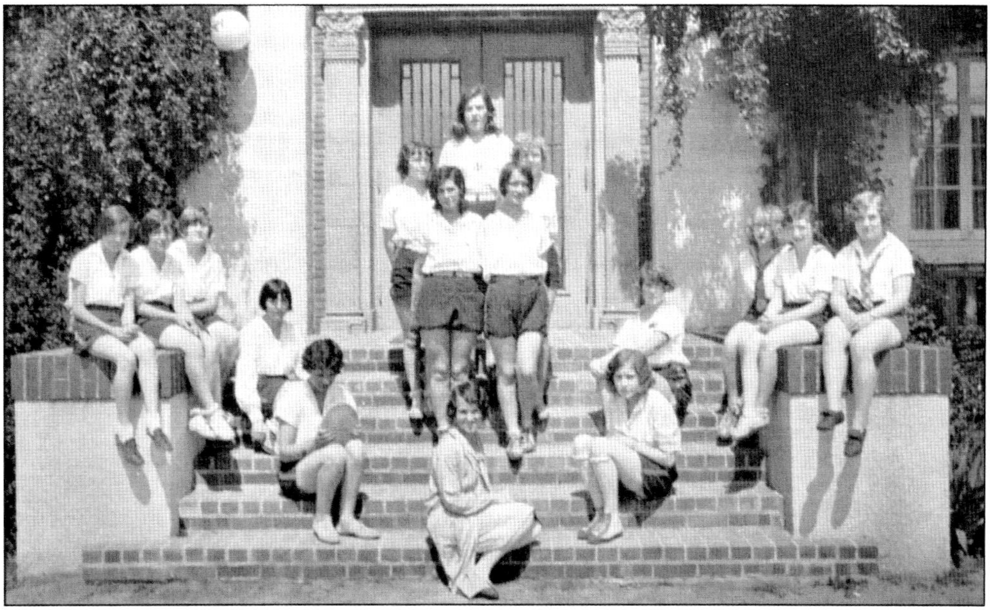

According to the 1942 San Juan High School yearbook, *Greenback Notes*, the girls' track team gave "promise of having an excellent track team." Likewise, "The 'tan skin' fad seems to entice them into taking up track work." According to the yearbook and in keeping with the World War II image of Rosie the Riveter, their slogan was "What man has done, *we* can do." (Courtesy Naida and Andrew Effinger.)

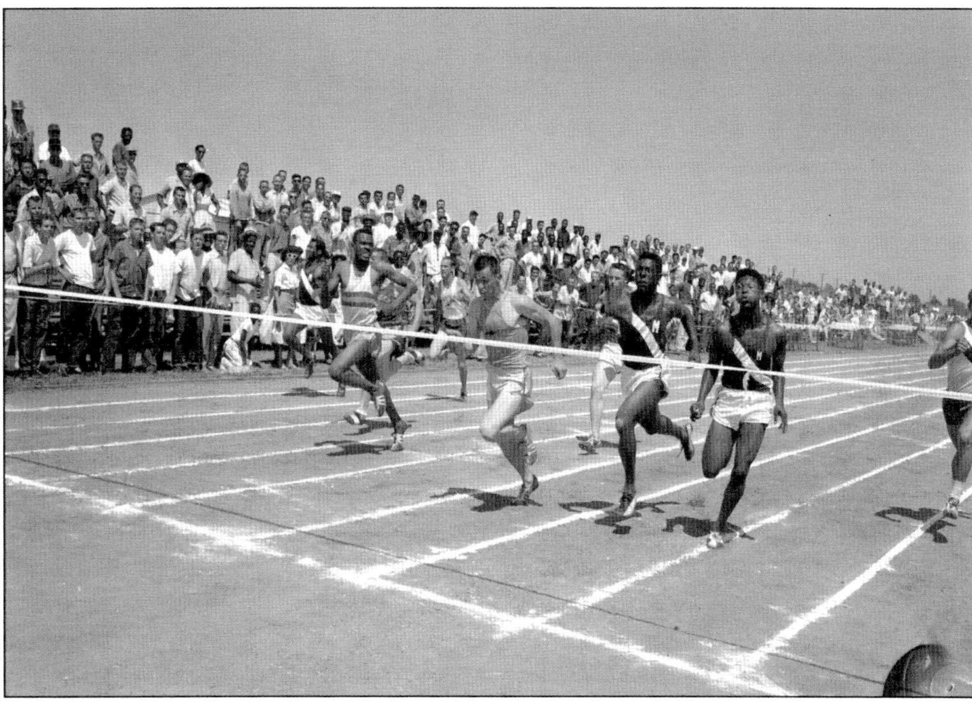

From May 11 to May 17, 1958, San Juan High School hosted a track-meet competition between the local high schools. Seen here is one of the many races in which students competed. (Courtesy SAMCC, Drawer 88, Row 5, Roberts, May 68.)

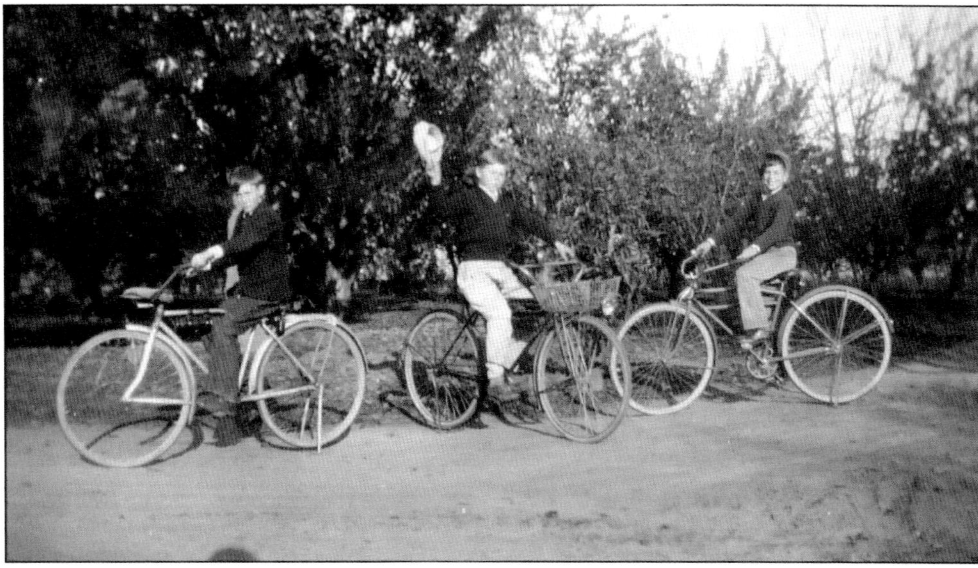

Riding a bicycle has been a popular means of both transportation and having fun for Orangevale residents for many years, as three young Tomich family members or friends demonstrate sometime between 1910 and 1930. The name of the modern vehicle dates from 1869, with various precursors known as velocipedes. In fact, crude two-wheeled vehicles propelled by the feet were popular as early as the second half of the 17th century. (Courtesy Fred Tomich.)

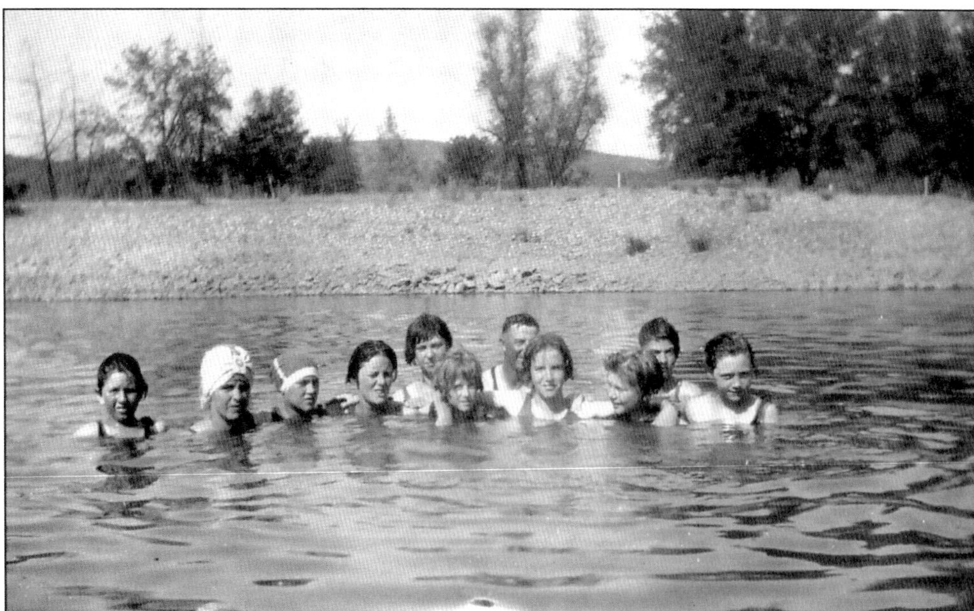

The American River has been a place of rest and fun for Orangevale residents since the 19th century. Marjorie Odlin (fifth from the left, with dark hair) and Ivie Odlin (in front of the man) enjoy a swim at Negro Bar in the 1920s. Negro Bar, on the south bank of the American River adjacent to Folsom, was destroyed by construction of the Nimbus Dam in the 1950s and is now commemorated on the opposite side of the river. (Courtesy Jean Kelly.)

The bluffs along the American River are some of the most beautiful in the country and Orangevale residents have enjoyed playing alongside them for more than 100 years. Here a young boy, like many others throughout Orangevale's history, jumps from the rocks of the bluffs into the river adjacent the Rainbow Bridge on August 11, 1970. (Courtesy SAMCC, *Sac Bee* Photo Morgue No. 1109.)

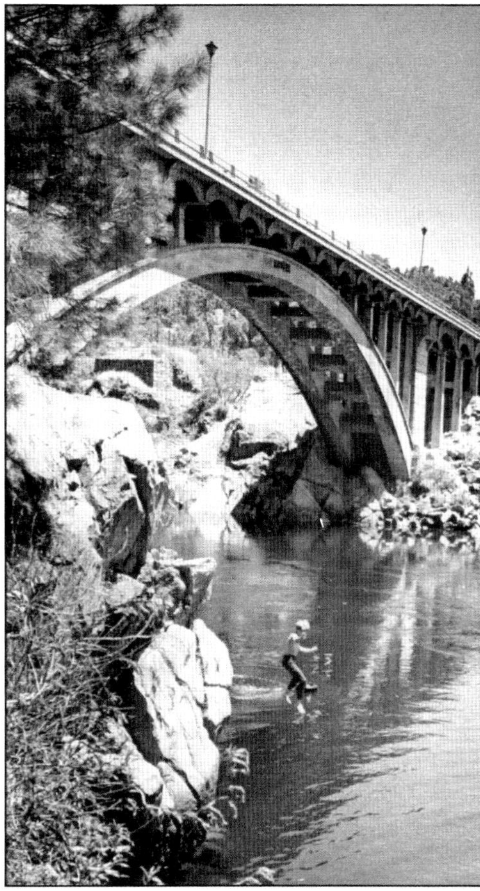

Sometime in the early 20th century, Tomich family members, including Nick and Frances (left), constructed their own crude type of go-kart, which they fashioned out of old fruit boxes. Go-karts have been around as long as the automobile. In fact, many top professional racecar drivers, including Michael Schumacher, Sarah Fisher, Darrell Waltrip, Tony Stewart, and Kyle Petty, got their start on the go-kart racing circuit. (Courtesy Fred Tomich.)

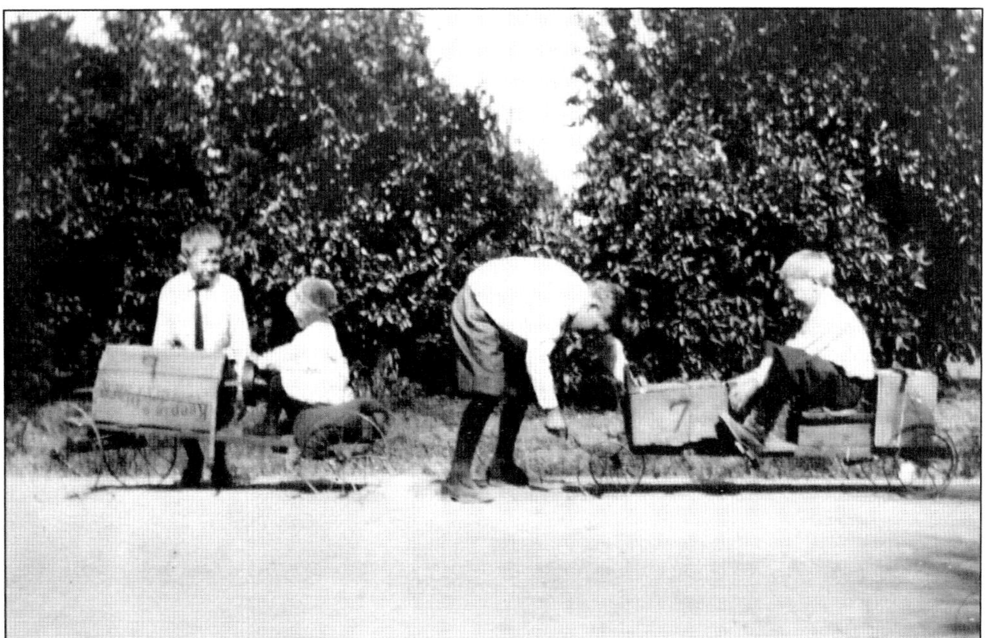

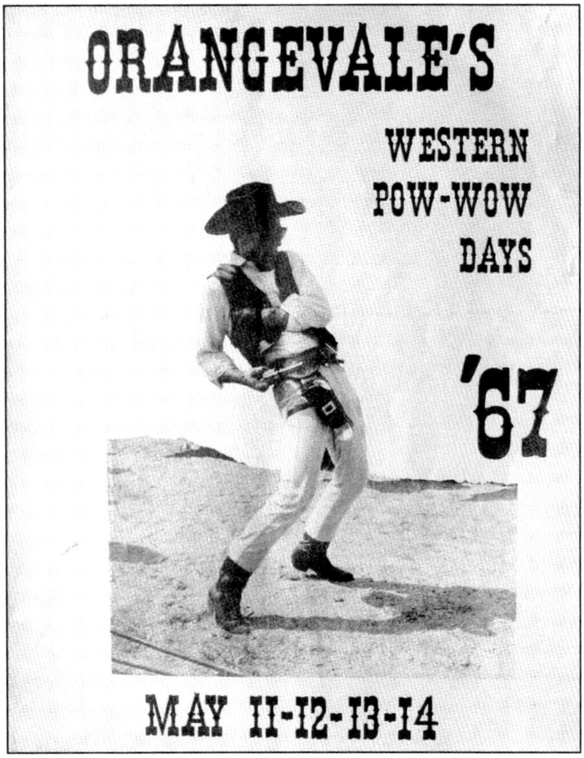

Pictured here is the 1967 Pow Wow Days program. The Orangevale Pow Wow Days celebration started in 1963 as Chuck Wagon Days. In 1964, the name changed to Fiesta Days and changed again to its name of more than 40 years in 1965, Pow Wow Days. Orangevale residents and visitors gather for several days of games, shows, food, and a parade, including a delicious pancake breakfast, horse show, and carnival rides. (Courtesy Glenda Lewis.)

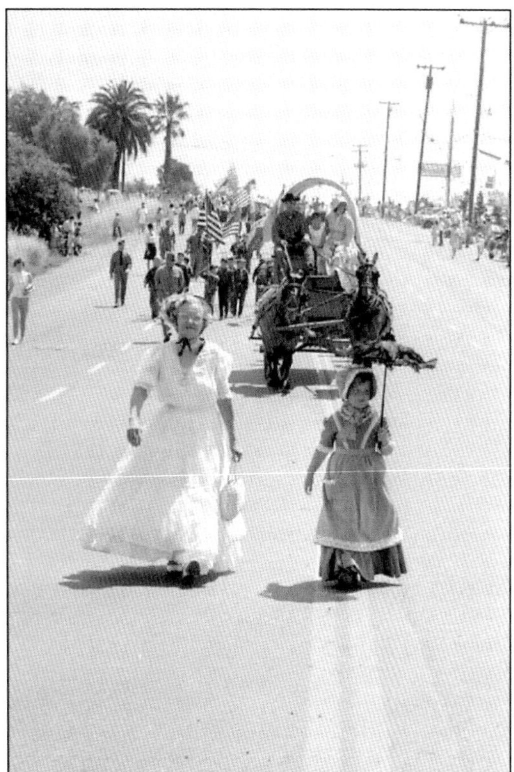

In May 1969, the Orangevale Pow Wow Days parade marched down Greenback Lane. Beginning in 1963, the route was originally on Central Avenue, ending at the Orangevale Youth Center on Hazel Avenue. The parade route moved to Greenback Lane by 1965 and then to Oak Avenue in 1971, returning to its current route on Greenback Lane in 1974. (Courtesy SAMCC, Drawer 85, Row 6, Neibaur, May 69.)

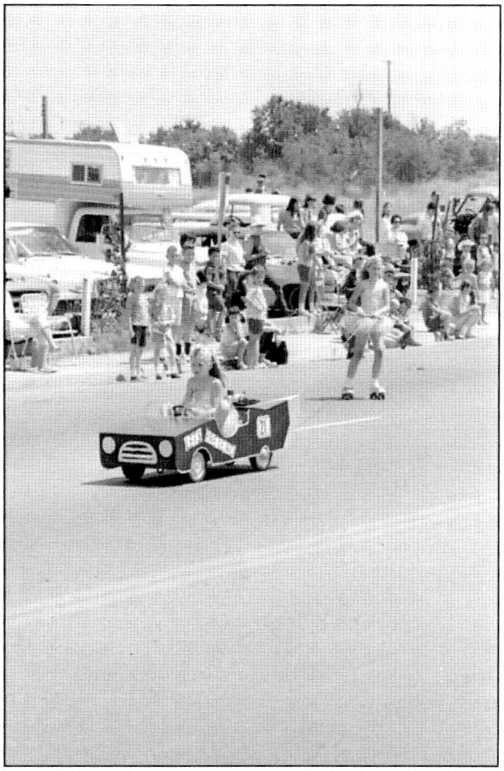

Orangevale Pow Wow Days parade members have included an astonishing amount of variety, including representatives from local clubs, emergency services, schools, sports teams, as well as children in the community. Pictured at right in May 1969, a more playful exhibit included two young girls, one driving a go-kart while, in tow, another reeled along on roller skates. Pictured below sometime in the 1970s, some young parade members rode down Greenback Lane on tricycles, one with a can in tow. (Above courtesy SAMCC, Drawer 85, Row 6, Neibaur, May 69; below courtesy Orangevale Grange.)

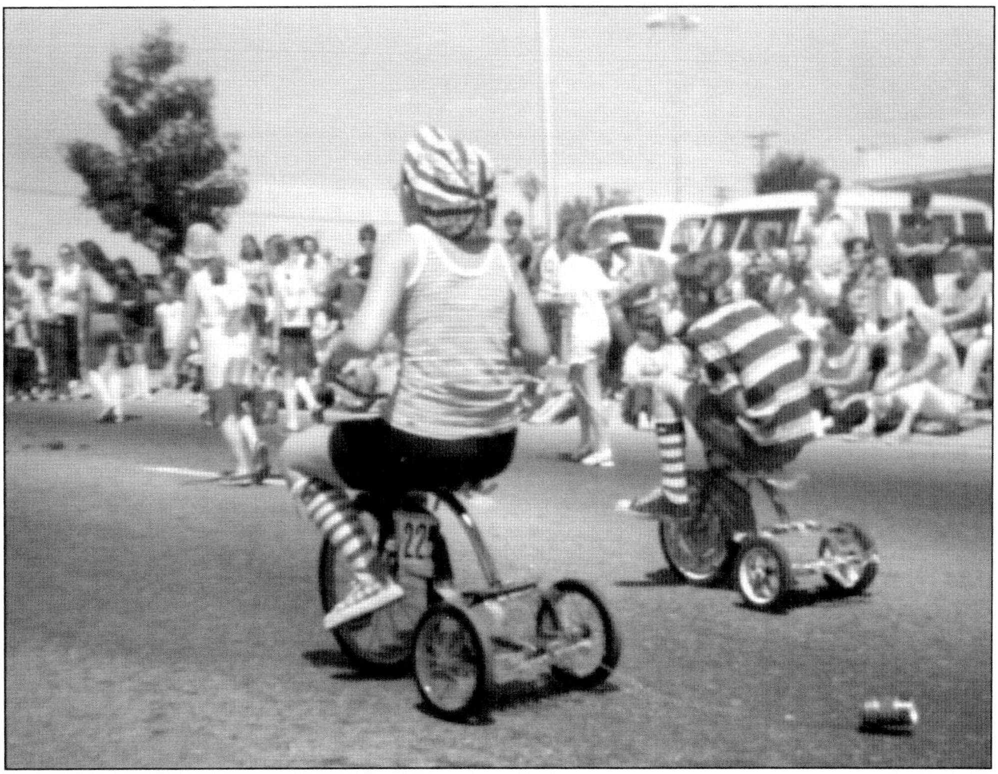

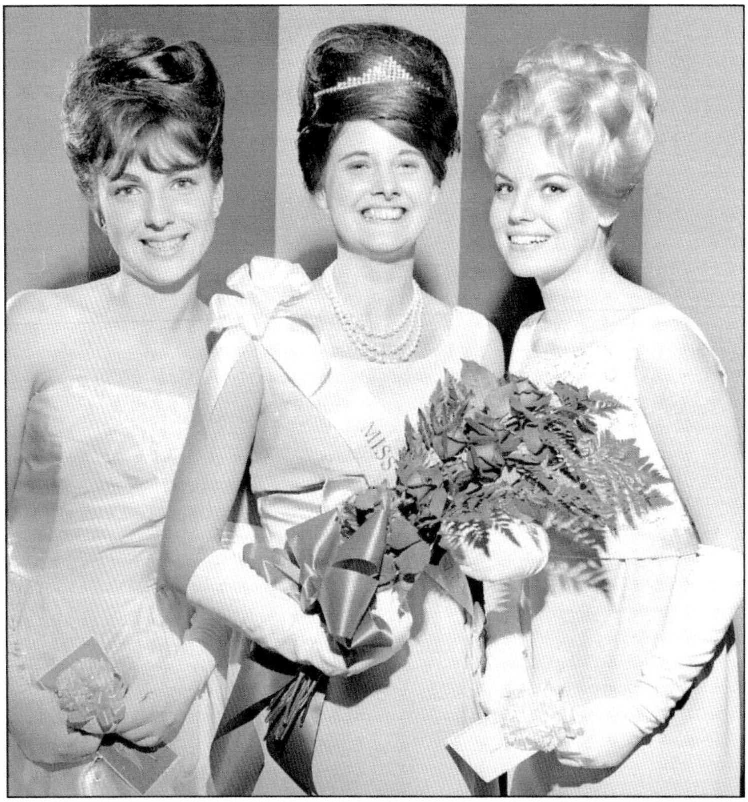

On May 8, 1965, Darlene Binning, daughter of Mr. and Mrs. Wendell Binning of Orangevale, was crowned queen of the Orangevale Pow Wow Days celebration. The Pow Wow Days queen contest and coronation kicked off the festivities. Serving as princesses were Sandra Rix and Carol Miller. (Courtesy SAMCC, Drawer 90, Row 4, Schmidt, May 65.)

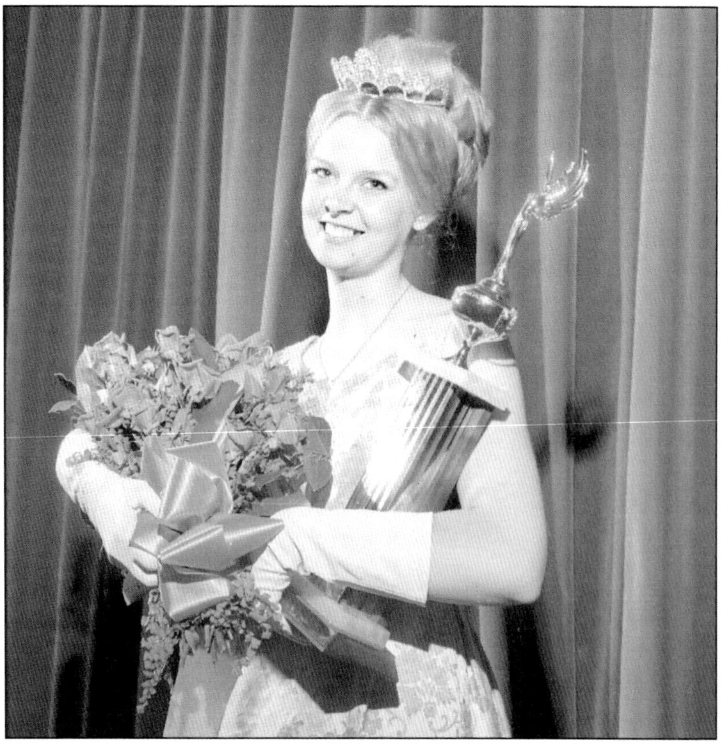

Susie Smith was crowned Miss Orangevale on May 7, 1966, to signal the beginning of the Pow Wow Days celebration. Susie Smith, a sophomore from Del Campo High School, was from Fair Oaks and was awarded a trophy and a $75 U.S. savings bond. She was picked from five finalists, which were narrowed from a field of 21. (Courtesy SAMCC, Drawer 90, Row 4, Schmidt, May 66.)

Selected Bibliography

This selected bibliography is a reference to some of the major works concerning Orangevale and is not meant to be an exhaustive or definitive list representing all sources consulted for this work. Sources can be found at the California State Library; Sacramento Public Library (Sacramento Room and Orangevale branch); California State Archives; and the Sacramento Archives and Museum Collection Center (SAMCC), as well as in articles in the *Folsom Telegraph*, *Orangevale News*, *Sacramento Bee*, *Sacramento Union*, and *San Juan Record*.

Primary Sources

McClatchy, James and Company. *Sacramento County and its Resources: A Souvenir of the Bee, 1894, Our Capital City, Past and Present.* Sacramento, CA: H. S. Crocker Company, 1894.

McClatchy, Valentine S. *V. S. McClatchy Letter Books.* Eleanor McClatchy Collection, SAMCC, Sacramento, CA.

Menefee, Selden, Patricia Fitzgerald, and Geraldine Fitzgerald, ed. *Fair Oaks and San Juan Area Memories.* Fair Oaks, CA: San Juan Record Press, 1960.

Sacramento County Recorder Collection. Articles of Incorporation of the Orange Vale Colonization Company, Sacramento, September 20, 1887, case file no. 505, SAMCC (SAMCC), Sacramento, CA. Articles of incorporation for many of Orangevale's various business and organizations are housed at SAMCC and the California State Archives.

Sacramento Record-Union. Sacramento through the Camera. Sacramento, CA: *Sacramento Record-Union*, 1901.

Sacramento Valley Sunbeam: Devoted to the Interests of Ideal County Homes. Sacramento, CA: B. F. Hulings, March 1909.

Secondary Sources

Heck, Catherine. *A History of the Orangevale Community. N.p.*, 1990. Found at the California History Room, California State Library, Sacramento, CA.

Laucher, Mary E. *History of Orangevale. N.p.*, 1962. Found at the California State University, Sacramento Library.

McGowan, Joseph A. *History of the Sacramento Valley.* Vol. 1–3. New York: Lewis Historical Publishing Company, 1961.

Orange Vale Water Company. *One Hundred Years of Service.* Orangevale, CA: Orange Vale Water Company, 1996.